# YOU ARE NOT ALONE
## (Organisation Management: Selected Essays)

## Books by the Same Author

- Enterprise and Society: A Study of Some Aspects of Enterpreneurship and Management in India (1979)
- The Communication of Ideas (1980)
- Essays in Longitudinal Thinking: Managing Change with Continuity (2005)
- Organisation Development System: Including Essentials of Organisational Behaviour and Organisation Management (5th Edition) (2011)
- Longitudinally Speaking: The Best of Drishti (2013)
- Lifelong Learning: Seeking, Meaning, Relevance and Self-Renewal (2018)
- Echoes (2021)

---

### About the Author

**Dr. Vinayshil Gautam**, often seen as a legend in the field of management is widely recognised for his writings; institution building efforts and as a thinker, teacher and researcher.

Dr. Gautam was Founder Director of IIM-K and Leader of the consulting team at IIM-S. He was the 1st Head of the 1st statutory Management Department (at IIT-D) in the entire IIT pantheon. He has served as Senior Advisor to KPMG and as Senior Managing Director and Principal Economic Advisor of the global consulting firm Protiviti (I) Member Private Ltd.

He has been adviser to several governmental departments; private/public agencies and corporations. He has been a visiting faculty at Universities of: Sussex, Brunel, Dominican, etc. and delivered lectures at Cambridge University, University of London; Toronto University; University of York; Duke University and various other Universities across five continents. He is currently the Chairman of D K International Foundation and the Leader of the Task Force of Jubilee Celebrations of International Federation of Training and Development Organisations (IFTDO). A recipient of over half a dozen life time achievement awards, his contributions have been recognised across several domains such as Management, Sociology, Public Systems, Education etc.

Dr. Gautam's work in the area of Organizational and Human Resource Development is widely respected and used in India and abroad.

# YOU ARE NOT ALONE

## (Organisation Management: Selected Essays)

Vinayshil Gautam

CONCEPT PUBLISHING COMPANY PVT. LTD.
NEW DELHI - 110 059

**ISBN:** 978-93-5594-677-5 (HB)

First Published 2024

*Published and Printed by*

Since 1974

**Concept Publishing Company Pvt. Ltd.**
A/15-16, Commercial Block, Mohan Garden
New Delhi-110059 (India)
*T*: +91-11-41101460
*E*: publishing@conceptpub.com, *W*: www.conceptpub.com

**Cataloging in Publication**--Courtesy: D.K. Agencies (P) Ltd. <docinfo@dkagencies.com>

**Gautam, Vinayshil, author.**
You are not alone : organisation management : selected essays / Vinayshil Gautam.
pages cm
Includes index.
ISBN 9789355946775 (HB)
ISBN 9789355947178 (PB)

1. Industrial management--India. I. Title.

LCC HD31.2.G38 2024 | DDC 658.400954 23

For
Dr. Ahmed AlBanna
President,
Bahrain Society for Human Capital Management

# Preface

This book is divided over 12 chapters: Organisational Behavior; Economics; Communication; Quantitative Techniques; Organisation Design; Operations Management; Finance and Accounting; International Business; Information Technology; Human Resources Management; Managerial Skills and Business Policy. Each chapter has a selection of essays approximating that theme. These essays have been published earlier in the Business Manager; The Daily Pioneer, etc. over a period of ten years or so. In this book each chapter's essay is captioned by its title. And each essay is a self contained text. The date of the original publication is given at the end of each piece.

These texts have sometimes been revised. In all they are a faithful reflection of the author's understanding, insights, and interpretations of the contexts.

One of the advantages of regular writing is the contextualization of concurrent trends, and this book has had the rich experience of the reader's feedback. Methodologically, the way this book has grown is an innovation and a testimony to the times.

These 10 years have been important in the nation's life, and it is a privilege to have the opportunity to reflect on some experiences and bring them out in a book form. (The readership will have an opinion on the extent this has been a worthwhile effort, and how it resonates with them). Thus, this methodology hopes to respond to a felt need in management literature. It is a book of its type which is simultaneously a testimony, a commentary, and a live interaction with live issues of the times.

As one goes through life whether in joy, or pain or simple plain experience one often feels that its unique to that person's life. This is often not the case. A careful look around would show that someone else or indeed many people have gone through such experiences. This realization helps to give a more balanced reaction to that particular experience or episode (personal or collective). In itself it is a sobering thought that "you are not alone". Not only does a better balanced approach emerge but options for coping or indeed dealing with situation get widened. Indeed, as Shannon L Adler once said "one of the most important things you can do on this earth is to let people know they are not alone" An intensified maturity is a great asset in life. Hopefully the underpinning of these writings will be of value to the reader towards the possibilities of a more mellowed approach in general

In the years to come, it will serve as a concurrent evidence of how certain concerns of the decade rolled out in the context of the times and what did one person have to say about it.

**Gurugram** **Vinayshil Gautam**
**April 9, 2024**

# Acknowledgements

Any book of this order stands in the debt of a very large number of people. It is always challenging to identify them comprehensively. That, that it covers a period of nearly 10 years makes it all the more difficult. However, it is satisfying to acknowledge the helpful approach of people such as Chandan Mitra, Anil Kaushik, Shobori Ganguly, and a whole host of people besides them, who have over the years encouraged me to write and express myself. My colleagues and acquaintances in different institutions that I worked with or was associated with during this period are gratefully remembered for all that they did to create a supportive environment for me. Amongst them, people at KPMG, TRIFED, FORE, IIT, Delhi, ISTD, IFTDO, and more deserve special mention. In particular, I am delighted to acknowledge my sincere gratitude and appreciation to Dr. B.B.L. Madhukar, Chairman, FORE. I also remember with joy the friendship and supportiveness of person such as Dr. Ebrahim AlDossary of Bahrain and Dr. Helmi Sallam of Egypt, Dr. Patti Philips of USA and Mr. Chenraj Jain from Bangalore. Mr. Ranjan Mohapatra, Chairman, IFTDO Board and Dr. Uddesh Kohli, Secretary General, IFTDO have always been encouraging.

In particular, I would like to express my happiness in dedicating this book to Dr. Ahmed AlBanna, President, Bahrain Society for Human Capital Management. It is an index of his temperament to reach out to quality wherever he sees it.

I am happy to acknowledge the support received from Mr. Nitin Mittal of Concept Publishing Company, whose diligence and professionalism I have always admired. They have an excellent editorial stuff who have rendered good service whenever required, as indeed, my colleagues from FORE, such as Dr. Prakash Gouda, Ms. Sonika Verma, Shri Plavila B. Saji, Shri Mohammed Nadeem, and others. I am grateful for the interest that Shri Vijay Gopal Pande and Prof. Subir Verma have taken in my work. I would also like to acknowledge my gratitude to all the libraries and repertoires that I visited in course of writing this text. They are far too numerous to identify individually. The help of person and holdings there, was immense.

No acknowledgement of this order can be complete without a reference to the many obligations and support efforts extended by my wife, Mrs. Shobhana Gautam. Much that I do is nourished by her patience and diligence. Dr. Tanvi Gautam and Ms. Saumya Gautam have been the best in-house critics of all my efforts, and it has been enriched by their inputs. I am proud and delighted with daughters such as them.

Finally, to my various readers and publishers, a deep acknowledgment of debt for holding my hand and being kind and nurturant to me.

**Vinayshil Gautam**

# Contents

# 1

# Organisational Behaviour

## The Cornerstone of all Relationships

The essence of life is credibility. There is a story from the *Mahabbharata* where there was an announcement in the battle to the effect of "Ashwatthama Hatow" (Ashwatthama is dead). The play on the name Ashwatthama was intended. There was an elephant by the name of Ashwatthama, and the name of the son of Dronacharya was Ashwatthama. Therefore, it was not clear from the announcement who died: was it the man or the elephant? In the middle of the battle, Dronacharya heard this announcement and is reported to have opined, Let Yudhishthira say this.

The essence was simple: Yudhishthira being the 'truthful' man, was expected not to tell lie on this. When evoked by the Dronacharya, Yudhishthira said in a loud voice, "Ashwatthama Hatow: ha Iti, Naro va Kunjaro va naiw Janamee" (Ashwatthama is dead, whether it is a man or an elephant, I can't say). Shri Krishna knew that Yudhishthira was going to say this. To fool Dronacharya, strategically, as soon as Yudhishthira said Narova... he blew his conch. In the sound of the conch, the rest of the sentence of Yudhishthira could not be heard. The negation of Yudhishthira added that he did not know whether Ashwatthama, declared dead, was a man or an elephant. That is another story. Just to complete it, Dronacharya closed his eyes to see with his far sight whether Ashwatthama, his son, had died. Then, Krishna prompted Arjun to shower arrows on Dronacharya to kill him.

The story brings out very effectively, the power of credibility. That the story had its twists and turns is another matter. More to the focus of this write-up, the emphasis on credibility remains an important part of one's personality. Whether lying gets you to hell or purgatory according to Christian philosophy or hell according to Hindu philosophy is a separate point. The truth is that trust and credibility are the foundations of all relationships.

Be it a husband-wife relationship, a father-child relationship, a relationship between friends, and more, the point remains. If there is no trust, there is no relationship. Unfortunately, not enough attention is paid to this aspect of character building in the formative years of a child's life, or, for that matter, even the life of a teenager or pre-adulthood.

No reference is made to the adult stage because it is presumed that personality is fully formed by the time one reaches adulthood. Be that as it may. Like many aspects of life, the value of credibility and trustworthiness is what one inherits from the values of the environment in which one grows up. In the latter years of one's life, credibility becomes progressively more critical and more difficult to acquire (as one walks through the corridors of life), if one does not have it already.

One of the most common responses of a person who does not believe in trustworthiness in a situation where he lies is denial. He responds with an elan: "I said what I did, so what?" This is a tricky question to answer. It is tricky because it strikes at the foundation of relationships. It's trivial, if, in any case, one does not value one's word.

That such an attitude could shake the foundation of any relationship is a matter of grave enough. But many people do not consider it so. The long and short of this is that it is difficult to carry on any social relationships without credibility. As one observes,

"Even the thieves do not like each other, because if they did, the whole 'profession of theft' would be in jeopardy! So be it, but as the actual relationship with one's life with oneself goes, it's difficult to change habits.

Something is missing in the education system where we talk about many things but, also, miss many things. One of the critical things one often misses is the centrality of the practice of credibility or integrity. This should be an outcome of education. To this, no one would disagree. However, it is rarely seen as a deliberate or conscious outcome choice of education.

This matter needs thought. It needs to be thought out because anyone who is not credible can hardly be considered 'educated.' He could be very knowledgeable; he could be very successful, but certainly not educated! It would be akin to attempting to write a play named "Hamlet" without the Prince of Denmark. How can one be educated without being trustworthy?

There is no easy answer to this dilemma. In effect, there are no easy answers to most of the serious dilemmas of life. They are left to be handled by personal choices. Difficult as it may be the matter needs serious attention. Society needs sound individuals with sound values, to have a sound society. This may be a no-choice situation.

November 23, 2023

## Creating a Robust Future for Planet

In modern times, there are certain critical points of change that get flagged. The French Revolution, the American War of Independence, and the Bolshevik Revolution stand out. Each of these defines a critical point in human history. Whether the list of the important events is complete or not is a matter of perception. That it espouses a euro-centric view of human evolution is obvious. There is nothing wrong in such a narrative, except for its incompleteness.

There are substantial parts of the world across which the European races spread. This covered the world from Latin America to Australia. The approach from the African world, Western Asia, South East Asia, East Asia, Australia—all went by default. Australia for example has had human habitation running into multiple centuries, almost from the Palaeolithic age onwards. Yet very little connected narrative is available about Australia before the Europeans arrived there.

The present dominance of the euro-centric view of learning perpetuates this approach. It has been institutionalised through the curriculum of educational institutions. The trouble is deeper, as there is little or no institutional attempt to modify and evolve this perspective to completeness. The current international bodies of the United Nations and more only perpetuate this bias.

Newly emergent nations follow the Euro American pattern of curriculum planning and seek eminence through conformity. Through a serious study of anthropology and an extension of its approach much of this can be countered. Also, studying human evolution from the vantage point of identification and utilisation of energy resources may serve a purpose. The human evolution from using human muscle power for energy purposes to the present status of using atomic energy may help in settling right many of the aberrations in the periodization of human history. India has a narrative, of its present level of evolution, generally taken to be of about 15,000 years of antiquity. Evidence exists of human presence on this subcontinent even prior to those 15,000 years or so. It is just that the history of the times before that is not amenable to the tools used for writing the narrative of what is termed as 'history' in the current values of the academic world.

A gradualist approach would help. A general awareness has to emerge about recognition of the assumptions, governing action of the people whose history is being written. In India, for example, thinking about the so-called other world of spirituality and 'abstraction' is central from the *Rig Vedic* times. This kind of orientation is not present in many parts of the world such as Europe, Americas, etc.

What could work is talking of 'alternate approach' to human evolution and history. This 'alternate approach' need not require a negation of the present attempts of history writing. It would require emphasis on the elements which emphasise a spiritual or a more than material approach to human evolution.

The Indian approach is about the conventional mind that looks at plants, animals, nature and more. A cursory recall of the richas of *Rig Veda* or the writings of Kalidas reveal sensitivity in depiction of plants and animals, which is missing in the writing of the text of those times in European languages.

Steps need to be taken towards understanding the alternate assumptions of human actions in different parts of the globe for real understanding of the evolution of human species, which may set a more realistic direction to compass human development. It will be real, rooted in local traditions and helping to create a robust global future.

December 06, 2022

## Coming to Grips with Human Reality

Life is a complex process. Living through it requires many skills, all of which are perhaps not even listed. The human life span is less than 50 man-years for effective work. This itself would be a generous figure if one factors in the time spent in sleeping, rejuvenation, looking after daily needs, etc. To calculate this for all the human groups inhabiting the planet is a daunting task. People learn what they can in what their circumstances and talent enable. This can only go so far. The time spent in earning a livelihood and 'keeping the body and soul together' is yet to reach the calculation table. The reality of the planet Earth runs into numbers which are demanding to comprehend. Life has existed in some form for billions of years on this planet. It evolved gradually from the living cells to amphibian life to separation of creatures that lived on the land and water. The present version of *Homo Sapiens* has traces, in some parts of the planet going back to 70,000 years or more. In the meanwhile, land movements took place, volcanic eruptions and more shaped the geography of what is today the plant Earth. Pushing of the weaker landmass against a more stable earth structures like the Tibetan plateau caused mountains to rise.

Rivers flowed and river valley cultures, emerged over thousands upon thousands of years.

The history of the world as taught and learnt in curricula around the globe, in the best of cases, do not even cross 10,000 years. Clearly there is so little that we know of how the *Homo Sapiens* arrived to be where they are on this planet. Planet Earth itself is a very small speck in the solar system of a galaxy. Our galaxy is one of many. A galaxy is a gravitationally bound system of stars, stellar remnants, inter stellar gas, dust and dark matter. To comprehend the figure, it is important to recognise that in 2021, data from NASA's space probe was used to revise the previous estimate to roughly 200 billion galaxies. This was only with reference to the observable universe. Most of the galaxies are approximately 3,000 to 3,00,000 light years in diameter. Most galaxies are 'gravitationally organised into groups, clusters and super clusters'. The speed at which the so-called stars of this galaxy system move is even more complex to comprehend. Galaxy of 'Milky Way' includes the solar system with the name describing the galaxy's appearance from Earth.

It is estimated to contain 100 to 400 billion stars and at least that number of planets. The solar system is located at a radius of about 27,000 light years from the galactic centre. The above description would be enough to flag the super microscopic reality of a human existence on this planet. Yet, this super miniscule existence is something 'super' in its own way. It has life and an intelligence which is somewhat evolved. It is important to keep the above in mind to have a sense of proportion about the significance and value of human life. It is important to understand how precious a super tiny life expression can be. It is important to get a sense of proportion and depth to our thinking and endeavours. All measurement is not just a measurement through figures. It is also a measurement by experience. It is also a measurement by potential. There are several narratives available of the powers some evolved *Homo Sapiens* succeeded in achieving. All this needs to be built into our curriculum planning and so-called school, college and beyond education.

October 09, 2021

## Creating Shared Mindsets

There are some common elements of mind and temperament across the human species. This is notwithstanding the history of physical anthropology which has studied all parts of the human body and highlighted differences which arose out of extended use of topography, exposure to climate and even water. The colour of the skin, height differences, shape of the eye are among the more obvious differentiating features between races.

Though all humans have the same organs, their size and intensity of functioning varies, too. For instance, the size of the brain of some groups is open to differentiation. This brings in the role and scope of abstraction in human life. Neurology at the present stage cannot explain all levels of the functioning of brain cells. However, one thing that is clear is that the ability of the brain to think is an important characteristic. Another aspect of life is the different ability among people to experience different emotions. For instance, all human beings at some point of time in life have felt let down. Everyone seeks support and, in moments of emotional upsurge, everyone claims one can do it alone. People who are low on confidence have nagging doubts that they could have done better and so on. The list is endless.

Two things which are almost universal are seeking happiness and wishing for help and support. Human behaviour has more in common than has been generally recognised. This has been reflected in poems, fine art, folklore, proverbs and more. However, this is not seen as a valid input to management theory. That is a loss. Some will recall a famous poem titled 'Three Coins.' The coins became three hearts and each of the hearts was seeking happiness. That may be quite another line of exploration and probably another story.

In the bid to understand what is common to human species and what is differentiated, there are hurdles and there are facilitations. The most important objective remains creating shared mindsets. This is aspired for between lovers, among family members, work groups and, indeed, where the spirit of nationalism is concerned. Herein lies the problem. How is this symbiosis likely? Or how can it be created? Creating symbiosis is at loggerheads with human aspiration for identity. This leads to dominating behaviour. Husband and wife go through this; parents, children and siblings go through this. In the workplace, any group of two or more has individuals genuinely believing s/he/they are capable and ought to dominate. This is the route of much conflict and worse, heartburn. The existentialist thinkers tried to solve this problem. They came up with the theory, "One can do whatever one wants, provided one allows everyone else also to do what everyone else, also, singly wants to do."

Critics of the existentialist theory argue that its logic takes away with the right hand what it gives with the left. One thing which is true is that the act of loving requires responding to needs. These needs can be physical, emotional, creative or, indeed, networking. Some people just like to talk. It does not occur to them that the more you talk the more vulnerable you become, because who knows with what purpose the person is listening or will ultimately use the input? Yet, all this is a part of creating shared mindsets. The core which surfaces is friendship. Each relationship is a special class of friendship. Various thinkers have tried to define it differently. The Freudian approach has used the psychoanalytic thrust while the Marxist approach was rooted in material requirements.

Adler's approach was power play in relationships. All of the above total up to an unfinished story. That is the challenge of behavioural sciences.

March 15, 2021

## Be Resilient in Order to Survive

No matter how one adulates the ability to face ambiguity and no matter how this capability is seen as the fundamental characteristic of an innovative person, the truth is somewhat removed. Whereas dealing with uncertainty raises resilience, like in everything else, one could well say "thus far and no further." Equivocacy ensconced in certain clear-cut parameters works. Ambiguity as a constant and dominant feature of life can be corrosive. The present times are unique in human history because of the almost endless and all-pervading ambiguities the pandemic has generated. One does not know where the virus originated from or the logic of its transmutation. One does not know much about its antidote or how it could strike. It is true that much poetry has been woven around the theme of subtle, calculated or not so calculated ambiguity. That kind of romanticised writing is conspicuous by its absence in the present case.

By a rough estimate, there are about 250 million children worldwide who do not have access to schools. For them, staying away from formal education was a no-choice situation. Of the children who have access to schools, 1.6 billion students across 93 countries have faced disruption due to the outbreak. The sheer magnitude of these numbers cannot be comprehended in terms of the impact of an invisible virus that can be so disruptive.

As of now, there is no certitude regarding where it will resurface and how long the contagion will last. The limitations of science and technology stare human existence in the face. It cannot be a subject to be trifled with. Notwithstanding the gravity of the situation for those who understand and for those who try to understand, there is a general sense of gloom in the environment, if not a sense of tentative trepidation. This is bound to have a long-range effect on frames of reference, the ability to understand and interpret interpersonal dynamics and cope with adversity. The whole world is at different levels of lockdown or reopening.

News has just been filtering in of the Coronavirus having reached a remote tribe in Andaman and Nicobar islands. Of this tribe, only about 50 members survive today. Reportedly, nearly a dozen of them are affected. Obviously, there will be any number of hypotheses of how the virus got there. The more relevant part of the story is the enigmatic one: Where else will it travel and how?

In the meanwhile, the vaccine story has its own drama, thrills, hopes and reality checks. The bare truth is, as of now, nobody knows exactly how far away, in time, is this vaccine. If an election has to be won and if one can do it, one obviously invests public money in buying up stocks of a vaccine, the availability of which is an enigma in itself. The media is busy with claims and counter-claims. One particular country is also reported to have the vaccine and has been ostensibly using it for a month at least.

The Indian version of this pandemic has the typical stamp of the Indian way of problem-solving, as some quarters are known to practise. First the lockdown came in less than four hours. That it followed a voluntary curfew and beating of cymbals and so on, was also characteristic, in parts. Literally, an endless stream of people termed "migrants" started trudging back home. The first response was of disbelief, then bewilderment, then an attempt to contain, cope and finally reconcile to the processes. The hardships of this odyssey of wanting to return to the place of one's origin can only be believed by those who witnessed it. Then came the closing and opening of many kind of borders, picking up the sick from their homes and rushing them to hospitals. And finally, the inevitable clarion call, "Learn to live with COVID-19."

Characteristically, a few notables offered adulation to some nations for successful handling of the virus and how much Indians had to learn from foreigners. That many such places experienced a second and a third spike was forgotten. The crisis has its crests and troughs. India is in the top three affected regions. The politician and the public figure with glib logic now peddle "cautious normalcy" with masks, sanitisers and, of course, social distancing. One would like to believe this would be a panacea.

In the meanwhile, the Government has rolled out an education policy of unprecedented dimensions, complete with slogans of digitisation, online learning, hybrid education, academic credit banks, digital citizenship and, of course, how a 'New India' will be born. Maybe it will! In the meanwhile, the institutions, which will deliver this education policy, are yet to be fashioned. This will be the most critical of all "unlocking" efforts. Resilience would be needed.

August 31, 2020

## A Search for Some Answers

One is living almost cocooned in an equilateral triangle. One arm of the triangle is the terrifying COVID-19 situation, the second arm of the triangle is an economy in a tailspin, with little understanding of how deep the dive is going to be or how it can be brought under control. The third arm of the triangle is made of the travails and trials of an ordinary life. The Covid age—for want of a better phrase—that the world is currently passing through, is known to have just as much of an impact on the psyche and lifestyles of people as the Coronavirus has on the human body. How long can one survive in a bottomless pit of anxiety is a question to which there can be no definitive answers. Even history is silent on this very vital issue of human endurance.

One wonders if people are actually suffering more from being infected by the virus or from almost driving themselves over the edge by the fear of being infected by COVID-19. The governance process itself seems to be in a trial and error mode with a hands-on situation. A few weeks ago, a locality of a major district of an important State was claimed to have no place in the listing of containment zones issued by the District Commissioner's Office. Yet, when the police department was contacted, they claimed it was still in the containment zone. Similarly, a Chief Minister asked the people to come out in large numbers and promote the economy. He said the weekly bazaars and hotels would open and much, much more lay ahead. The Lieutenant-Governor negated the instruction and the hapless citizens struggled to understand what the content of Unlock 3.0 was.

There are millions of questions about the virus that remain unanswered. To what extent is surface transmission of the disease real? Do the envelopes received in the mail pose a risk? One former director of a major national medical institute says he keeps the mail and packages in the sun, for a while, before opening them. He didn't have an answer on what to do when it rains. A doctor from England advised the use of gloves while opening envelopes received through an agency, or at least sanitising the hands after opening the mail. However, the World Health Organisation (WHO), in an advisory says that it is safe to receive a package from any area where COVID-19 has been reported. So, who does one believe in a situation like this?

Then there is the case of newspapers. Epidemiologists say newspapers are safe while others have their doubts. It is difficult to identify which is an authoritative source of information in so many aspects of the so-called Covid-era. And then, what happens to currency notes? The packaging of the kitchen ingredients which any household would need? Or the milk packets brought from the dairy?

As noted above, one side of the triangle is that of one being currently caught up in the actual experience of acquiring the Coronavirus infection. The other side of the triangle is the kind of collateral experience when trying to live a normal life through a pandemic.

Even if one forgets about the vaccines, the high and mighty of the medical profession are still not unanimous on the nature, extent and the reality of the actual infection.

If one is not clear there, one can only keep washing hands, sanitising surfaces, not go out of the house beyond a certain point and hope for the best. Therein comes the third arm of the triangle. The ways of earning, while staying at home, (the ordinary life) are limited by class and profession. The circulation of the service class is so large and unstructured that contact tracing can sometimes become like trying to put together a ten thousand-piece puzzle.

Add to it the travails of real life. The other realities don't disappear because the Covid-era is in focus. Where does one find a safe dentist? In the rainy season one will contract cold because of change in weather. How does one find out whether it is the first stage of the Coronavirus or an overheated imagination? One of the estimates says that over 16 lakh Indians have fallen ill in the last three months of the pandemic from the Coronavirus. Is there any figure available of how many people fell ill from diseases other than the Coronavirus, in the same period?

During the same period, the number of unemployed rose by 10 crore. Even milk registered a lower availability by 30 per cent. One of the news channels ran a random survey, where 11 per cent of those surveyed were found to be suffering from mild depression and another six per cent from depression. Reportedly, in a Parliamentary Committee proceeding, there has been reference to an addition of 12 crore to the number of people who have, further, sunk below the poverty line. The auto sector has registered loss of jobs to the tune of 30 per cent and the retail sector up to 60 per cent.

More statistics can be quoted. The relevant part is at least to ask whether the Coronavirus is the bigger malaise or the collateral damage done by it? For a solution in either case, a scientific method and its comprehensiveness will be the acid test.

August 03, 2020

## Many Lessons to be Learnt Yet

There is one widely accepted cause for an avoidable personal disaster. It is rooted in the simple belief that "it cannot happen to me." The propensity of drivers to take undue risks on the road is also rooted in the same belief. There are enough studies on accidents and in traumatology which establish this fact.

It is a similar story where contagiously-transmitted disease is concerned and HIV/AIDS is a classic example of this. People believe that it will happen to someone else, somewhere else and not to them. They manage to convince themselves that a brief indulgence cannot lead to such disastrous consequences. But, as they discover to their peril later, this is not always the case and they have to pay a heavy price for negligence.

An obvious one next in the list is COVID-19. A quick visit to/from somebody one wanted to see surely can be undertaken without fear of infection. We do not want to be accused of overreacting so we would rather take our chances. Such things can happen, do happen and several people do escape unscathed. But lightning is also known to strike when least expected.

The news of an employee in a bank contracting the dreaded disease has a salutary effect. That branch itself may have to be shut for a week/fortnight. When one hears the news, it has a disconcerting and sobering effect. But as time passes, the memories fade and the impact dims. Life goes back to normal and the inevitable rationalisation sets in: How long can one take precautions? Some day the workers/domestic helpers will have to be let in? If it has to happen, it will happen and so on.

Else the logic which Duryodhana used on Karna to get him to use that "invincible" arrow on Ghatotkach sets in. Karna was reluctant to use that unique arrow as he had saved it up to kill Arjun. However, Duryodhana is reported to have argued, "That day may never come if Ghatotkach is not killed today. Ghatotkach is going to wipe all of us out." Karna yielded to Duryodhana's logic, Ghatotkach was killed and Krishna had the last laugh as he once again saved Arjun from death.

The use of illogical reasoning to appear rational is a common human failing. It comes out very strongly in times of emotional exhaustion, social tiredness and most of all an exasperated mindset. Unfortunately, there is very little in our learning strategies which gives us the antidote for such failings.

The present phase of the passage of COVID-19 on this planet has seen different types of popular and common practices grow. More Zoom meetings have happened in the last 90 days than in perhaps any other comparable time frame. There has been more talk of online education in the last several weeks than has been ever before in much larger units of time.

Working from home, once considered an innovative fringe in organisational management, has now almost become a routine and accepted practice. The human mind and human nature are allergic to "inactivity", hence a location for work has to be found, even if it means disrupting the work-life balance and the sanctity of home. Man is described as a social animal and being gregarious is a human trait. So much so that solitude is taken as one of the biggest forms of punishment. Stretched over a period of time and the subject himself being rendered helpless in responding or exercising a choice about solitude, can be a devastating experience. People in such situations have been known to suffer psychiatric disorders. Social distancing and the lockdown necessitated by the pandemic has locked us up in our individual cages and we have become wary of each other.

There is so much talk of the "new normal", "nature taking its revenge" and the "costs of indulgences" and more. This is an understandable line of thinking as a sense of guilt at one's indiscretions feeds such thoughts. The environmentalists are gleeful and are boasting how they saw it all coming. They are right in saying so and this pontification has to be permitted and learnt from. We would not have been in this mess if we had listened to their wise counsel earlier. The fact of the matter is that with all the forwards masquerading as "philosophy" and "knowledge" on social media, there is no attempt to give content and form to this marketplace philosophy, for the making of better and wiser human beings.

The next generation of pre-teens, when they graduate to teenage and more, may well be behaving just like or worse than their parents or ancestors did at that age or phase of life. This is a loss.

The global tragedy of the pandemic has the potential to recast learning processes. A universe where mature consideration supersedes trivial indulgences; where a due consideration of risks can result in the application of brakes before our actions unleash punishment too severe to capture in words.

If the pandemic can create learning formulations for a more sober, thinking and sensitive human being, capable of self-renewal, then truly this period of agony would be a blessing for the human race. Humanity would have evolved to its next stage of growth.

June 08, 2020

## Endless Protests and their Fallout

There's a feeling of disquiet among segments of the cross-section of a news-aware people across the country. They consume news either in print or television, which is dominated by private players. This has led to a situation where financiers view their broadcasting channel to be a surrogate of their own political, social and economic inclinations. This is a fact of life that is seldom flagged. By and large, the so-called public is unaware of the political slant of the promoters and protectors of the medium who carry the news. Hence, the distinction between facts, comments and commentary often becomes dubious.

Comments parade as facts and commentary often becomes the explanation thereof. This makes the job of the reader—to understand what is actually happening—even more complex. The result is that rabble-rousing often gets mistaken for a vibrant democracy.

The current atmosphere of agitations for and against an issue has raised some fundamental questions. One of them is: How significant are street protests as a counterfoil of a dominant majority of parliamentarians, who in their wisdom, took a decision on a given topic? It is generally assumed that given the total voting population of the country, a parliamentarian represents approximately 16 to 17 lakh voters. No single demonstration ever approximates that number. What makes a demonstration great is the media coverage it receives and how for hours, certain shots can be repeated over and over again. That some people get animated and get prone to posture in an excitable manner is no secret.

Thus, it is that process give a slant to a situation represented by a selection of facts. Repetition of this approach across more than one forum serves as a drumming up. It goes far beyond the wildest dreams of the sponsors of that limited agitation on the crossroads.

Brigades of two types of professionals then descend upon the location. On January 23, an aspiring leader-to-be descended with a mike on the crowd of protesters in Shaheen Bagh to encourage them. He promised that he would create 500 or better still, 5,000 more Shaheen Baghs across the country. The same day, while delivering a memorial lecture, a now retired VVVIP lauded the very act of protest as something very encouraging.

Whether it is encouraging or not is another matter. The bald truth remains that it raised several unanswered questions. For instance, protest is a desirable process in a democracy but the concurrent question is: What form should it take? How should the theme be chosen? What is the mode of protest? Is it disrupting the life of an average citizen, who is interested in nothing more than leading a normal, quiet and ordinary life? The questions are numerous but answers are few. At the end of the day, any protest that has to last beyond a small fraction of sustainable time needs the support of sponsors. Somebody has to promote it and that person would not do so without a vested interest.

Across world history, from Paris Commune to Bolshevik Revolution, lessons are easy to identify. The Paris Commune collapsed when organised sponsorship withdrew. Perhaps, there would have been no Bolshevik Revolution if the Germans had not smuggled Lennon into Czarist Russia. In such circumstances, serenading protest for the sake it, especially by the young and distinguished professionals, who have no track record of having participated in a significant populist protest movement, can only be pandering to the gallery. Such episodes cannot be overlooked because they tend to feed upon themselves, get drummed up and projected. The ultimate spread effect cannot be a gain to anyone or any process. There are innumerable cases where protest movements have fizzled out because of the absence of a sustainable agenda. That, too, would be a tragedy because protests or any process should be an input to be more robust. The danger of throwing the baby in the bath water is too risky to sustain or even consider. It would have made sense if some leader of standing, credibility and past records made a headline by pointing out how protests can get out of hand.

Besides, there are ripple effects, too. Reports have it that a lady enumerator of a certain, totally a political social intervention, while dealing with a community of people of her own faith in Kota, was summoned back to the colony after she collected data of names and addresses. She was threatened not to use them. This kind of contagion is highly infectious. A little later, hundreds of miles away from Kota, a programme run in the aid of internet awareness by Google India and Tata Trust got into foul weather. The reason was that enumerators were asking for the names and addresses of the trainees. The upshot was that the programme, at the end of December 2019, was halted in all the five districts of West Bengal because the trainers faced trouble. Is this right?

January 27, 2020

## Systematic Destruction

The current social environment in India has some distinguishing characteristics. It is a high decibel environment. Whether it is the television chat show or the public opinion leaders in action, the pitch is high, the language is sharp and moderation is conspicuous by its absence. Tilting at each other using extreme expletives and incoherent logic seems to be the rule of the day. This cannot be a sensible way of either individual of social discourse.

When accusations fly sharp, logic is the first casualty. So the subject or the topic becomes irrelevant and aggression becomes paramount. It is becoming commonplace with some to say that our institutions are under attack. The question automatically arises: From which quarter?

Consider the case of the Supreme Court, which is the ultimate custodian of collective morality. Not so long ago the Chief Justice of India (CJI) was being threatened with impeachment. This is a grave matter on more than one score. Since 1947, there has never been a case where there was a threat held out of impeaching any constitutional authority. Then came the judgement over the number of days that would be granted for voting in the Karnataka Assembly to prove one's majority. The Supreme Court judge, under the chairmanship of the then CJI, decided to close the matter by reducing the number of days given by the Governor of Karnataka to prove majority to 48 hours. The rest is history.

The purpose of these remarks is not to comment on the judgement of the Governor or the wisdom of the Supreme Court bench. The focus of this narrative is merely to highlight the strangely quiet way in which, after this judgement, the proponents of the impeachment of the Supreme Court Chief Justice in the Rajya Sabha allowed the matter to lapse. To the layman, there are only two options in drawing a conclusion. One is that the proponents of the impeachment had a sudden change of heart and the overlap of the timing with the vote of confidence in the Karnataka Vidhan Sabha was a coincidence. The second option is that the movement for impeachment was essentially a political act aimed at warning the Chief Justice to 'behave himself' as seen by some. Once the key player read the message that was delivered, the select Opposition did not find it necessary to push through their demands. It stretches the imagination to talk of the first option at face value. The protagonists of the impeachment move are sharp people with good legal mind and great ability at marshalling a given argument. They acted deliberately and buried the hatchet, when the Chief Justice was interpreted as serving their purpose. If the latter was the case, as seems likely, the damage done to the institution of justice is something to ponder about. If this was an isolated case, not too much need be made of it beyond a point.

However, the story goes on. The statutes have it that the Director of CBI will be appointed on the recommendation of the Prime Minister, Chief justice of India and the leader of the biggest Opposition party in the Lok Sabha. Nearly two years ago, Alok Verma was appointed as the Director. The leader of the biggest Opposition party at that point of time put in a note of dissent. Around 23 months later when circumstances led to the consideration of removing him, the matter came up for discussion to the same committee. The committee deemed it desirable that the serving director should quit. The same person in the committee, who had given a note of dissent at the time of the appointment, said Verma should not be sent away. In this case, too, two possibilities are there. First, the similarity in two notes of dissent is coincidental. Second, the notes of dissents were dissent for the sake of dissent. It is for anyone to judge what this kind of behaviour indicates.

Several other examples can be cited but this collective indication of damage to institutions can't do anyone any good. Never the less juggernaut rolls on. The Prime Minister of the country has been called a 'chor' more than once by the president of a major national party. It has been repeated over and over again. If indeed the Prime Minister is a *chor*, then he should have been proceeded against in Parliament. Name-calling may be yet another novel way of strengthening the institution devised by this particular person but that is not how public institutions are normally built. In this case, the options of interpretation-coincidence or otherwise, raised in other two instances above, are not available. Alas, the apparent observation seems to be: There is more to map on how institutions get destroyed.

January 21, 2019

## Consolidating the Indian Narrative

There are a few national endeavours that are shared, as closely, by billion plus Indian citizens, as elections. The country is almost continually discussing or organising elections in some part or the other all around the year. The print media contributes to creating these images and the electronic media takes it far afield. After both lose steam, folk statements and word of mouth take over. But the dominant influencer group across Kashmir to Kanyakumari and Kutch to Kamrup is clearly the political class. They fly, use the rail or other means of transport or depute their foot soldiers.

Over a period of time, many conglomerates of the political class got fragmented and lost their ideology to demagoguery or head count. Obviously, there are exceptions but the bulk, which constitutes the exception, is clearly receding. In the pre-Independent days, predominantly, the literate and the well-educated led populist movements.

Be it Subhash Chandra Bose, Mohandas Karamchand Gandhi, Jawaharlal Nehru, Bhimrao Ambedkar—all had some social connection and education abroad. Foreign travel and education was much more of a rich man's indulgence then than it is now. That a lot of them learnt their basic lessons in nationalism after a social snub during the sojourn abroad, is another matter.

When they came back to India—Bose after getting into the Indian Civil Service, Gandhi after his mixed experiments in South Africa, and Nehru after his lack luster performance in Harrow and Cambridge—all of them adopted different shades of nationalism. One must hasten to add that this narration of facts is not rooted in irreverence but in an attempt to push the boundaries of understanding closer to the real world and indeed, the making of the modern Indian leader. The full range and spectrum of style and intellectual anchorage was under heavy foreign shadow.

Landing in India and being invited to lead the indigo struggle in Champaran saw Gandhi shedding his barrister's apparel for the trademark *dhoti* and occasional *kurta*, which gradually gave way to *chaadar*. Mohammed Ali Jinnah made sure his English conditioning showed and pitched himself as the opposite of Gandhi. In-between there came a series of nationalist leaders who, though outstanding, never actually made to the grades of Jinnah, Gandhi, Nehru and others who developed their intellectual orientations abroad. In this would be a number of persons, such as Rajendra Prasad, Vallabhbhai Patel, Sheikh Abdullah, Periyar Ramaswamy Naicker, among others. The scene of the narrative, however, continued to be British India.

There is no regular history available of Arunachal Pradesh, Mizoram, and Nagaland even today. Being far-flung cannot be an explanation. This is equally true even for the interior lands of Nizam in the then Hyderabad State. Their chronicling was left to the tender mercies of Verrier Elwin, Christoph von Fürer-Haimendorf and a host of other anthropologists. Subsequently, attempts were made to make the British the villains of the piece and heroes out of those in the tribal population who resisted.

The happier territories of Travancore—Cochin, Baroda, Patiala, Cooch Behar, not to overlook some principalities of Odisha—were clearly not a part of the social discourse or institutional curriculum. Even Jammu & Kashmir had its own cocoon and no 'national leader' bothered too much about the territories of either Gulab Singh or Hari Singh.

Educated in Aligarh, Sheikh Abdullah travelled to Srinagar to begin his career as a school teacher. He tried to be on the right side of the Maharaja by wanting the audience to celebrate the birth of his son. Not getting the welcome he hoped for, he walked the way which led to the setting up of the National Conference.

To put it simply, to be recognised as a top ranking leader of India, one needed Western connect and recognition by British rulers. Some mass base helped in this direction.

Gandhi was unique in attempting a first-hand familiarity of the country by travelling across the Indian railways network. Nehru never quite understood Dravidian politics or Malayalee tapestry of cultural patterns. However, supported by Gandhi, he became the 'numero uno'.

By this token, the core task of consolidating a political nation fell to the leadership of post-50s. In this adult suffrage, elections to Parliament and Assemblies had an important role. Unfortunately, local self-Governments went by default for a long time.

Thus, it is the political class far more than any other class that holds the key to multiple dialogues and strengthening of political identity. There needs to be a serious movement to educate, orient and liberate the political class of its baggage. Simply assuming that good sense will prevail and nationalism is a part of everyone's DNA may not suffice.

An approach of advocacy and dissemination of ideals of acknowledged heroes of ideas and action, from all periods of Indian history, all parts of India, needs to be adopted country-wide. Consolidating the Indian narrative is too serious a theme to be left to randomness of political groupings and a few articulate and mass savvy politicians.

July 23, 2018

## Quintessence and the Role of DNA

Whether we like it or not, we are all significantly ethos driven. We are born with a genetic code which carries selections from the DNA of 16 people, eight from our father's side and eight from our mother's side. The DNA components of one's personality has been well researched and established. In many parts of India with many communities, it is practiced as the *pind-daan* ritual as an ode to immediate generations of ancestors.

In all cases, four generations of ancestors on both the mother's side and the father's side are remembered. This is something scientific and many appreciate it as a purposeful gesture.

However, the processes of selection from the DNA is not quite clearly mapped or understood. For example, if somebody in the fourth generation of ancestry was colour-blind, somebody among the lineal successors may be born colour-blind. This symptom can be genetic. Yet, we cannot say which generation will inherit colour-blindness or if at all. Hence, while we know something is there, we are not quite sure of either its contents or coordinates.

'Inheritance' is an equally significant element in understanding the architecture of 'ethoses'. In certain ways, it can be tempered by the genetic code and certain other factors. The other factors include the physical and psychological state of biological mother. Early childhood impressions gathered through the eyes or other sensory organs such as the ear (sound), tongue (taste) etc. can play a role in defining the ethos which the individual operates with.

As the Homo sapien grows up from the infant stage his/her ethos can also be impacted by the early socialisation process of the person. The individual's values to some extent get determined by what one witnesses, what one perceives as an encouragement in getting a positive feedback or discouragement with a negative feedback. There is enough empirical evidence to prove that wolf children never have the consciousness of gender the way a human child has. Thus it is, that ethos is central to the making of an individual.

The same can be true of communities. The way parts of the *Jaat* community behaves is clearly so distinct from, say the behaviour of a specific Naga tribe. Even religion is not a leveler in an absolute sense. The difference between a Ramgarhia Sikh and a non-Ramgarhia Sikh is significant enough to give a level of comfort or discomfort, say in a marriage, even amongst communities of the same religion. A Syed Nazibuttarfain Muslim is clearly distinct from an Ansari Muslim. Forget the larger distinction between a *Shia* and a *Sunni*. A hierarchical structure of ritual acceptability is there in many religious communities.

In such an environment, the issue of national ethos is as complex, sociologically as perhaps any of the other sociological complexities. Irrespective, there is such a thing as a national ethos. Man-woman relationship of a British couple is not necessarily of the same ethos, as the man-woman relationship in Koeri community. This is not to a fault but to recognise that there are defining characteristics and identifiable behaviour patterns of communities.

An Indian, irrespective of caste, religion, community through a normal law of averages, does talk with ease, of fate as an explanation of his lives experiences. Referring to *kismat* or *bhagya* or pointing to the forehead to highlight the principle of pre-destination is quite common in India. This does not happen in a similar fashion, say in a Teutonic community. This is ethos. Understanding its fundaments contribute to nurturing realistic nationalism.

Of course, the anthem, the flag, other symbols and forms help. What strengthens a national identity is the recognition of the binding factors which put the group together. It helps to reach a consensus and make it a part of the narrative of nation building.

This can be done empirically. The sooner it is done to the satisfaction of a broad number of the citizenry, the more robust would be the feeling of nationalism.

This need not necessarily make one community superior or another inferior. It only helps to read the writing on the wall and spell out the obvious, to achieve the goal of nationalism in a more realistic manner.

May 22, 2017

## Too Many Opinions, Not Enough Facts

The quality of public discourse has been steadily declining and needs to be arrested. The quality of enquiry, the quality of interrogation, interpretation of the data which normally precedes discussion, is poor.

One is not referring to the number of public denigrators of Prime Minister Narendra Modi who have now turned vocal adulators. One is not even talking of the new found enthusiasm of media personnel who now see him in a 'sunny' mode.

Some persons 'discovered' within days of Mr. Modi assuming power that the Prime Minister is going to put India back on track. Books under print were re-labeled and re-packaged. 'Rewards' are yet to come! Headings and sub-headings touched fresh depths. Some magazines even captioned stories as: "Modi embraces poor". But they were only trying to make a living. They can be forgiven.

The cause for concern is much deeper. In the last two years, public discourse has progressively moved from name calling to heckling.

As public life stands today, there really are no major controversies. Hence, controversies are being created. Public bashing, duly aided and abetted by untalented anchors, continues. The examples are too many to critique but some reflections on the quality of enquiry and the quality of marshalling of argument is essential.

To begin with, let us take the Rashtriya Swayamsevak Sangh. For several people in the country anything which originates from the RSS is wrong and has to be debunked. Hence, the industry of RSS baiters is feverishly working over time.

One may or may not agree with the RSS on all the solutions that it proposes but then again, is there any agency with which everybody agrees? What is beyond doubt is that the RSS is devoted to the Indian nation and has a stake in how to work for the country's welfare.

The organisation has the right to project its solutions, within the constitutional framework, just as much as anyone else. What is regrettable is the uncouth argumentation of adversaries that is presented without due research.

Consider the controversy over the word 'Hindu'. There is no concept of the Hindu in any of the ancient Indian texts. Those who are now labeled 'Hindu' mostly believe that they belong to the *Sanatana Dharma*. *Sanatana* means eternal. Unlike many other religions, *Sanatanis* do not believe in a prophet, in that sense of the word. It is their way of communion with the divine consciousness. They are entitled to it, just as anyone else is entitled to their route to 'godhood'.

The point to be made, however, is different. Those who have studied the past of this country, not necessarily just professional historians, are aware that the word 'Hindu' came into the lexicon after the Greek learnt of the Sindhu river, which is know as the Indus to the anglicised.

Facts, however, show that phonetically the sound 'S' does not exist in the Greek alphabet. The Greeks cannot pronounce 'S'. So wherever there is the 'S' sound, the Greek pronunciation converts it to a 'H' sound.

When the Greeks learnt of the Sindhu (Indus) river, they referred to it as the 'Hindu' river, much in the same way as the Sindhu river became Indus to the other Europeans.

In their imperial quest, when the Greeks from Macedonia marched through the Khyber and the Bolan passes, they found it convenient to refer to all those who lived across the Sindhu (Hindu) river as Hindus. Thus, a new word was added to the vocabulary.

To the many hoards of foreigners who travelled through the region, this trend caught on and those who lived beyond the Sindhu River were labeled Hindus. The land where such people lived became Hindustan or, literally, the land of the Hindu.

Positions can be taken on any debate through predilection and prejudices. All one is pleading, here, is for an informed discussion.

As far as the argument of the Congress spokesperson that the Constitution of India talks of a Bharat, not a Hind, there is little to say. Perhaps he should condemn the first Prime Minister of this country for having given the slogan of Jai Hind from the ramparts of the Red Fort. Jawaharlal Nehru did not say 'Jai Bharat'. It's the Congress that launched a movement to correct this aberration.

September 05, 2014

## Beyond the Divisive, Identity Politics

The 16th Lok Sabha is unlike any preceding Lok Sabha, in many ways, small and big. That however, is another story. The important thing is that the way of looking at the Lok Sabha certainly seems to be in the need for some change.

It is not going to come easy because the mental constructs of analysis have been ingrained over decades of practice. No easy answers are possible. A word in explanation will help focus on the argument.

It is natural to look at the composition of the Lok Sabha or even the Union Cabinet and ask whether there is anyone from one's own sub-caste, caste, religion, region or State.

However, everything which is natural and understandable does not necessarily become the right, suo motu. The manner in which the issues are formulated and debated also go a long in making for positivism.

The trouble is further compounded when identity politics is carried by the hot air balloon of prejudices and popular rhetoric. In other words, when prejudices for or against a situation, aided by the gift of the gab, raise decibels of noise which are not only capable of drowning other voices but also create a false impression of huge base, then the danger and the damage are compounded.

It also prevents the birth and growth of alternate paradigms, which may help the growth of a more robust nation. For decades, the Congress practiced tokenism in sensitive matters of religion, caste and more. Questions such as, how many minorities are in the Cabinet, or how may followers of religion X, Y and Z are in the Cabinet, or, what is the caste equation in the Cabinet have no place. And similar investigations of this type are essentially divisive constructs, even if drummed up in the name of inclusiveness.

The matter doesn't end there. Banal divisive constructs, carried by prejudiced rhetoric, becomes more subtle and less pertinent depending upon whose cause the commentator wishes to serve.

UPA 2 had no Minister from Bihar. It didn't seem to bother anyone, not even the Biharis. Of the two Bihar MPs who were popularly elected, one was installed as the Speaker of the lok Sabha and the other was packed off as a Governor. Somebody could have been included from the Rajya Sabha from Bihar in the Union Cabinet but it didn't happen.

Now, suddenly with the new BJP-led NDA Government coming to power, commentary is flourishing on who has not been included and who should have been included in the Modi administration.

If no minister from a particular State has made it to the Cabinet, and that is considered important, there are ways of handling it in a democratic system. Similarly, to keep asking how many minorities are there or what is the nature of the regional composition, queers the pitch of public discourse.

It cannot be a flaw to have a view at Cabinet formation which transcends these stereotypes.

The new Prime Minister, like all Prime Ministers, has his hands full with contentious issues, problems and the realities of a power game. But surely, if he attempts to pole vault through all this in his own style, and gets lampooned in the process, then others have a question to answer.

The question is of responding to perennial demands for change; exasperation with the banalities of the prevailing system and yet when faced with the option of moving things forward, having a compulsive urge to going back to business as usual.

Whether one likes Mr. Modi or not, the issues at hand are bigger than any individual or even a collection of individuals. The threatening inefficiencies of the banking system, the atmospherics of a tehsil office where chaos is tolerated like the inevitable sweat; the quasi trained drivers at the wheels of heavy vehicles tearing down the road, may not get the headlines like statements on Article 370, but the corrosiveness is huge and affects everyone across caste, creed, religion and region.

We have put up with much of this with incredible inanity and with patience that cannot be explained. We now have an option to set things right. It is the future of all of us, which stands at a crossroads. We owe ourselves a chance.

May 30, 2014

## A New World Order is Now Emerging

There are few phases in human evolution where change is not just symbolic but seminal. To capture the first is easy because it involves tokenism and has external indicators. To understand the second is central to all acts of *Homo sapiens*. This is because, if that phase is not consciously worked upon, it passes unnoticed and a great opportunity is lost.

The times that we live in are essentially of the second variety. It's not just the hauling down of one flag and hoisting of another. A new global order, both at micro and macro levels, is in the making. The contours seem to be shifting and the contents are not always clear. The patterns are variegated and difficult to map. This is happening with reference to inter-generational relationships, the nature of business, the pattern of financial transactions, frameworks of governance, gender relationships, currency usage, territorial delineation, styles of living, modes of communication, digitisation of time, search for identity, leadership patterns, logic of aggregation.

The Indian scene is especially complex. No where in the world do so many centuries co-exist together as they do in India. From pre-historic modes of production to the space age in its bloom, can all be found in Bharat. Change in such an environment, therefore, means a myriad things to myriads of people. Some have a level of comfort with status quo, others want to move from one level to the other.

No individual has an isolated life. What is required in the act of living is to go along with others. This involves recognising that we need each other and must adapt our aspirations with those with whom one has to lead shared lives. The art lies in knowing with whom one has to share one's life and for how long.

These questions are not easy to answer. They are even more difficult to operationalise. Such a situation is contributing to a almost universal sense of restlessness and a state of anxiety in recognising the inevitability of the present. We have not even begun to address these questions because we have not formulated them with clarity.

Running an organisation in such a context is an act of courage, embedded in unpredictable outcomes. The organisational man and organisational theorist grapple with this reality to understand how many organisations fail while others sail along and few succeed.

A new world view is emerging. Not so long ago, elections were fought on the merits and demerits of an ideology. Today, an election can be won on a projected humility of "we are simple people" or some notion of corruption or problems of daily living. Oversimplification seems to sell.

A little over a decade ago, a political party of this country went through a debate on what works better—ideology or strategy. For a time it seemed that ideology mattered only to a few. A number of the participants were happy to align with strategy. It enabled wielding of power.

It is not clear if that debate holds true today. The last 20 years of national evolution have shown that even the basic tenants of constitutions are evoked selectively as per political exigencies and with almost little or no serious application or adherence to the collective principles. The Constitution talks of a sovereign, democratic, socialist and secular republic. Even parties whose name contains the concept of socialism do not evoke it anymore!

The contradictions are many, the confusions are large. The act of fumbling along cannot be rarified into a principle. The time has come for clarity in everything. It should begin in the act of governance. The clutter needs to be cleared.

January 10, 2014

## Era of Gloom and Doom is Upon Us

To say that there is a general sense of gloom in the environment, is to state the obvious. What is amazing is how life continues to be as usual for the high and mighty of the land. The high-end restaurants continue to run packed, the airlines are full of business-class passengers, the roads are clogged with expensive cars and the political elite with, some notable exceptions, continues to be inaccessible, aloof as if to say that such things keep happening.

The public domain is full of tokenism. There is an air of nonchalance. Official and classified files tend to disappear and when an occasional catch is made, alibis are available more easily than ever before. If there is a police encounter, it is fake; if there is a grisly act at the border, there are strenuous efforts to underplay it. Matters of rape and murder do not any longer make shrieking headlines. The response is a shrug or reconciliatory stoicism.

The attraction for Western degrees remains unabated. Even for an academic to be recognised in the country, he must have foreign publications and foreign jaunts to his credit. How a nation as talented as Bharat and as populous as it is, has come to such straits is inexplicable!

There was a time when the country had a moral reference point—be it in Mohandas Karamchand Gandhi, Vinoba Bhave or Jayaprakash Narayan. But that list has almost disappeared. Once in a while, one hears a name like Anna Hazare. His description by the serving Minister for Information and Broadcasting over a year ago, as the spokesperson of the ruling elite, would be in many memories. Statements like that are not made off the cuff or as an emotional outburst. They are carefully rehearsed and deliberately mouthed. The Anna Hazare movement finally split, not without some help from quarters who did not wish for it to be around.

Baba Ramdev's movement, apart from the episode wherein state forces descended with full might on unsuspecting protesters in the dark of the night, is an unprecedented event in the annals of history. Yet, there was applause in some quarters for the 'firm action' taken.

The citations can be large, the examples numerous, and they can be found in all parts of the country. The reason is simple: There are elites in all parts of the country, they are entrenched, they are powerful and there is nothing random about their behaviour. The battle is no longer for the minds but for the ability to get away with anything.

If the Comptroller and Auditor-General raises questions, he is accused of crossing his constitutional mandate. If those without a voice take to the street, it is desecration of parliamentary democracy. If there is a hue and cry about poisoned mid-day meals, it is suggested that the resultant deaths were part of a political conspiracy. If somebody is caught in the act of corruption, it is a frame-up. The skill to spread confusion has become a fine art. Corruption has been so professionalised, that the corrupt may as well run degree and certificate courses.

It is possible philosophically to argue that this too shall pass but then so will generations. In an era where ineptness raises no hackles and efficiency seems to be the choice of a miniscule minority, it is not surprising that the lack of capability and concern is an enduring reality. Electrocution from naked wires in public places or accidents by untrained drivers is merely the more dramatic expressions of the lack of concern for capability and competency.

In an era where jobs and skills stand disconnected, and new wrongs are being institutionalised to right the old ones, optimism can only be a compulsion. One can only hope that these testing times, of which most of us are simultaneously victims and perpetrators, will come to pass as a generational tragedy.

August 23, 2013

## Some Realisations of Institutional Efficiency

Institutional building can be a tricky affair. Much depends on the type of institution, the age of the institution, the extent of formalisation of the system, the processes that has taken place in the institution, the environment in which the institution is embedded, and above all, the kind of periodic reviews the institution has undergone. This list can be added to, and it is not necessary to attempt to be exhaustive.

The truth is that many people in a large number of institutions believe that the system plays favourites, makes demands, and does not adequately recognise the need for competitive compensation. Many employees also believe that they need to be on the right side of the power to be to get what they need, or else the system, doesn't always give them what is due. In other words, the process of institutionalisation leaves much to be desired. This leaves the overall atmosphere of any institution somewhat less than optimally happy.

Indeed, none of the statements made in the earlier paragraphs can be universally true, but even if they were true to some people for some time, enough damage has been done, to the institutions concerned.

The quest has always been to find the ideal, while realising that much of it is feasible with difficulty. Nevertheless, hitting the bull's eye remains the objective. This text is devoted to looking at some of the issues which can mitigate some of the failings in the efficient and fair running of institutions and what can be done to raise the overall quantum of satisfaction with the state of affairs. The attempt is also to be realistic and look at the feasibility of the aspiration to have "perfect institutions."

One of the biggest failings of institutional efficiency is the failure to realise that all institutions need systems and procedures that are clear, actionable, and futuristic. There cannot be a situation where the powerful are allowed to get away with what they want from the system without some accountability. In fact, any institution of this variety is bound to come to grief sooner than later. Ultimately, what will make an institution run is the power of its inner members to keep the system going and operational. This could be broadly termed as "institutional culture." The basic truth is that those who allow the powerful to take advantage of the institutional system are as responsible for the aberrations as much as the ones who take advantage of the institutional resources.

It is popularly believed that those who take financial advantage of the institution or its resources are the ones who are really guilty. This may be partially true, but the truth has other components. Any institution which has individuals without some kind of judgement or concern about the use of institutional resources and decision-making develops its own antithesis, which may manifest itself in dissent, loose talk, and worse. Gradually, the institutional capacity to handle the weaknesses, likes, and passion for power emerge. Mutual competitiveness and fault-finding become the hallmarks, and what is popularly referred to as institutional politics emerges.

July 01, 2023

## Changing for Success

Change is a natural process. It is a part of life. Even the inanimate without life undergo change. The difference between the change in a live entity and a non-life entity is simple. A life entity has some extent of choice in the direction of change. Choices, amongst other things, will be exercised in terms of the nourishment it takes, the waste it throws out of its body and the way it copes with the impact of the environment. A non-life entity has no such directional change. It is under the effect of a simple physical and chemical process.

Contemporary lives across the planet have been changing through the last nearly two years, periodically. In effect it has meant significant changes in the known ways of life.

The media and indeed the 'word'—whether written or oral—has tried to capture it, the best it can. The viewership of the electronic channels has exponentially increased. The printed word has not raked in the same kind of experience. Anxiety and the ability to cope with change and stress has become a touch stone.

Effectiveness lies in the capacity to cope with anxiety. Coping with anxiety is easier when the facts are known, the physical and chemical processes are clear and there is a near consensus in the ways of coping. COVID-19 experience belies many of these assumptions. Hence, there are local, regional and other variations within the rubric of governance. The governance process may itself be ill informed; it may be well informed; it may be political. It may take direction not from internal strength but the resultant of the impact of the forces operating on it.

One doesn't have to go far. The current Afghan experience date lined 17th August, 2021 is typical. The Taliban forces are yet to form the government. The serving President of the country has fled. The serving Vice-President has declared himself to be the interim President. It is not clear from the media where the, so estimated, over Three Hundred Thousand Afghan army is of today. Some are reported to have joined the Taliban, others are reported to have moved over to neighbouring countries and clearly there are others whose identity and inclination is to surface in the media. As of 17th August, two or three countries have announced their intent to recognise the Taliban.

Hopefully, dear reader, by the time you read these lines, the situation would have, perhaps, become clearer or would be on the way towards some clarity. That is another issue.

This text is devoted to the theme of change. Change is eternal, it is the shape, pace and direction of change which needs to be comprehended and acted upon. The role of human will in this whole process is at the best of one of the impact making factors. In spite of a very worthy emphasis on the role of 'will power' to set directions, the ground conditions have a more embellished story to roll out.

Iron will power, no matter how indomitable cannot generate resources; it can lead to generation of options and possible innovation. The truth of life is innovation works many a times but it is not a guarantee to success. There is a whole constellation of factors which generate change and a whole host of factors which help to cope with change. Whether it works or not and in which direction, is a complex interplay of forces which may be at times very difficult to forecast, extrapolate or even visualise.

Wisdom lies in working on oneself to keep oneself a functioning whole. If one adds the spiritual element, life becomes easier. The total interplay of energy and life has its own sequence. There have been attempts to decipher it by the *rishis*, the seers, the sage etc. Those which have the ability to realise that being alive is, as yet, an incomprehensible process in its totality of matter and spirit, would have a point.

Those issues cannot be resolved here. What however needs to be registered is that since human physical life has a beginning and an end, change has to be wrought within that frame. Human capacity to change is limited between the givens of the factors which impact the individual's personality and the persona. This has to be taken together with the capacity to change.

In all this, the mind plays a very powerful role. That may be a matter of still further exploration.

The issue however is simpler when focussed on the business of the Business Manager. Change requires ability to sense and seize opportunities; it requires the need to grow and the need to harvest the results of resources and ingenuity.

Continuous change in synergy with the external world can and often does spell success.

September 01, 2021

## Higher Education—When Comes the High Tide?

Many may not have listened to the Economist Radio on Facebook. The Economist Radio carries the brand of an on-demand social listening platform. It enabled listening, sharing and perhaps endorsing the Economist audio content. Magazines like *The Economist* had clearly a stake in it. That's understandable. In the present day and age most points of view which survive and circulate, ride on the shoulders of somebody who stands to gain when the objectives of the move are achieved. To facilitate this happening such person(s) often dip into their coffers. The ranking of executive MBAs is an integral part of the game. The serious thinker often, vainly, hopes that what he believes as a cause will gain currency on its own. There are several revolutions that have been kept alive and have survived because of somebody's or groups' vested interest in the cause.

Even COVID-19 has not been able to prevent the few business houses known to be in proximity of the powers that be–from making their unusual profits in these difficult times. There does not seem to be many apologists around either. This brings the discussion to the state of the world in the rolling era of COVID-19. Even the oil industry may have its troughs in the chain of value addition. However, in the phase of resurgent demand after the blackout of the lockdown, at least the oil refineries are doing well. The tyre industry is racing ahead—nobody quite knows how! In fact, the question itself is tautological.

The same applies to the fate of education which is forever being talked about and nothing much has changed, in any real sense, at least in the domain of higher education. The University Commission which D.S. Kothari headed, lent strength to creating an Indian version of the University Grants Commission in Britain. Over 60 years down the line with multiple threats to its very existence, the University Grants Commission, comfortably chugs along. It is one of those institutional wonders where almost everyone has some fault to find with it, and be it the UPA or NDA governments, nobody has got anywhere near shaking its foundations. Someday somebody will write the history of the UGC typifying how mediocre institutions survive in a sea of almost near ineptness.

The UGC has a charter of upholding the standards. Nobody quite knows what the lowest common multiple of these standards, are, cutting across, as they do, so many disciplinary faculties and so many versions of undergraduate and post graduate education. Every effort, in their operational domain, is meant to be consecrated in upholding the UGC standards. For good measure Medical education, Pharmacy, Architecture, Agriculture and some others have their own sacrosanct empires. The performance track record of their regulatory agencies is not very different from that of the UGC. This may not be the best place to get into that story. It will be reasonable to assume that research outcome is one of the legitimate fallouts of the kind of ambience. UGC has tried to be nurturing and put a frame to it. Be it the sciences, engineering, law, social sciences—and the list can be added to—there is hardly any school of thought originating from India that has merited attention as a major contribution to its profession globally.

The route to fame, comfortable social ambience, political visibility and perks which go with it are still available largely to those who have first gained some recognition in some non-Indian locale to be read as that as 'the west'.

Once someone has achieved that visibility, powers that be in the government or the corporate world shower patronage on them and such 'distinguished' persons visit India at personal convenience to distribute wisdom and ingratiatingly get lionised. Discipline-wise copious names can be found of dignitaries who when rejected in the Indian system migrated abroad and developed height king-size.

Is this because the Indian system is somewhat less and does not recognise talent or the Western system is something more and transforms the mediocre to a glittering icon? So much has been talked about in the last few weeks beginning 25th March that there is almost a competitive bidding for time in the webinar circle.

If any webinar has discussed the achievements of the Indian system of education led by the UGC, it is one of the best kept secrets.

The proposition is simple. If the outcome of research of higher institutions has this kind of international recognition, there can be multiple reasons for it. Some of them are well known and some of them have created vested interests for keeping them outside the pail of discussions.

Taking a look at the employment outcome of higher education, the outcome is not very different. The burgeoning numbers unemployed, underemployed and aspiring to be employed–without serious credentials is a story written large on the wall. If higher education was creating focussed skills, competencies and doers to aid national development, the number of aspirational applicants for each advertised job from directors to that of peons would not be so disproportionately large.

There is something not quite right in the state of education in general and higher education in particular. The least it should attempt to do is to create a cadre of graduating students who can, at least, understand and have a sense of identification with the many legitimate achievements and outcomes of higher education in the country, through its many millennia.

August 01, 2020

# 2

# Economics

## Towards a Logic Beyond Consumerism

India is a land of festivals. By the Gregorian calendar, each of the twelve months has some major festivals celebrated in some part of the country. It has to do with anything, from a collective memory to the harvesting season. It is a welcome sign because it feeds the spirit of joy and merry making. It also breaks the feeling of drudgery and boredom from the routine. If Holi was to be celebrated in a particular way, that is the way it had to be celebrated. The same was true of Eid or Christmas or for that matter any festivity. It is only in the last decade or so that the governance regulatory framework started entering the method of festive celebration. A classic example would be how some agencies have put a frame on the bursting of crackers during Diwali or the way colour is to be applied and with what 'intensity' during Holi. The purpose of referring to these instances is not to pronounce judgement (which may be valid in its own right) but to flag the essence of an approach to how festivities are to roll out. Clearly, governance processes have not been bashful about venturing into certain expressions of 'festivities'. Another analogy, at an operational level, can be cited. Any number of Hindu places of worship, from Kerala to J&K,

have been taken over by the government. The revenues which are primarily from donation of Hindu worshippers are used as per government's preferences. Interestingly, no such intensity of attempt seems to have been made to regulate the management of income of the places of worship of other denominations, which could involve, Islam, Jainism, Sikhism, Christianity or whatever else.

The purpose here is not to enter into that debate but to ask if there is a selective approach in regulating denominational efforts? The argument is simple: if the approach of managing the 'governance' of certain types of festivities and places of worship is 'beneficial' then the benefits of that approach should be made available to improving the festive spirit and efficiency of all denominations. If the approach that is being followed is not so sound, then it should be improved; applied even-handedly in every similar case. Consistency is a virtue in public dealings. The entire situation, reference festivity styles and governance, is quite complex. Commerce rides many waves of the festivities. And if volumes are significant, consumerism wins. Illustratively, consider the way Christmas is celebrated. By an estimate, in US alone, the retail industry during Christmas is worth around $3 trillion.

The cutting of the pine trees in Europe is a business of $60 million. In the UK, the slaughter of Turkeys during the festive season is worth $10 million. Obviously, consumerism is at the driving wheel. This means there is intense lobbying, advertising and whatever else goes with it to keep the business rolling. There is a close linkage between popular sentiments and consumerism which if 'commercially' tapped can be, operationally, a very 'enriching' and profitable process. One cannot handle these issues just by moralising. The response in the name of 'sustainable development' is not proving adequate in causing effective rethink, let alone reversing the depleting impact of consumerism. The time has come to fall back upon the eternal postulates of fair play, even handedness and sound judgement, to rethink how the human race can manage its material pursuits. This is the need of the times. This needs to be done before the current trends of selectiveness and 'consumerism' become too devastating to tackle in a sensible way.

December 30, 2021

## Grasp the Situation

Staying positive is not the same thing as the inability to read the writing on the wall. The first is as necessary as oxygen is for life. Experiencing the second, is, not recognising the fact that ignoring the obvious can only lead to a roadblock. The situation is compounded in an endemic environment of anxiety about health and receding frontiers of income and opportunity.

Pointing this out is necessary because if debt repayments are necessary for survival of intermediary financial institutions, approaches which are likely to push firms into bankruptcy can be equally dangerous. Under such circumstances, topping it all up with understandable but untenable social objectives is only going to make confusion worse. Consider the situation of ordering Small and Medium Enterprises (SMEs) with less than 100 workers to pay full wages. On the face of it, this appears to be a laudable approach, yet there is a flip side to it. From where will the SMEs find the money to pay when they are not earning anything themselves? If they go bankrupt, the employees will not even get what they could be getting in a reduced manner. This is not economics. It is common sense.

When the reality is grim, appealing to "resilience" or "dynamism" can only lead to an echo situation. One can hear oneself over and over again but nothing is going to change. What is required is overcoming the crisis with a genuine ability to develop alternatives and indeed lower the sights. Consider a situation where all this is ensconced in an administrative environment of further tightening processes to a still more rigorous tax regime.

Governance, anywhere, works on many wheels. One of them is committee work. The Covid era has no dearth of committees, with many of the members of such panels being busy bees in the corridors of power. Apparently there is also a 'COVID-19 economic task-force.' If it has not made any Earth-shaking recommendations till now; they must be among the best-kept administrative secrets.

What one finds in columns and discussions are phraseologies like "transformative economic opportunity" or exhortations for "meaningful and effective" action. What does all this add up to? Having a compass, which has a needle with no marking of the North, is not the normal process. This is not the normal way of finding a path.

Mergers of banks were announced with great flourish; however, for this to work, there had to be a preparation for a conscious redesign of their architecture. What was needed was a framework of reference. Perhaps an activity for which no one has time when everyone is in a hurry. There are many ways of writing off a good suggestion, which one is unable to understand and the best is to term it theoretical/intellectual/unrealistic. The Covid era may have changed many things but the area on which it has still to make an impact is clichéd responses.

To consider the severity of disruption of economic activity, banks find it difficult to meet singly, either a demand shock or a supply shock. When both come together, the people in authority, having a limited understanding of the triggers of the situation could mistake activity per se as the solution. It takes an astute administrator to realise that one can be very active, just jumping up and down at the same spot but you will not be going anywhere.

One of the reports terms the situation arising out of COVID-19 as "economic asphyxiation." This is a particularly difficult phase to go through for finance-related institutions. Several international ratings have revised India's outlook downwards. Fitch ratings of a month ago are particularly devastating. Add to it the high public debt India is burdened with. For one thing, even the weekly game to meet, partly, the situation by hiking fuel prices seems to have exhausted itself. By itself this could be ignored up to a point but this is the lowest investment grade India has had in well over two decades. Foreign currency issuer default rating can be an important indicator in getting funds.

A distinguished friend of influence in Government circles made the argument that such ratings are "red herrings", because indicators of normal times cannot be used to measure abnormal times like the Covid era. This kind of a debate is interesting to toss around but unhelpful in working for an economic turnaround. In the meanwhile, the much-maligned and little-understood people factor continues to get weighed under the realities of commodity prices, spiralling expenditure through populist doles and receding fiscal revenues. The solutions could possibly lie in a package of approaches, which would include lowering public rhetoric, recognising that economic crests and troughs are unrelated to political gains and losses, recognising that in a universal pandemic situation most economic segments will have to redefine their life sourcing strategies. Political rhetoric may be understandable but when it ignores fully the realities of life, it only sharpens the pangs of distress.

August 17, 2020

## It is Time for Focussed Action

COVID-19 is probably one of the topics about which more has been written and spoken than perhaps any other subject in the last several months. The subject itself would be suffering from some kind of "author's fatigue." Content-wise, the articles have little more to say than perhaps reflecting philosophically or administratively on certain categories, policies or more. All this is a part of life and several media fora flourish on this. So be it!

On May 25, in a write-up titled 'Impenetrable Barriers' in these columns, a description had been put forth on the logic and birth of the concept of the National Capital Region (NCR). It pointed out how an over-anxious administrative zeal on the part of some in the affected NCR States had created impenetrable boundaries, barricaded with permits. For weeks, misguided zeal, an ill-informed search for solutions and an urge for seeking applause had created a state of competitive "statism." Uttar Pradesh, Rajasthan, Haryana and Delhi took turns to make the life of average law-abiding citizens hapless, forcing them to try and build bridges in an attempt to integrate divided lives across barricaded State borders.

There is at least some data on faulty test kits, alternate test kits, the number of people tested and the number of people who ought to be tested but there is no data available on how many suffered and in what manner, (all in the name of containing COVID-19) due to the closure of State borders. It may be recalled that much of this was post the lockdown phase of COVID-19.

Bless the Home Minister of India, who announced from a forum on June 18 that NCR for the purposes of the present concerns and more, should be seen as one unit. In matters like this, no credit needs be claimed but one needs to count one's blessings. Since the Home Minister made this announcement, at least, the comparative babble of containing the virus through entry passes seems to have receded. What the future will bring remains to be seen.

The truth is, that as of now, the only instruments of containing COVID-19 are the common sensical ones of basic hygiene, social distancing, wearing masks, avoiding crowded events and the like. This is no rocket science. All diseases would be better controlled with these measures. Only in the case of COVID-19, they seem to be the only route. The drug and pharmaceutical options are clearly months away even though there has been some progress in the right direction. Of course if you are rich and powerful or both, you can get into a hospital where your influence or money could move the treatment from one to the other of the five-six options available and hopefully, something would work.

Earlier in this text, there have been references to a kind of fatigue that is setting in with all Coronavirus-related issues. A similar fatigue is setting in on social media platforms too.

Messages and jokes on strained husband-wife relations on account of the "absconding" maid are becoming fewer, wisecracks on domestication have significantly reduced and spaces so vacated are being taken over by China-bashing and posts on rejection of Chinese made goods and so on.

The kind of leadership shown by the Home Minister could be emulated by the Finance Minister. Few will doubt her attempt to try but it becomes more effective if the attempt is focussed. Doling out money in its various incarnations, including in the so-called bailout plans for the banks, in the past, did not work. Now the fond hope is that if you cut down the EPF share of the working individual and thereby put more money in the people's hands, the economy would boom. Even an undergraduate student of economics would know that this is the classical case of misconceived economic correlation. There are other options of course. Clearly, all is not lost on the economic front. Some of the sectors of the pharma industry are poised for big gains. That gain itself may be coterminous with COVID-19. The important thing is to select lines of pharmaceutical industry, which are prone to multiple drug formulations from an assortment of drug research streams. Those who have dealt with technology-oriented start-ups know that it is doable. At the policy level, both at the Centre and at the States, this could be done. It could be done by channelising of funding in a sectoral mode. However, this can only happen if focussed policy frameworks modulate the propensity to chase the last wagon of the train.

Now that it is obvious that, whether officially accepted or not, 2020 is a "zero year", there needs to be some attention on a proactive policy effort focussed on the realities of the economic potential. Our success in the motorcycle sector, especially in the manufacturing of its component parts, is a good example. It establishes what Indian acumen can do with a little bit of support and some encouraging policies.

June 22, 2020

## Marketing New Perspectives

The change in nature of markets has created several universes within its fold, so as to almost require an interpreter to talk from one segment to another. Yet in a country like India, all marketing instrumentalities, from hawking to internet communication, seem relevant. Their pertinence in the social segment in which they operate determines the robustness of that economy. Each segment has its own significance and it determines to a large extent the prosperity of the region where it operates. This economic growth is central to the community's welfare because livelihoods depend on that. However, there remains a catch-22 situation as each marketing method in a socio-economic segment can and does evolve. Leaving it frozen at a given level is unwise for the overall well-being of that division. Nature, being what it is, will induce change and its own evolution does not need a policy decision. But this progression may be slow and may be excluding migrant segments of that given economic division from returning to it for their livelihood and with a level of comfort. Thus, it is that remaining migrant groups are reluctant to go back to where they originated from and settle down where they have moved to. Thereby they almost delink themselves from the base community from which they emerged. Marketing methods are a major determinant of this process.

Just as it is difficult to visualise a so-called avant-garde marketing method in a remote village cluster which does not even have proper amenities for food and shelter, so also the marketing methods have to be at peace with lifestyles and communities. The catch-22 referred to above, can be worked out by resolving this dilemma. Instruments of change have to carry out the upgradation of the affected communities without disrupting their livelihoods. This requires thought and proactive designs of intervention. Unfortunately, this is a perspective which many social interventionists seem to miss altogether. The crescendo of modernisation does not help the case of graduated and gradual change.

People often mistake the toolkit for substance. In the course of participation in many planning processes, it becomes evident that the interventionist paradigm of the leader, especially if he is a powerful one, gets smoother endorsement with the powers that actually control that segment. The result is many square pegs in round holes. In view of the competitiveness, India is often seen to adopt a method which appears prima-facie acceptable but undoable with immediate effect in many contexts in which it is attempted.

India is not the only country where periodically such interventions have been attempted in different pockets. Turkey, under Kemal Ataturk, attempted mediations which were not confined to economics and livelihood but also covered social engineering, where the national leader attempted to catapult the country into European social norms from the more conventional Middle Eastern ones. In many cases, these intrusions did not take root and created a self-defeating environment where social practices lapsed into the original mould from where the political intervention had sought to leverage the community. In-built levels and echelons of hierarchy which were going to be affected by the changes, fought hard against them. It would be useful to remind ourselves that in a country as large as ours, it is possible and even desirable to have a certain degree of economic modeling, common at a pan-India level. At the same time, the economic diversities are so large that regional models of development will have to be crafted, evolved and practiced. Work in that direction is yet to begin in earnest. The overarching dominance of the Planning Commission and subsequently the NITI Aayog, coupled with the penchant of continuously highlighting emotive issues like caste, religion and language, have blurred the focus on regional development. It is difficult to conceive how a river valley culture of say West Bengal could be the receptacle of the same kind of economic philosophy which would work in the woodlands of Mizoram. The limited ability of economists to visualise a sociogram good enough for our agro-climatic realities and the wealth of soil and land, had high prices to pay. It is true that there are literally millions of people below the poverty line but the definition of poverty line alone reflects an overarching emphasis on the monetised version of economic development. There are substantial parts of India where forest produces are the primary resource of livelihood and where the money economy has still to make its entry in a significant enough manner to affect and create social interventions which result in positive change.

A window on the whole process can be created by extensive fieldwork in trying to understand what it is that moves livelihoods in a given agro-climatic zone. The first step towards the initial documentation of the ground realities is to smoothen and strengthen the conventional process in a manner in which wastage is reduced, longevity of the products is increased and the awareness of its availability is universalised in a relevant social segment where it can be bought. Socio-economic engineering based on the fulcrum of the local productivity process can move the world quicker. The lever has to be the intention and the will to give this alternate economics, rooted in local conditions, a chance to prove itself.

February 03, 2020

## Disruption, Cohesion and the Way Forward

The world of economics and financial ongoings is an interplay of a number of variables at the same time. Singly, they are complex, put together, they are bewildering. When ensconced in a world which considers it fashionable to talk of 'disruption', confusion gets confounded.

Equilibrium amongst variables is lost, coherent thinking becomes improbable and savage noise-making takes over the role of cool collected thinking. Identifying the sane way forward, under such conditions, becomes more challenging. The time has come to flag these issues before the damage gets worse.

In the global world of economics and financial transactions, there are a few concerns that need greater attention. Of these, first is the need to recognise the difference between growth in central bank assets and nominal gross domestic product. Beyond both is the flow of 'real'/operational economy. The real/operational economy does not respect any logic save that of the flow of life. Accordingly, when asset prices are distorted, risk management goes in the realm of unprogrammed logic.

Recovery after the 2008 crisis was like a wound half healed. It led to an excessive focus on policy rates and balance sheets. The outcome was zero interest rates and massive asset purchase. India started walking that road much later and bank interest rates started getting lowered only a few years ago.

One thing was obvious: Traditional policy tools were not working. In a country like ours, with multiple economies rolled in one, there was a disconnect between the global economy influencing stock exchanges and village economy. In many village economies, services continue to compensate with grains and household aids. This creates unique contradictions, not solved by avantgarde economic theories.

Whatever the Goods and Services Tax may or may not have proved, it has certainly brought to the fore the contradictions inherent in multiple financial markets of the country. One wonders how many, involved in policy-making, factored that in the designing of the strategy. Globally too, there are other palpable contradictions. On one side there are the clear forces of globalisation and on the other, even more powerful, contrived calls for protectionism. Any social scientist with process insights, would be aware that this contradiction is a factor of increasing social-fragmentation-with-growth.

Going further, growth is not evenly spread across the income spectrum. Even a casual visit across the mega malls of new Gurgaon and its lanes of Sadar Bazaar would bring home these contradictions to even the persons of benumbed observational abilities. The distance between these two horns (malls and Sadar Bazar) of the millennial city and the economic planning headquarters of the National Capital could not be more than 30 kms. Yet, there is no continuum or plough back of experience and communication between the two.

This explains how disruption has destroyed interfaces and how so many segments of the national economy are on a trajectory of their own. The problem does not stop there. Along with 'financial relations', 'economic condition' is the third element of 'monetary policies'. Effectively, demonetisation was a child of monetary reform; GST is the child of the universe of financial relationships called 'taxation'. The real economy has a trajectory of its own. The results are evident.

When insights are absent and understanding yields place to assertions of power, the kind of social narrative which one witnesses in the shrill debates of the media is the result. The bald truth is that the old order stands disrupted. This is partly through a natural process and partly through a synergistic effect of well-meant policy instruments. Any way forward would require a dispassionate understanding of what one is doing to oneself and inflicting on others.

In a universe where ingratiation is seen as the way of careers being advanced, jobs, skills and wages will be on their own orbits round the economy. In the meanwhile, it will be soulful to realise that G7 economies have collectively grown at just 1.8 per cent annual rate between 2010 and 2017. The sooner India, as a thinking entity, registers the facts of the case and brings better cohesion to its policy instruments, greater is the hope for the future.

December 18, 2017

## From Maharaja to Pauper for Sale

The social discourse, like anything else, becomes painful when it is repetitive. Consider the case of Air India. The news has come of Cabinet approval of Air India disinvestment. Its form, character, proportion and more will need far more considered thought and many more resolutions on many fora. For several decades, the entity has been in the talk of solutions for its endemic bankruptcy, indifferent management, terrible aviation purchase management decisions and more. Several of these were caused by factors outside the fold of the core Air India management. Many interventions have been attempted. Indeed, apparently, there is not a solution which has not been attempted or at least seriously considered.

The merger between Indian Airlines and Air India is a great example of experimentation in the governance domain. Persons such as Russi Modi were wheeled out of their 'steel frame' to lead Indian Airlines; successful business leaders like Y. Deveshwar were summoned from ITC to lead Air India. Favoured bureaucrats were fielded by the dozen. The rest, as they say, is history.

One thing that did not change was the privileges of people in public domain, who, for years, have claimed priority on just about everything, big and small, with reference to Air India. This included preferential seating arrangements of the first two rows in all aircraft over the natural choice of a full revenue paying passenger, upgrades and more.

It set the operational priorities of the entity in question. Many are aware of the great drama which originated in Mumbai—about some VIP landing at the airport to discover that it was an aircraft which was all economy! So much for the constitutional vision of a 'socialist' India. Even outrage and anger seems to have become, convenient and selective.

Getting back to the theme of the discussion, namely, business propriety and organisational efficiency to make it worth the time for revenue efficiency, the story of Air India stays an instructive one. It has been stated that the repetition in public domain is painful, what's more it does not contribute to mitigating the loss of revenues in the business domain.

It may not be too much to argue that the guiding principles of Air India's operations have laid much emphasis on providing convenience to the powers-that-be in governance.

I recall a situation in mid-90s, where an Indian Airlines flight from Delhi to Patna was pushed ahed of schedule, from 7:30 am to 6:30 am of the following morning in the preceding evening at 11:30 pm. (Of course this can be, technically justifiable) It seems even a media announcement on the radio and television was made somewhere around midnight. When more than half of the 07:30 am passengers missed their flight, they were informed that the announcement about the changed schedule was made at midnight. If there were operational reasons for doing that, one could still understand. It turned out that two VIPs of the then ruling party had a programme in Patna which made it necessary for them to reach an hour earlier. Of course Indian Airlines obliged!

Getting into a debate on a topic such as this may not necessarily help unless it be realised that it is an outcome of an approach which belies any business or efficiency consideration. If there was not an Air India, the powerful entities of the day would not have attempted this kind of a behaviour.

The proposition is simple: When the assumptions are flawed the conclusions are also flawed.

One can go on repeating the options for efficiency in a cyclical manner. One can even mistake movement for progress but really speaking correct diagnosis is needed for managing change. If Air India is to take to wings again, be it infusion of capital; change in management; strong arm tactics; bringing in bureaucrats; bringing in people from the private sector or even disinvestment; the objectives are not very likely to be fully met, by this alone. Business must run as business.

A change of approach to aviation affairs, for Air India, in the real world, is needed. Convenience of the powerful shows, even when it is cloaked in the garb of the 'people's' power represented by a select few, nurtured by an ingratiating set-up.

July 03, 2017

## Understanding India and its Economy

The projected departure of Reserve Bank of India (RBI) Governor Raghuram Rajan has received unprecedented attention. I do not remember signature campaigns being launched in favour of any serving RBI Governor who was a potential candidate for another term.

The polarisation of such positions is a dangerous trend and it could have been a good idea for our liberal thinkers to take a position on the principles involved in such crucial governance issues. The facts of the case will, perhaps, forever remain a mystery. Who instigated what and what was the motive, remains a matter of speculation.

Meanwhile, the media, in its various incarnations, has been flooded with observations. It has been suggested that the real target of some of the comments was Union Finance Minister Arun Jaitley who had to rush back from his China tour. There comes a time in campaigns when well-orchestrated interpretations start parading in carbs of truth. So be it.

It may not hurt to look at some concerns or questions. The economy has paid its price for high interest rates. It was deliberate. Non-performing assets have never been so high. Regulatory measures contributed to the state of affairs. The real estate sector shows mixed profiles and it is obvious that high interest rates did not bring down inflation. There is one simple truth about the Indian economy: It is variegated and often unstructured.

When I used to say this in my sojourn at Sussex, some decades ago, I was called to produce evidence. I had to explain how there was only partial monetisation of assets in large parts of rural India. Payments for goods and services was often in kind. One effect of this process was throwing the statistical profile of income distribution in a tizzy. And when the Planning Commission chose to read this gospel, the results which it produced, are there for all to see.

Hence, what is good economics and who is a good economist remains a question, whose framework of reference still eludes definition in the context of Indian economy.

It is painful, but true, that in absence of clearly identifiable indicators, a status-driven society like India has become brand-driven in decision-making.

Getting a degree from Harvard University, Yale University, Columbia University, University of Wisconsin-Madison etc. or getting an employment in the International Monetary Fund or the World Bank becomes a passport to not only attain high ranks, but is also a platform to gain high attention. There is no correlation between the competencies of earning a degree and practicing economics in India.

Whatever one may think of China, especially in the backdrop of deliberations on the Nuclear Suppliers Group, the truth is that this communist country has developed operational models, rooted in the tested wisdom of past wisdom and is indeed showcasing it for economic purposes. Consider how medicines from China is packaged, exported and respected globally.

What have we done to Indian systems of healthcare, with many constantly ridiculing what they think, it stands for?

The Indian seamen ruled the waves for centuries and Rajendra Chola is merely one symbol of our prowess in seafaring. The current effort that is going on to put the ocean studies on the map of Indian psyche is not a day too soon.

In the meanwhile, China has been busy, since March 2015, in not only projecting, propagating, but practicing One Belt, One Road capability, infrastructure and economic development programme.

The new silk road echoes Economic and Social Commission for Asia and the Pacific's Asian highway. Asian Railway and Asian Economic Corridor fills in the missing link connecting China to the rest of Asia and Europe. The maritime components as the 'string of pearls' in the Indian Ocean extends westwards to Europe through the Red Sea and eastwards to South China Sea.

Ports have become the key in such infrastructure projects. Such forces are possible when driven and supported by capacities, manufacturing and measured returns, even if modest, to domestic investment. The opportunity of funds has to be enough to allow for some profit and high economic risk in foreign infrastructure that can support raw material supply and open market for manufactured goods.

Prebisch-Singer hypothesis of trade will explain this point. It was for the RBI to script the narrative. The future awaits us.

July 08, 2016

## Exploring the Ocean of Linkages in Our Country

One of the amazing elements of learning is that some common place items of information are not in the conscious domain of knowledge of people. The case of the ocean surrounding India and bordering the countries on the east African coast and of south-east Asia comes easily to mind.

To put this observation in perspective, it is important to note that the concept of a nation state is itself of a comparatively recent origin—not even two centuries old.

It is important to recognise this to understand the underpinning of the prevailing trade and commerce, not to forget business, in this part of the world. An illustration will help communicate this point.

Civilisational change is as old as rivers. There is adequate evidence to show that cinnamon was taken to Australia by sea-farers from south-east Asia about 45,000 years ago. Given that scale of sea-faring traditions, more recently (roughly over a 1,000 years ago) south-east Asia was known to have deep exchanges with South Asia.

Hence, that many sea routes were chartered and there are palpable similarities of customs, belief and language between different parts of south-east Asia and South Asia.

The veneration of Rama IX of the Chakri dynasty in the Kingdom of Ayutthaya in Thailand comes easily to mind. The reigning deity of the temple of Prasat Preah Vihear of Cambodia is of lord Shiva and Angkor Wat of Cambodia is dedicated to lord Vishnu. The influence of Tamil culture of the Sangam period on Maldivian oral linguistic and cultural tradition and customs has been significant.

The Jatakas and the Puranas show abundant evidence of maritime trade with this part of the world. There is evidence of similar traditional boat-building techniques. The examples can be multiplied through centuries. It will serve the purpose of this text to flag the significance of understanding the dynamics of linkages. These linkages are eched in the psyche of communities.

To develop appropriate trade linkages and to forge meaningful economic ties, it is essential not only to know of the modulating influences of culture, but also to learn from each other.

This reflects itself in modern times. For example, in India, a small percentage of the population carries a large burden of tax and it is worth asking if this helps with the overall prosperity. If so, to what extent?

Mauritius Seychelles, the UAE, in this region and indeed elsewhere in the world, like Bermuda Luxemburg, Monaco etc. are tax-free zones. China has more than 500 special economic zones.

India can create its own equivalent of a Dubai, Singapore or Hong Kong. If one were to consider special economic zones on our coastline and consolidation the eco systems, the gross domestic product (GDP) of India can grow by leaps and bounds in about a decade.

The proposition is simple. A framework is needed for good governance, calling for new paradigms. Typically: Can India be an investment destination in the Asia-Pacific Rim area? If so, India which has 17 per cent of the world population in 2.2 per cent of the world land mass, with a share of 2.6 per cent of the world GDP and 2.2 per cent of the world trade, has indeed 0.35 per cent of the world foreign direct investment. It's difficult to understand all this, let alone explain it.

The proposition is simple: Where so much is being said in celebrating India's diversity, the diverse indigenous economic structure is still to be mapped. Trade can become complementary only thereafter.

There is a need for a proper mechanism and institutional framework for harnessing regional savings and productive deployment of these resources. This has to be carried to its logical conclusion with a more evolved policy planning framework.

Policy debates need to be encouraged for identifying those core issues concerning infrastructure investments, evaluations of existing and prospective mechanism for channelising savings.

This is doable provided we can cultivate home grown or *swadeshi*, effective human capital. After all, India arrival day is celebrated in the nations of Caribbean, Mauritius, Guyana, Suriname, Jamaica, Fiji and the list is large. We in India have to also respect the talent that is in our country and is rooted here.

June 24, 2016

## Slogans Mustn't Cloud Development Horizon

Cloudy vision can take place due to a number of reasons. It can take place through faulty/dusty lenses, it can happen through cataract, through fog, bad windows. And the list is long. But perhaps the worst type of clouding takes place through empty/incomplete slogans. They cloud the horizon.

However, there are some all-time favorites. Popular ones include 'removal of poverty' or 'protect secularism'. Mercifully, ever since the NDA Government came to power, these slogans have been somewhat muted as popular psyche is registering new messages. Not that poverty or secularism is no more an issue, but it is just that people are realising about new elements, while others remain to be recognised.

There is a realisation about climate change, but there is not sufficient realisation that climate change impacts wheat production and the quality of wheat. As it were, with a rise in temperature, food prices too go high. As some people rise above poverty level, the availability/price balance shifts.

Worse, there is an increase in the population level, below the poverty level, (if not more) than the numbers that rise above poverty.

It is strange but true that there is a thundering silence among the political class across various segments on population control.

Be that as it may, it is important to realise that slogans too have their life. A good second line in the hierarchy of the over-used slogan includes the word 'inclusion'. This confounds even more than it confuses.

The truth is that the process of financial inclusion began in 1955 when the Imperial Bank of India became the State Bank of India. The next landmark was in 1969. This was followed in 1980. There was talk of priority sector lending; kisan credit cards and it still continues. Many Governments claim originality in repeating the past.

However, the truth is that in real world, some numbers do change, but percentages do not. New phraseology is not necessarily a revolution.

Take the case of Pradhan Mantri Jan Dhan Yojana (PMJDY) which talks of universal banking services. There is nothing wrong with it. Claims have been made about containing leakages through this instrumentality. There is truth in the claim, but one has to stretch a definition to see how it is 'inclusion', the way it should be, if those covered by it have not entered the main economic stream.

The life of a common man remains in a tizzy. Opening accounts is helpful, but it does not cause economic progress. Perhaps the process is being confused for objective.

The answer lies in encouraging demand-oriented savings. The number of accounts opened under PMJDY is large. Several of them have no significant deposits. Credit and remittances need to be customised to lifestyle patterns. Income streams of an average Indian cannot be just a matter of finding employment. There is merit in the talk of servicing, through the business correspondent model.

As of now, there is much heat over how to deepen the penetration of financial services into the rural areas. No prizes for guessing the post office system remains the favourite.

It is a well-known fact that India accounts for 16 per cent of the world's population and only four per cent of the global water resources. Whether it be the venerable wise ones of the Planning Commission or the Niti Ayog, both miss a point. Water shortage effects production of rice and higher food prices absorb the rise of purchasing power. Little is left for pushing industrial growth. The Reserve Bank of India continues to talk of interest rates.

Obviously, multinationals are also looking for their own kill, big four consultancy organisations remain the favourite of the institutions of the present Government, as they were of the preceding one. Financial multinationals including banks have their own take. They will come nowhere near the PMJDY. It falls in the lot of the public sector banks to keep pushing for financial inclusion while the cream of their assets stand hugely monopolised by the socially savvy and politically influential.

Some names of the leading luminaries are too well-known to be repeated. Putting it simply, a *desi* model is needed to solve the *desi* problem. The present Government cannot afford to lose the opportunity.

June 10, 2016

## Curbing Black Money is the Way Forward

I can understand the dilemma of the Union Government. After all the hype on black money in the election campaign; after eminent lawyer Ram Jethmalani deciding to go noisy on it, (not to overlook the frontal assault by BJP leader Subramanian Swamy) the Union Government is under no obligation to appear active on the topic.

The really powerful are so powerful that the ruling dispensation cannot afford to risk their wrath. The poor are so poor that they can barely subsist. So, both are a 'no-no' option.

The hapless 70 per cent of the 223 million Pan Card holders then have to bear the cross by atoning for the sins of others. Hence, the bearers of the tax code (pan card) are the obvious targets of the campaign against black money.

It cannot be anybody's case that those with black money should be spared, but it carries more credibility and conviction if the bigger advantage-taker is targeted first. Nowhere in the world, or at any point of history, hitting soft targets has really won a war.

There is a simple law of regulation, "Intelligently guarded freedom to anyone achieves objectives better than a closed regulatory regime." Those who have dealt with teen-age children will easily understand this principle.

Last few weeks have seen a spate of regulations. The Union Government has made pan card a mandatory input for any serious transaction. Of the 1.25 billion people in the country, 223 million are Pan Card holders. The number does not have the necessary critical mass to leverage the 1.25 billion out of the financial morass.

Incidentally, like many approaches in Indian governance, hitting gold as a soft target also knows no party divisions. India raised import tax on gold to 10 per cent in a series of hikes in August 2013.

February 05, 2016

## Rediscover the Ocean, Build a Blue Economy

To understand the evolution of India post-1947, it is important to grasp the significance of certain symbols. The national emblem came from the Ashokan Pillar at Sarnath. The national flag, reportedly, focused on the religious composition of the Indian polity in its selection of colours. The official calendar of the Government of India was the Saka calendar, going back to Kanishka, the Kushan king. He never had sway over any significant part of either the Indo-Gangetic plains or peninsular India (never mind that nobody used this calendar).

Ashoka was glorified by naming the first luxury Government hotel in Delhi, after him. The epithet of 'The Great' was bestowed on Akbar who is credited with having founded the cult of 'Deen-e-ilahi'.

Meanwhile, the Cholas, the Chalukyas, the Pallavas, the Cheras and the Palas were not seen as worthy of being etched in the psyche of the newborn independent state. Even the Guptas of Pataliputra were eclipsed from honourable mention. Those who have read *Discovery of India* will find it easy to trace the seed bed of these ideas. So be it.

The consequences of such an approach have been large and in many ways unrecognised. Few countries in the world have defined or practiced their identity in the way India did soon after its tryst with destiny at mid-night of August 15, 1947.

A significant fallout of this approach was the almost complete eclipse of sea power in the making of a post-independent India. Chittagong in the east and Karachi in the west, which were significant ports for Indian commerce, were lost to foreign sovereignty. Years later, Kandla was conceived to offset Karachi but it is a still limping project.

In the east, the silting of Howrah in Kolkata made the entrance of ships an even bigger challenge. The battle of the delta and its access has not been won by the dredgers. If Akbar could be the epitome of Indian grandeur, surely India could be great without sea power. This seemed to be the implied thinking of many individuals governing India including its coastal States.

Meanwhile, the world changed. Singapore, formerly a fishing village, became one of the biggest ports not only of South East Asia but the world. Dubai came into its own, and Colombo became the link between Singapore and Dubai. It reached a point where there was a grudging recognition of the fact that the 65 per cent of India's export-import containers are trans-shipped through neighbouring country ports.

Some statistics would show how Kochi should have responded as a possible Indian port to this challenge. It is 11 nautical miles from the Gulf-Singapore channel and 76 nautical miles from the nine degree channel from Europe to the Far East. All other Indian ports are much more removed from the trunk route. This multiplies the maritime routes. It was eminently suitable as a trans-shipment hub. The commercial significance of maritime opportunities was large. The plan needed policy support.

What has happened on the ground, however, is another story. The LNG terminal that has been constructed in Kochi works at two per cent of capacity. The pipeline-laying project, between Bangalore and Mangalore, by the Gas Authority of India Limited is incomplete. Only 40 of the 900 kilometers has been completed.

During a recent visit to Kochi, the writer was informed that GAIL has to appoint a new contractor. The International Container Transhipment Terminal remains the regional terminal to serve as the gateway of shipment traffic. Only 30 per cent of the capacity is, currently, utilised. It may useful to remind ourselves that ICTT is a special economic zone port. Some tweaking of the policy could change the scene. Illustratively bunkers could be given duty-free to coastal ship touching ICTT. Income tax exemption could be extended to the shipping crews touching ICTT. The examples can be multiplied.

The shape of things could be changed if only we could collectively rise to seize the opportunity which history has bestowed on us today. This would include the Union Government, the State

Government, the corporates, the consulting firms and the Indian citizens. Some positive indications are there. One only hopes the trend gathers strength.

June 12, 2015

## Catch the Reform Bull by the Horns

The urge for safety is one of the driving forces of human nature. The defining characteristics of individual behaviour are often found to be replicated in the behaviour of organisations. This is the reason which leads to the emphasis on the need for a synergy between individual and organisational goals. Closer home, the need for corporate revamp, across the full spectrum of the typology of organisations, is needed.

Selective, episodic and fragmented interventions across the range of Government entities, regulatory agencies and more seem to have produced bewildering results. Private organisations are no exception. Whereas the number of professional degree-holders among the owner-managers has gone up, the values and quality of their decisions are often rooted in traditional practices. Whereas the powerful and the influential very often get away with what they want to do, the honest and the compliant are inundated with forms, questions and investigations.

Taking the discussion to a higher level, the issues affecting the governance of enterprises and the corporate sector haven't changed much over the last two decades. And if the concerns haven't changed, neither have the positions. There has been no radical shift between the policies of one set of the cabinet members to another.

The process of economic reforms initiated in July 1991 has been fairly steady in the last 23 years. The emphasis has been on the external sector, fiscal policy reforms, reducing entry barriers for industrial investment and liberalising foreign investment. These are comforting domains where a lot of energy can be spent, without affecting the cosy comfort of the powerful or mitigating the misery of the honest.

Safety of the status quo, in terms of power distribution, is a significant driving force for the intelligent. Interestingly, examples of industrial restructuring, privatisation and/or nationalisation, not to mention the basic re-examining of the paradigms governing action, have been few and far between.

Over the last few years, one has heard arguments in favour of making India a low-cost economy. Now, with onions being sold at Rs. 70/kg, frugality is a fairy tale proposition. So much so that even the proverbs are changing. The old quip used to be: "I can survive on chapattis and onions". Today even that is lyrical. A basic transformation is on its way.

The facts are simple. Industrial re-structuring cannot be a painless process. It involves justification of each item of expense, often causing reduction of function-specific manning levels. Re-deployment of staff is also inevitable. It is not an easy job, with bulging figures of people seeking employment, and innovative definitions of poverty. And this is not to refer to the creation of a climate wherein claiming to be a person below the poverty line has large political and economic advantages.

It does not take a genius to realise that unviable industrial units must close. State-owned enterprises and private ones too must streamline their operations. But this means re-defining the rights of workers and enabling growth in viable areas. It is significant that that in the recently concluded general election, no political leader, no political party found it worth their while to raise the issue of population control or advocate family planning.

The logic of unfettered expansion of the supply side cannot be ignored, in practical terms, if we want to create a safe India. Many measures are possible including monetary compensation to a re-trenched worker. The Ramanujam Committee reports, produced decades earlier, had dealt upon this. A National Renewal Fund has been talked about, employment assistance centres had been talked about, and unemployment insurance fund has been talked about. But talking apart, no action has followed. Perhaps the 'genie' defies control.

The simple proposition that population control will need to walk hand-in-hand with improving the employability and skill dimension of those already in the labour market, and those wanting to enter it, has been talked about as well. Now, it needs action. To be a nation of achievers we have to discipline our instincts. We have to work on the paradigms that govern our productive forces. The mind-set of getting by on contacts and privileges is unacceptable. Reality abhors evasion.

July 25, 2014

## India Needs its Own Set of Standards

August 15, 1947, was the fulfilment of a dream. The country's woes could be laid at the door of colonialists. Highly resonating phrases on the 'tryst with destiny' were lyrically pronounced about that midnight when the world sleeps and when India awakes to freedom.

What changed post-1947 was the formal expropriation of the surplus of Indian productivity to foreign lands under the British Crown. A Constitution was, in the course of time, framed; a democratic process put in place; and a governance pattern institutionalised in a fairly uniform manner. We got several things right and some not so right. The actual, credible, balance sheet is still in the making. Among the many remarkable things that happened in the immediate post-independence era was the operational marginalisation of many of the Mahatma's wishes.

Gradually, the white masters were replaced largely by brown masters of the same genre. Several thinkers of the Independent liberal Party, including Fenner Brockway of the UK, had warned of such an eventuality. What followed is too well known to need recount.

In the name of change, a Soviet model was put in place and the Planning Commission created as the instrument of the Union Government's will. The impact of such interventions is yet to be evaluated.

Irrespective of the evaluation, the Indian dream was still anchored to some mythical space abroad— presumably somewhere in the geography of the UK/US/Europe or even Japan. There was little, if any space, for patterns or models that were Indian in nature. The Indian dream about career was fashioned abroad and the high watermark of social evolution remained 'London-return'. As time passed, these archetypes were strengthened, and respectability became a synonym for foreign association and, success, a matter of foreign acceptability.

The dream of the average Indian mother, gradually, became that of acquiring a son-or daughter-in-law with an NRI status, or at least a foreign residence permit. For a while, India became a land which had only three categories of people: Those who had migrated; those who wished to migrate and those who did not have any idea about migration.

Bright young persons were queuing up outside the embassies of prosperous Western countries for visas. Gradually, the dream of *swadeshi* was sacrificed to at the altar of the argument 'there is no need to reinvent the wheel'. The economy in the heydays of the Planning Commission was always forecast for takeoff 'after 15 years'. The number of 15 years never reduced. Only the forecast ceased.

By the early 1990s, the foreign exchange reserves reached such a level of credibility that, literally, the Union Government had to transfer its gold to British vaults. Contemporary history, with its usual twists and turns, brought a Narasimha Rao on the scene who, while heading a minority Government, still bit the bullet. Historical processes were reversed.

I.G. Patel, invited to lead this transformation, preferred to migrate to the directorship of the London School of Economics. Mr. Manmohan Singh experienced his second windfall and became the Union Minister for Finance. The political fortunes of Rao prevented him from getting full credit for the economic renaissance. But one thing remained constant: The preeminence of Western centres of learning.

The Jagdish Bhagwatis of the West toured India exhorting and extolling the virtues of a free market economy. The flash in the pan lasted for a while and the 'India shining' slogan eventually gave way to the chant of 'India emerging as an economic superpower'.

The intellectual habits of six decades, emboldened by the ineptitude of the administrative processes, metamorphosed to more contemporary patterns of transference of assets abroad.

Scams, one bigger than the other grew under the stewardship and leadership of 'a very honest person'. It is said that the national psyche of a people stirred to a point of despondency can strike back with incredible vigour. The 16th Lok Sabha may prove symbolic of the vigour.

The need of the hour is an Indian standard for the economy, in education and industry and much else. For this, everyone will need to pitch in. This is a national endeavour. The identifiable indicators will include the emergence of an Indian currency that is respected as an international currency of exchange; an Indian passport that is treated with the respect it deserves, making Indians proud of India.

June 27, 2014

## India cannot Operate in Parallel Universes

Sigmund Freud is credited with the theory of the conscious and the sub-conscious. The conscious mind is what the individual is aware of and what he deliberately deals with. The unconscious mind deals with everything, just that the 'subject' himself may not be aware of it. However, analysts claim that individuals are often influenced by their sub-conscious even without being aware of it. It is well acknowledged that organic systems often behave like individuals with similar life cycle experiences. Societies are no different.

A large part of Indian society today deals with what can be labelled as the documented and the undocumented part of financial transactions. Sometimes one gets the feeling that it is the undocumented part which is dominant in financial transactions. Be that as it may, not everyone has the skill to operate at two levels or in parallel universes. Those that are deft and can carry out what could be called 'duplex transactions' seem to forge ahead. But the story does not end here.

In macro-economic terms, the dominance of one over the other can be a critical determinant of national, societal, and organisational health. It also determines robustness of the country's currency and investment potential, not to mention, its international prestige.

The present fall of the rupee in the currency exchange market is not entirely unrelated to this rather strange equation between the real economy and the official economy. It may even be argued that many persons in positions of dominance in governance processes survive because of their position in the unlisted economy.

However, the process of governance itself enables interventions only at the official level. It holds to reason that interventions in areas of the economy cannot aspire to impact the whole. Unless this situation is formally accepted and ways found to bring the unlisted economy to some modulated position, reversal of the present tragic path that the nation seems to be treading may be difficult.

September 06, 2013

## Chanting 'Secularism', Ignoring Development

One of the things which needs to be reconciled before this nation can afford to talk of development with confidence is the use of contradictory categories. Irrespective of pretentious claims, glibly-mouthed, it is no news to anyone that secularism defines much of the current political demagoguery. One should ask how secularism is the cornerstone of development. Development is an economic concept. It can also be a social concept but how it can ever be stretched to become a religious concept beats imagination. Hence, there is the confusion of categories.

I only have information that's in the public domain, but till date I haven't heard a political leader of any standing claiming to be anything but secular. The battle-lines are about secularism, pseudo-secularism and the like. However, the bitterness with which this battle is fought seems to be only deepening. One wonders if the battle is about secularism at all or is it about something else that no one wants to accept.

By definition, secularism is an emotive word. It generates more heat than light because it stokes the embers of righteousness. It is a condemnation of all points of view which are not that of the speaker. Even if there are differences in the understanding of secularism or disagreements on the origin of the concepts in the Indian ethos, a democratic framework is expected to work through *samwaad* (dialogue) and a healthy exchange of ideas.

Instead, one is not only noticing undignified accusations but indeed virulence which could lead to violence. This can be dangerous—at any day, anytime, anywhere. It is doubly worrying if it starts contributing to the corrosion of institutions which are the pillars of civil society. The price of such corrosion can be so high that it may be self-destructive for the perpetrator and anarchical for future generations. The astonishing thing here is that, barring a few media channels, nobody seems to be speaking about this. Is it because apathy has numbed our sensibilities? A wise friend told me that these were the "signs of the time". Be that as it may, it does not mitigate the extent of catastrophe which it could cause.

Mouthing gross statements, expressing opinions which are positively wild and then trying to camouflage it as only posing a question, does not reduce the negative impact. To believe that such gamesmanship will be positively rewarding is naïve.

On July 12, the 17th flight of the Indian Space Research Organisation's versatile Polar Satellite Launch Vehicle, PSLV-C15, was launched from Sriharikota. It was a huge success and a matter of national pride. It placed into orbit the remote sensing satellite, Cartosat-2b (an advanced remote sensing satellite built by ISRO), and four other satellites after a perfect lift-off from the spaceport. It was a 54-hour countdown for the 44.4 metre-tall, four stage, PSLV-C-15 costing Rs. 260 crore. All the satellites were put into orbit one after the other. Yet, this did not merit any major national reference, let alone public celebration.

The launch took forward a worthy tradition. The multiple spot scene imagery gathered by the satellite will be useful for village-level resource assessment and mapping, detailing urban infrastructure planning and development, transportation systems planning, preparation of large scale cartographic maps, preparation of micro water-shed development plans, and monitoring of conditions in remote areas.

July 12, 2013

## The Indian Century

India in modern times, broadly understood as the 18th, 19th, and 20th centuries, and beyond, has been a geopolitical mass of tremendous significance. The 18th century saw the colonial powers struggling with each other and with the local powers, to establish their dominance in the sub-continent. The English began in the Ganga Delta moving upwards through Ganga. The French began in the south via Pondicherry, and the Portuguese, after an early start, kept pushing the boundaries of territorial dominance around Goa. The rest, as they say, is history.

That the English succeeded more than other colonial powers was as much about the entrepreneurial spirit of the race as it was about not getting mixed up with the socio-religious sensitivities of the local population. The Portuguese kept pushing for conversions and was succeeded to certain extent whereas the English (with the East India Company being their economic and administrative face) was happy even to serve as the dry nurse to God Vishnu. Thus, they fulfilled the roles which the past rulers had, say in some of the temples of what is today, a version of the then East Bengal.

The operational roll out was significant to the extent that the French exchanged some influence in the territories on the Tamil coastline for giving up their claims in Bengal region, the Dutch confined their influence to the south east island archipelago. The local rulers were so busy fighting each other that they were not able to face the technological might of the European powers.

There were occasions when, given the global contest for empires effected key decisions. Typically, the French gave up some advantage in India to the English to gain leverage on the eastern coast of North America. Indian territories had become a part and parcel of exchanges of land and influence contests around the globe.

The Indian sub-continent was important and so it remained even after the English East India Company surrendered power to the British Crown. In 1857, the trading company from India was wound up to yield power to the British Crown working through the British Parliament. The period between 1857 and 1947 witnessed one of the most un-abashed economic exploitations of a colonial region by the dominant colonial powers. The shame of that period has progressively gained attention, but the sensitive analysis of the same, not the compensation, is still a matter of incomplete research. By the same token, a very poor understanding of the brazenness of exploitation and what it did to the Indian economy, remains to be appreciated in its fullness. The 'Permanent Settlement' of the Bengal Presidency led to the ruins of many lands of economic production. The history of the Bombay presidency, also referred to as the 'Western Presidency', was substantially different. Be that as it may, India remained the source of much of the might of the British imperial muscles, while Indian goods, silver, and more add to the wealth of the island referred to as the United Kingdom.

The Indian soldiers fought for and protected the British empire through World War-I and II, and more. What they got in return was an arch on what is now called the 'Karthavya Path.' The arch of stone has names of Indian soldiers etched on it in a manner in which a few can decipher, but that's another story.

Many of the Indian elite so identified with the British form pomp and glory that they became more British in mannerism than say, the British themselves. The rich intellectual tradition of the Indian sub-continent got labelled as the 'Hindu tradition'. The labelling may have been technically correct because much of the Indian tradition was subscribed to by the followers of Hinduism. But practically it did a great dis-service because a common heritage got labelled as a sectarian heritage. The ripples of that strong belief, on the surface, are still making the waves.

In Israel, ethnic Jews from all parts of the world acknowledge a common heritage of Judaism. In India, the cultural identity of a universal character got labelled in a sectarian manner and was mischievously pitted against, say, Islamic heritage or a so-called post-modern Christian heritage.

These historical constructs, even though mischievously and ingenuously perpetrated, are not easy to undo.

It will take a long time for a general appreciation to emerge that intellectual traditions have a lineal heritage and that there is no competitiveness, segmentation and paganism amongst the intellectual traditions of a land.

Once this is achieved, the Indian century would have truly begun.

October 01, 2022

# 3

# Communication

## Language: Emotional Connect and More

Communication is central to all living entities. Plants communicate; creatures and animals communicate; and, of course, human beings communicate. They communicate not only amongst themselves but also across different categories and species. The examples are many, the illustrations are numerous, hence, there is no need to overemphasise this aspect of communication. The big concern is not with the act of communication but with the modes of communication.

For example, the uses and anatomy of communication among plants are well mapped, but there are not many who attempted an extensive research study of plant communication.

There are some exceptions, especially in the form of references and awareness. Illustratively, Kalidasa, in his epic drama 'Abhigyan Shakuntalam', would have us believe that when Shakuntala was leaving the 'Tapovana' (the hermitage) of Sage 'Kanva', the creepers of the jungle wrapped themselves around Shakuntala to bid an emotional farewell. What Shakuntala said would probably never be known, but it was obvious that sentiments and expressions were involved. The creepers wrapped themselves around Shakuntala as a kind of embrace and communication medium. Like an electronic system, the system of communication points requires encoding and decoding, and there is a thought process behind it.

Plants don't make sound in the way that animals, insects or some other creatures do. This makes the act of communication between insects and animals somewhat more sophisticated. The chirp of the insects of one variety or another is an act of communication, as indeed is the howling, barking, whining, and such acts of the animals among themselves and across species.

All these creatures make sounds through their throats and mouths, and depending on the kind of noise that comes out of the animal, it is encoded and decoded. There are sounds of fear, just as there are sounds of invitation. There are sounds of anger and the sounds of nothing more but peace and the invitation of an attempt to put together a group or give an alert about a danger. All put together, the derivation is obvious: 'communication' is not just a human phenomenon. It is as rich as the mind of the entity.

A dog, for example, communicates in multiple ways and is capable of sounds of aggregation, mating, warning, and more. The sound of a dog varies from species to species and from one breed to another. It is another matter that not many texts have been scripted on this theme, and hence there is little available on the language of the dogs.

Amongst human beings too, all races don't have a script, yet within the race, they communicate. The matter does not end there.

Amongst human beings too, as indicated, there are a large number of variations among those of human species that don't have a script for their language but still communicate with each other. The difficulty with such a situation is the lack of standardisation and communication that the group needs when dealing with a new group. Thus, there is a geographical limit to the expanse and range of languages. In the more evolved type of human species, a script is available, and after a period of practice, the script is comparatively evaluated. In the times of yore, there was a Roman script, there was a Dravidian script, a Devanagari script, and there were Chinese scripts; there may have been a few other scripts that are no longer alive but must have existed. As time passed and the human species moved, mother scripts of Latin, and Sanskrit, acquired prominence and thus many modern languages were sprouted under their impact. It is not clear how many human languages exist on the planet today or, for that matter, how many languages are dead today.

Literature, as we understand it, is available in some of the languages.

The coming of writing was another phenomenon. It is reported that in the earlier stages of writing, the writing was on palm leaves, and pointed tips of hard material like bamboo branches were used to sketch an imprint on the leaves. The growth of writing is a specialisation in its own right, it is not feasible to attempt to document different stages of writing here. Put one clear thing, if that is the only clear thing, that the writing of the language adds to its durability.

Language is a binding force between individuals and groups. It also attempts to integrate a range beyond the sounds of languages and written scripts of languages.

In most parts of the world, among all human beings, there may be a struggle between human groups for dominance, but certainly no struggle over the value of any language. Any language within its range, growing along with each other, should be a binding force. It cannot be a force for mutual exclusion and antipathy. Put simply language is the vehicle of the mind.

November 08, 2023

## Resolving Life's Dilemmas is an Art

Another New Year, in the form of 2023, is on our calendar. As usual December 31 marked both verve and spirited celebrations. Nothing is wrong with that; however, a simple question about the celebration on December 31 is inherent in the situation.

How was December 31 different, say, from November 30, or coming January 31? It is the same diurnal circulation of the earth. The sunrise of January 1 was not any different from any other day!

A calendar is clearly a manmade division of time, marked by a convenience for time calculation. There are different calendars around the world, of which the Gregorian Calendar, the Vikram Samvat Calendar, the Saka Calendar are only a few of the many variants.

Be that as it may, celebrations and measurements play a significant role in human life. Thus it is that concepts and everyday living have to be blended together for a healthy lifestyle. The art of doing so is the art of effectiveness. Ultimately, it is the mind that shapes the understanding of the world and relationships.

Art lies in resolving life's dilemma and seeing 'meaning' into things. This happens even when does not formally realise it. It is this 'perception' and 'reality' that affects behaviour.

All human expressions of love, hate, attraction, depression and more are, therefore, also, sensory experiences. And it is this iteration that creates human civilisation with its linkages to 'territory'.

It is important to realise that values provide the link between self and the external world. It is this connect, also, that is a challenge to unravel. Be it philosophy, be it the arts, or whatever else, it is embedded in matter and driven by spirit. To be in sync with this relationship, is the requirement of life.

Art of life is, also, embedded in values and the ability to redeem one's word. This is why organisations are formed to deliver as per certain known 'standards'. To organise this is the route to success.

It is this ability to generate, sustain, and implement standards that is at the core of organizations. It covers everything from individual demeanour to societal relationships.

The word "organisation" has a rough Sanskrit translation, "Yojana". This word is derived from the Sanskrit root word 'yuj'. Translated it means to "organise". In the Vedas, there is a dictum which roughly translated means "it is difficult to find someone who can organise".

To organise, one must have standards, fair play, and the ability to articulate forms. The Sanskrit dictum clearly says that to do this is difficult. A look at the history of institutions of all kinds reveals that only those with the ability to 'organise' survived. To organise, therefore, requires the enunciation of principles and the ability to follow these principles.

To organise is, in other words, a high form of human relationship: the relationship between matter and spirit, the relationship between matter and matter, and, ultimately, any activity that needs to be goal-driven.

A calendar is a link in this ability to organise, and it is central to any assessment or measurement.

This approach has to be made a part of the training to the individuals and training of groups. This covers everything from the private to the public sectors, it includes the local governments, state governments, the national government, the army, the cooperative movement. The day one realises this, one will really usher in a 'New Year', in a manner of speaking.

January 04, 2023

## Dealing with Others

The ability to work with others is one of the basic requirements of life. It precedes things like climate change, nuclear disarmament, world peace, or indeed handling a virus. The moment a child feels hungry, it instinctively knows how to ask for a feed. This means sending a message to whoever is willing to listen. Usually, it is in the form of crying or making a sound seeking attention. If the child didn't have this capacity to deal with others, it would never get feed.

Gradually, the individual learns to communicate with gestures and movements. Sounds begin to fall in a pattern. Language competencies emerge. People learn to respond coherently and a dialogue begins. Language is embellished with an expressive and larger vocabulary. When needed, body language or facial expressions replace words to make communication subtler.

The purpose here is to reflect how dealing with others is basic to human existence. Moving beyond childhood, the infant grows into an individual with identifiable preferences. The individual enters a higher level of personality development and is conscious about how one can gain support. A person needs clothing, a place to rest, and begins to look for comfort. The person's range of relationships grows.

In teenage and adulthood, the individual recognises some people are easy to get along with and some are not. The issue is not of pick and choose. It is basic and bounded because the needs of food, shelter, clothing, and resources are limited to finding it from a bounded environment. This is often an institution such as a school or college or a social set-up like the family. The realities of society start surfacing. It becomes obvious that institutions and social groups are important. However, there is also a need to have contact with 'strangers' and the need to handle random, short-term interactive situations. One has to go out shopping and deal with a person at the billing counter for acquiring goods or fulfilling a need. One cannot risk being abrasive but one cannot also always marshal the necessary patience, attitude, or even the words to gain compliance. The art of dealing with others gets larger and bigger.

Each individual has a distinct personality and expressions vary from person to person and even situation to situation. This is what makes dealing with others a craft.

Summing it up, one has to learn how to 'read' others and navigate very carefully to achieve one's goals without disrupting or annoying. However, temperament, ego, vocabulary, and above all the competency to think and talk becomes increasingly critical. One deals with others through words, gestures, eye contact. The list is long and dealing with others becomes complex. Tune and meter come in. Music and songs emerge. They get embedded in an environment of light and shade, comfort, and discomfort. The interplay of so many forces makes it challenging to stay in control.

Indeed, the only dimension one can have some control over is oneself: the choices of words, gestures, timing, voice inflection, and intonation matter. To be in total control is difficult but remains the ideal.

Gradually, dealing with others becomes an interplay of reflex actions and conscious choices. Communicating slowly could help at times and communicating effectively requires a mellower personality. It requires a capability of simultaneously assessing the environment and consciously conveying what one seeks to convey. The range of excellence in doing so is often the discriminating factor between the quality of failure and the quality of success. This continuous journey is inherent in keeping life going. It requires skills of dealing with others.

August 09, 2021

## Integrity of Thought and Delivery

Everyone experiences life. Over the years, every individual has developed connect, some are cherishable others would be better forgotten. We all believe we deserve better. The list of experiential attribute, common to all human beings, can be a lengthy one. What distinguishes one person from another is his/her ability to interpret experiences and internalise the learning for a more evolved self-conduct. The last two verbs are also almost universal. Experimentally, one could ask anyone if he/she interpreted his/her experiences. The answer would be yes. Ask anyone if he/she learned from this exercise and the answer would be yes. So be it.

For the sake of the narrative, one can move away from self and focus on the other person. Love turns sour, colleagueship in the place of work gets dented and community connects suffer because deep within, one finds the other person to be deficient. Some say it, some don't. Those who speak about it are almost universally labelled as plain spoken at the mildest and abrasive at the worst. Almost everyone talks of desirability of a feedback and yet, when it is provided, very few welcome it. Results are there for all to see—there is almost a universal disruption of bonds that once kept couples, families and communities together. The fashionable thing is to talk of social safety nets, self-reliance, universal healthcare and the list can be long. This is far more fundamental and far reaching today than the effect of disruptive technologies.

The fact of the matter is that greater the distance from one's given location and technology orientation, more glorious and attractive it seems to the distant vision. Even though a friendly doctor in the neighbourhood has disappeared in certain urban environments, it is possible to dig out connect of some variety with him, be it through school-day relationship of yesteryears. Concurrently, there is a romanticised version of medical care of the so-called industrialised West. Short-term stays in such environment have one set of experiences but longer ones are another matter altogether. Those, who are long-term residents there, have imponderable waiting schedules before they can have an appointment of specialist medical advice. The only step short of that is emergency care.

However, the space of medical needs, between emergency care and needing specialist advice, is large. When this is topped up with stringent pharmaceutical regulations governing the sale of over-the-counter medicines (including drugs and medical compositions which one knows to be friendly to one's body system), life can be a nightmare. This writer is allergic to Kiwi. A decade ago on a visit to Melbourne, he developed high sensitivity on the skin. The narration of what happened next would be seen as a criticism of Melbourne, Australia, or one's lack of planning and more. That is not intended, however, as they say, it's another story. Nevertheless, it was a challenge to find a suitable antidote.

The theme of this writing is essentially, to keep things simple. One might ask: Is being truthful so difficult? Is taking care of the assurances one gives, so elusive? Is honouring one's word so difficult? The answer to these questions may raise a whole school of philosophy, much gyration and even ridicule. One is left wondering: If by a process of evolution, certain parts of the world, by definition, are only capable of dealing with each other with a ruse of facades. When they converse among themselves, they keep making statements which they know are not true, or hold out assurances being fully aware of the infeasibility of whatever they are proposing. The amazing part is that this is lauded by some as 'being diplomatic'. One fails to see how calculated inaccuracy and worse could pass off as diplomatic.

The message is as simple as the writing on the wall. If one took oneself seriously, one would happily be simple, straightforward and honest. That would give him/her the capacity to receive the truth, deliver with conviction and contribute to a sense of gross happiness or at least help diminish disillusionment. Communication would also be authentic. Perhaps, one deals with facades and almost develops deftness in it because of the limited ability of individuals to receive the truth. A constant urge of wanting to come across others better and more glorified than they actually are, is destructive.

Realistically, it's easy to see how one can trip up oneself, it's equally plausible to be kind to oneself and accept the facts of one's life just as one accepts one's height, place and year of birth.

These are things nothing to brag about or to be embarrassed for. One way of alleviating pain is to keep things simple. There can be no substitute for integrity of thought and delivery.

January 07, 2019

## Need for Information

We live in an information determined era. The complete set of indicators of what constitutes information are unknown. The space for information identification and dissemination is filled by the media. The norms of the conduct of affairs of the media, do exist, but are far from complete.

This state of affairs could constitute a civilisational crisis. The situation is worsened when some of the favourite topics of some select stakeholder groups are serenaded and there is so much noise created about it. The noise itself becomes news. The upshot is discernible but is not being flagged.

The confusion is worse confounded when it passes through the prism of political biases and interests of the media groups. The refraction of news is also influenced by growth theories, the views of economists and indeed the biases of certain perspectives which have achieved cult status like the views of the Italian economist Vilfredo Pareto. This is not likely to be reversed in a hurry.

In the meanwhile, the situation at the survival level of the planet and at a national level for a country like India continues to escalate. Some illustrations will make the statement clearer.

Water is a major global concern. It is basic to agriculture and human living. Land masses have been defined by the quantum of availability of water. The fact that an overwhelming surface area of the planet is covered by it, is irrelevant to life and crop. This is because of its saline nature.

On June 14, in one of its few policy level based surveys and analysis, NITI Aayog made a statement on 'water'. It is reported that about 600 million people face high to extreme water stress and about 2,00,000 die every year because of inadequate access to safe water. This is a deeper crisis than any known epidemic. NITI Aayog went on to do what it enjoys doing, rank states on how well they use and manage water resources. This was understandable because the document is entitled, 'Composite Water Management Index'.

There is obviously a need to enhance the quality of our understanding of water resources.

In the meanwhile, it is recognised that underground water level is receding. However, if this realisation has helped better monitoring of tube wells, it is still to show.

The above statement notwithstanding, there are other yawning gaps in the developmental discourse of India. Consider the shortage of teachers at all levels of formal instruction. It hasn't reduced the zeal for setting up and approving more institutions.

A shift in scene will help to amplify the contradictions. Prime Minister Narendra Modi has a penchant for coining accurate and pithy slogans. At the Maritime Summit of 2016, Modi gave the slogan of 'port-led development'. The slogan was dutifully picked up, orchestrated, and choruses were sung in praise and confirmation of the same.

Consider the situation two years down the line. In the report card of the Government so meticulously prepared and so widely disseminated, there is not a page to what happened to the slogan 'port-led development'. The thundering silence may be at a far bigger cost than even the media is willing to flag. One is not talking of the biased, the paid and the sponsored media. One is talking of the basic straightforward media as media.

There can be no maritime activity without shipping. The state of the ship building industry, in India, is conspicuous by its absence. In the meanwhile, there is ceaseless talk of competiveness with China. let's take shipping. COSCO Shipping Aries, China's first domestically built 21,000 twenty-foot equivalent units (TEU) container vessel has been officially put into service as reported by CCTV news on June 12, that very day.

The 400-metre vessel has moulded beams, a draft (underwater depth) of 58.6 metres and free board (above water depth) of 33.5 metres. It can travel at a projected speed of 22 nautical miles per hour and has a cargo capacity of 1,98,000 tons or 21,237 TEU.

It is built by a state-owned corporation.

Did our media notice this? Did it merit any relook at the state of the slogan 'port-led development'?

June 18, 2018

## Getting to Grips with Indianness

India is in the process of celebrating the 75th year of independence. The 'band baja' of G-20 has joined the crescendo.

Several speakers are dwelling on India's achievements and talking of the great things which have been done/can be done. Integrity of intentions can sometimes supersede some operational flaws.

The purpose however should, also, be to strengthen the Indian sense of identity while flagging the significant achievements which Independence of mind enable. These break free efforts are valuable.

Typically, they range from achievements in space to near elimination of Polio. In the same breath, it is necessary to recognise that there continue to be many and significant areas of potential improvement. Not to think of them and not to attempt to tackle them would be naïve. The objective here is not to create a balance sheet.

The objective here is to flag some of the distinctive concepts and manifestations of Indian identity and how it makes India a truly unique experience. A few illustrations may help.

Consider the proposition that India probably is among the few lands in the world where *mauna* (silence) is celebrated and idolised. There are many amongst us who observe silence for a given day or parts of the day. There are others who choose when they want to keep silent and will communicate only in writing. This is often seen and experienced, among other things, as route to mental peace and coming to terms with oneself and one's surroundings. It is well known that spoken words are like a shot of arrow and cannot be taken back. Unthinking utterances can, sometimes, cause more damage and pain than perhaps even broken bones. Yet communication is such a basic urge that people talk sometimes even when the other person is not listening. Give a mike to a speaker and the chances are he will exceed the time in the fond notion that even if many people are not listening, he needs to say what he has to say. A recognition of the significance of *maun* and its projection as a trait would be a worthy contribution to the seminal components of Indian identity.

At a different level, consider the concern of brother-sister relationship. India is probably the only culture where a man-woman relationship has been sublimated to an asexual level. It is not only its sublimation but its ritualization that is a matter of higher level of consciousness. Relationships have been created across many seemingly unsurmountable hurdles by the sending of a *rakhi* by a lady to a gentleman with whom she would seek a connect. The reciprocation of that gesture of sending *rakhi* is celebrated with much social approval. Some stories about this circulate and many still practise it symbolically. This component of Indian identity needs to be projected with far more vigour to the edification of all who may wish to be more knowledgeable.

Other examples of Indian uniqueness, are many. The listing of the type attempted above can only be illustrative. Mythology and folklore provide a rich treasure trove for those who know how to seek and interpret.

In an era full of climate talk and resetting of developmental objectives, the approach would be incomplete without a look at the uniqueness of Indian-ness in an ecologically related context or indeed the non-human world.

In India we have recognised life in a unique way amongst animals, trees, plants and more.

Two examples would help illustrate the point. In India, even beyond the symbolic value of an elephant, the reference to a *Hathi* (elephant) can evoke images of the *Aeravat hathi* (elephant). In other words, the celestial elephant with many divine virtues. In the pragmatic world, in India, elephant enjoys unparalleled images of prosperity and wisdom. The rest of the elephant lore is another story. From Ganesha-jee's head to the fields of battle there are many stories.

Coming to the second example, the reference is to trees. A concept is thereof a heavenly tree called the *Kalpavriksh*. Belief has it that wishes come true under the shade of this *Kalpavriksh*. How can then, one practice thoughtless felling of the trees? The targets of climate change, be they of 2030 or of 2070, apart, would qualitatively improve if the prism of looking at the issues were also to be modified.

Be it business or *Amritkal* of independence or a G-20 event what is unique about India has to understood. stated and projected.

The road to rediscovering Indian identity is clearly arduous and needs sharpened ability to think. It is worth the effort. The new education policy would hopefully serve as a cataylist.

March 01, 2023

## In Defence of Truthfulness

The caption of this text may appear strange to some. The question would be asked as to why truth should need defense?

This is a good question. Truth in itself should be self-sufficient and stand out for itself. Indeed, all communities all over the world teach their children to be truthful. Notwithstanding this obvious practice in operational terms, truth is often a casualty at the level of convenience.

Human interaction is often spent in trying to be pleasing to each other. This is so because no one wants to be the "foul guy' to the other. An illustration will prove the point.

If 'A' asks 'B' "how am I looking?" the chances are more than likely that the reply will be irrespective of the truth. The reply will be "You are looking fine". The person so responding may not mean it, but he will still say it.

Hence, in interpersonal dynamics, pleasantness becomes the guiding force, and this is often at the cost of 'truth.'

In fact, a person who is truthful is seen as tactless and often meets with some reservation on the social front. The person who is pleasant, "no matter how untruthful", scores over the truthful person. It is then that the 'truthful' person's parents, spouse, children, friends, and more, all start persuading him to be pleasant and not just truthful. In fact, being truthful is almost taken to be unacceptably blunt.

If the matter were to end at a social level, there would not be much to talk about because, socially, what one would lose on the round and one gain on the swing.

When the matter goes beyond social platitudes, it becomes serious and has deeper, more basic implications. Recently, there has been much media space taken up by detection of people's wealth earned through other than truthful means. The role of the CBI, CID, and Enforcement Directorate is not the theme of this text.

These agencies do their job just as any other agency is meant to do their job. The subject of 'truth' in this text is more commonplace and more of every day usage than the role of financial probity in life.

One of the bigger problems of being 'un-truthful' is to keep track of what one said to whom. If one says one thing to 'A' but does not say the same thing to 'B' in a manner that is replicable, then consistency becomes a causality. While talking to 'B', one has to remember what one said to 'A.' And, if the number of people increases from 'A' to 'B' to 'C' to 'D' and more, the problem keeps getting more and more complex.

The truth is, memory is never perfect and if the framework of reference is not truthful, then even the change in emphasis or a few words can alter the meaning and the impact.

Hence the proverb, "Honesty is the best policy." In that case, one does not have to strain the memory and keep reminding oneself of the version of the truth one has presented. The truth has a way of standing out.

Nevertheless, as already mentioned earlier on in the text, for many conveniences is more comforting than the truth.

As time goes on, more and more people are seeking comfort in ancient texts, which have withstood the test of time. Be they *Vedic* in character, or the *Gospel*, or the *Quran* or the *Guru Granth Sahib*, and more. These are treasures of humankind and have sustained the homosapien species on this planet over millennia without letting them get lost. They may have varying prophets and more, but all of them unequivocally have supported the wisdom and the necessity for 'truth'.

In the culture of the Indian sub-continent, the dictum is 'Satyameva Jayate.' In a free translation, it would mean 'truth alone triumphs'. What is to be noted is that the statement does not say simply 'truth triumphs'. It says truth ALONE triumphs. The meaning is so simple; it needs no explanation. This is empanelled in our national emblem. The wisdom of this choice is unexceptionable, it remains the ideal framework of the societal development of India.

And that is for good reason.

Like anywhere else, practice of truth in business, as anywhere else, is critical. That is what brand building and sustenance is all about. That is the essence of basic business transaction. Following this route, business too will be successful.

Empiricism is the testimony to the fact that any other route is not only risky or sub-optimal, but basically unwise.

Falsehood may appear fashionable, but truth and faith in it, are also as old as the seas. And that is the 'defence' of truth, if any, be needed.

November 01, 2022

## Between Emotions and Relationships

Attempt to understand human nature and motivation is almost as old as 'history of ideas'. At different points of time, different theories have emerged and attempts have been made to ascribe relative weightages to it. Depending upon the context one or another point of view has been appreciated, received adulation and held out as the key mover of human action.

Management literature has a surfeit of writings on motivation. The assumption being, if you understand motivation, you understand it all and there is no need to delve deep into any other domain for getting results. This is a palpably consoling thought. Like all consoling thoughts, it has its limitations. Whether it is Maslow, Herzberg or whoever else, one cannot move the world on the lever of motivation. The lever would need a fulcrum. It is this understanding of the nature of the fulcrum that has progressively occupied more space in management literature. The fulcrum may come in the form of opportunity, resources, timeliness of the action or indeed the skill of the doer. The list of components that go into the making of the fulcrum can only be non-exhaustive. With the passage of time, the list changes, evolves and acquires definite contextual overtones.

To put it simply what works and what does not work can be a matter of many variables other than just motivation.

This is a perspective which has, in many management contexts escaped due attention. To make the domain of application of management theory more actionable, it is important to recognise the cognate elements which arouse motives and will sustain it over a period of time.

No motivation can sustain itself unless it is linked to certain basic traits of the person and the context in which it has to operate. Illustratively, motivation theory is heavily rooted in the material needs of the context. An arid zone needs water and an area which is frozen in ice needs warming. There cannot be 'motivation of water' in an icy area! Thus, it is that motivational theory is context specific and is linked to the key characteristics of the key personnel involved.

Management theorists would do well to create an algorithm of motivational forces across contextual variants of universal trends.

An illustration would help. Many theorists have believed that man is a social animal and therefore is gregarious in character. A human being cannot live alone and needs people around him. People are needed not only in material terms but in emotional and cognitive terms. This creates dependencies and relationships. To understand what moves people, situation and contexts, one has to recognise that at the core of human action are relationships.

Relationships evoke emotion and very often emotions are nurtured by material conditions. Emotions are bred by contiguity, communication and resonance of one variety or another. Put simply, emotions are that inner feeling of attraction or repulsion that are not necessarily driven by any equation which can be fully explained by analysis. Emotions come like a surge and can sweep like a flood They can demolish logic and can propagate self-preservation and self-destruction with equal intensity.

Emotions are very often rooted in identity and nothing appeals more than whipping up that wave of identity to a point of celebration.

These are complex emotions sometimes described as 'love' which popularly is ascribed to the heart. What got this identification of the feeling of love with the functioning of the heart is difficult to explain. A good scholar of logic once told me that it is the heart which supplies blood to all parts of the body and hence the correlation between 'love' and 'heart'. What one didn't cross-examine the scholar of logic with, would be the proposition of a possible substitution of the reference to the 'heart' by that of the 'lungs', as the place where 'love' is lodged. There are two lungs in the body and there are always two people where love is concerned. The lung provides oxygen to every cell of the body in a far more profound way that what the heart does by the supply of blood. If this is physically true, then why not say that 'love' is lodged in the lungs?

This, however, is a moot point and need not be shredded too closely. The important thing to remember is that relationships are at the core of human action. Emotions are a subset of relationships.

Once this is understood, it will be easier to organise action which would include business. Ultimately, business also survives on relationships.

April 11, 2022

# 4

# Quantitative Techniques

## Pandemic and Seminal Experience

Periodically, the *Homo Sapiens* pass through a seminal experience that affects the very core of their existence. Millions of years ago, when the wheel was discovered, it was a seminal revolution. Human civilisation and culture depended on the outcome of this experience. All this happened so long ago that there is no record or information on where this revolution began or did it begin parallelly in many parts of the globe at the same or at different points of time. One doesn't know whether the wheel was one man's idea or a collective effort. So distant it is in the hoary past that no one has ever thought of even celebrating this breakthrough. Similar is the story of fire—again, a basic revolution. Not much is known about the discovery of fire. The list can be added to. Similar is the issue of discovery of iron or the invention of firearms. Given the brevity of a human life, the active years are less than half of one's existence. Given the millennia that have passed in human growth, a human lifespan would occupy even less space than a speck on the canvas of time. Imagine the level of insignificance when compared to the evolution of a planet.

Notwithstanding this truth, seminal times have been many in human history. They have even varied from region to region and few of them have had global impact concurrently.

The last century and the first two decades of the present one have been transformative. August 6, 1945 is etched in glass because of the dropping of the atom bomb on Hiroshima. Along with Nagasaki, both are a grim reminder—if any be needed—that human beings have no limits to what they can wreck on one another. There is no record of any regret having been expressed in words or behaviour to the civilisation-altering, conscious effort at human devastation. If anything, it led to a global race for possession of atom bombs, hydrogen bombs and more. Human civilisation lives today with 'bomb-mines' with a magnitude which belies comprehension. There are nobler sides of the human effort too. And if the earth still rotates around its axis, it is because human beings are capable of equally elevating efforts. Many could possibly conclude that human effort in history is a strange mix of banality and benevolence.

Be that as it may, the present Covid times are a grim reminder that everything that happens is not necessarily within the domain of human comprehension to begin with. The human species has to grow to comprehend this. Here is an experience the logical origin of which is unknown. The parameters of mutation stand very largely unprogrammed, the responses, be it of prevention or the antidote by way of vaccination, etc., have areas of grey. There is no knowing when it will end. Surely, these are seminal times. It may be an error to believe one thing or another. This virus may never fade away or indeed it may continue in a more transformed manner. The core message is to develop a realistic vision of human competence and capabilities; to have the wisdom and fortitude to recognise one's own divinity but with a modesty of recognition to its reach. Human beings need one another. They need to do the best they can to keep the species evolving and growing.

Today, that message to the *Homo Sapiens* who began their journey with the wheel may be as significant as any revolution this planet has seen. The sooner we wake up to this truth, the better we will cope with the pandemic.

August 31, 2021

## Scientific Thinking & All That Goes With It

There is much emphasis in scholastic dialogues on the scientific method. This has roots, since ancient times, in many disparate, unlinked traditions, existing simultaneously.

Confucius in the Chinese tradition, Chanakya in the Indian tradition, Socrates in the Greek tradition, laid emphasis on the scientific method. It requires evidence-based reasoning. In many cases, there is no choice because without reasoning it is difficult to set direction with confidence. Even so, it is equally important to realise that reasoning has its limits. Take the case of the theory that there is a God particle in every atom. An atom can be identified but the God particle cannot be. *Sanatana* theology for millennia has propounded that there is 'Godliness' in every element. It was dismissed as 'hocus-pocus' by the ultra-rationalists. Reconciliation of the two vantage points of perception in the preceding paragraph—'the presence of God particle in every atom' and 'Godhood in every particle' is yet to take place. Given the focus of this text, there is a need to examine the strengths and the limits of the scientific method. This is specially so in the current pandemic context. The globe is enveloped in several contradictions in understanding the pandemic situation. The origins of the pandemic are unclear. Worse, it has been politicised. The near-obsession with sanitisation involving masks, washing of hands, social distancing, etc., continues to be serenaded. There are parts of the world today where combat and conflict are rampant. Afghanistan is a good example. It would be interesting to know the views of the Taliban on COVID-19 or is it that coronavirus cases are 'non-existent' in Afghanistan? Under such disturbing situations, the locus standi of scientific thinking becomes severely nebulous. So many aspects of the pandemic are under ceaseless debate. To what extent does the virus travels across surfaces? What is the antidote to the virus, at what stage of virulence? How does the reversal of the disease get organised?

What are the collateral damages of the disease on the human body and to what extent can it be reversed, if at all? How effective are the vaccines? Are booster doses needed? Of what periodicity? The questions are endless.

The answers are limited. The confusion is extensive. Family, social, national, global debates are all over. Even maintaining sanity in domestic situations is up for grabs. The wonder is not that there is so much stress, anxiety and worse. The question is the sheer miracle of keeping a semblance of logic afloat. But the basic question remains, what is the strength of the logical force? To what extent can scientific thinking provide the answers? A prolonged period of home isolation has its effect on healthcare. Exercises and skincare would be only two of the several platforms on which the health dimension would have an effect. The solutions have to follow the scientific method. Whereas doctors, therapists and healthcare workers have attempted heroic levels of lateral diversification, the mismatch between the number and skills required to the response is huge. Whereas there is a progressive movement towards some clarity, there is also a lot that still looks like 'fiddling with wires in the dark'. With all the connects that the scientific method is entitled to, there is a need to reinforce it with extrapolated experience, faith and spirituality. This would help in navigating the uncharted domain. Scientific thinking has to be reinforced with applied creativity. Applied creativity needs to include experiential reasoning. One has also to extrapolate distilled experiences. This may not be a matter of choice in certain areas. It may require a well-thought-out Delphi approach and more to navigate.

August 19, 2021

## Understanding Energy Concerns

Each social grouping has its mythology. The sense in which the phrase social groupings is being used in this text refers to human aggregations popularly clubbed as a category, such as "the rich", "the poor", "the professional", "the sailor" and so on. The rich have a sub-category that is derisively referred to. This sub-category is called "the nouveau riche," which is supposed to be loud in its display of recently-acquired wealth. Whether as a characteristic this is true or not has never been empirically tested, however it is believed to be true. Similarly, many professional groups such as engineers, doctors, et al. look down upon history as a discipline. A professional historian is neither taken seriously nor referred to with the mellowness which any "serious" professional would have been. So be it!

Applying this yardstick of traits to the profession of energy specialists, the same kind of syndrome can be found. Unexplained professional myopia prevents many of them from recognising that the need for green energy is not a first energy shift that has ever touched the human civilisation. Energy shifts are as old as humanity. When the physical energy of human beings was used to break down aggregations of natural material, such as branches or boulders, the substitution of physical human energy by power of draft animal energy was a major energy revolution. For any kind of traction or movement being substituted with the use of animal energy, there was an equally big revolution.

Ostensibly human beings took a long time to recognise that they need not walk to move from one point to another but they could instead ride an animal. This too was nearly as big a revolution as any. Lions remained untameable, elephants lost on speed what they gained on bulk. The horse was the clear winner and its popularity became so much that horse power became the unit of measurement and even today the strength of an engine is explained in terms of how many horse powers it represents. The message is simple. Each source of energy was a process which had its era of dominance. The shift from one era to another was as fundamental, drastic and dramatic as the shift one talks of today for an aspirational or needed change from fossil fuel to green energy.

Be that as it may, any such shift needed a change in technology. Other collaterals followed in the process of evolution: Size of the circle (often referred to as the wheel) and the concomitant size of the case which would contain the machinery (called the equipment).

This meant change in the service industry and indeed the full gamut of ancillary skills. Hence, to understand green energy and the era in which many front-edge communities are locked in today, in a module of learning, is a complicated process. In the prevailing dominant social culture of "fast food", few have the time to pause and consider the nature of the problem.

There isn't any serious dissertation available on how long any era lasted before it gave way to the next era of energy usage. To recognise and change this framework of reference to a more holistic one is the need of the hour. The present obsession with one form of green energy or another, be it solar, wind, hydro, oceanic or biomass is proving good almost only for talking shop and the industry. There is a clear need to get our perspective right on the significance of power, per se. Energy is the underpinning of human civilisation. Its characterisation determines the periods of history. Understanding the methods of transition in the past, from one energy era to another, will help us to find solutions to the current energy concerns better.

February 15, 2021

## Impenetrable Barriers

Any territory around the world, right from a street to a State to a city or a region, has its characteristics. The word "territory" has one of its most common usages in the field of sports and athletics where identities compete from a defined piece of land without having a sovereign status. Thus, it is that Scotland, as a territory, can field a team without having a sovereign status. However, this cannot be the place to resolve these concerns or indeed debate them. The use of the word "territory" in the first sentence of this column is in terms of identity. COVID-19 has changed many things in our world. How many of them will remain altered and how many will relapse to their original form once the virus leaves us is anybody's guess. However, if one can survive the stress of the possibility of being a Coronavirus suspect and being put in quarantine, then there are some very interesting processes at play.

A former civil servant, who for some reason had to travel by car from Almora to Delhi, thus traversing through the three States of Uttarakhand, Uttar Pradesh and Delhi, expressed genuine anxiety at being stopped, grilled and monitored for the virus at the numerous checkpoints he was bound to pass during his journey. He was quite worried about the possibility of being put into quarantine as reasoning usually does not work in such cases. He was convinced that given the state of mind prevailing around the country regarding the pandemic, even his status as an ex-Secretary of the Government of India would not change anything and he would be put in isolation. And given the horror stories coming out of quarantine centres, one can quite understand his reluctance to be put in one. But that's another story for another day.

More to the point, for the first time ever, in modern Indian history, State boundaries have acquired the status of a phenomenon. Consider the birth of the concept of the National Capital Region (NCR). The city of NOIDA came up in the late 60s in select sectors, as a retreat for the rich and famous, especially the ruling class in Delhi. Freelancing educational entrepreneurs and others, particularly the three forces, also penetrated NOIDA. It became a "hub" of sorts.

Subsequently, when commercial spaces in Connaught Place, Khan Market, Nehru Place and others started running short, the done thing was to move to Gurgaon, now known as Gurugram. Corporate offices moved to places such as Cyber City, which coincidently had no special "cyber" identity save being a fanciful noun. Many multinational corporations moved their offices there and those who couldn't get into the cyber bubble, lined up National Highway 8. The Big 4 consulting companies, Price Waterhouse Coopers, Ernst & Young, Deloitte, and KPMG, were not far behind. Pioneering zeal and everything else in between led the way. The Metro followed and a modest four-lane link between Mehrauli and Gurgaon was created. The price of real estate skyrocketed, with many of the rich and powerful boasting of substantial properties in Gurugram. It became a centre of high living, much spending and social standing. A new "territory" was born. Some people lived in Gurugram and worked in Delhi because "the gram" gave the veneer of country living. Others lived in Delhi and worked in Gurugram because Delhi had the advantage of being a social hub where the movers and shakers of society did the rounds of the Delhi Gymkhana, the Delhi Golf Club, the Delhi Race Course, the India International Centre, the India Habitat Centre and much else. In these havens, life pulsated and social elitism flourished. Art and culture were not far behind.

In fact, this intermingling and frequent commuting between the two territories reached such a crescendo that even toll plazas had to be abolished. Straight roads were converted into multiple U-turns. Few if any, complained. And then suddenly, COVID-19 struck the world and walls went up across the country almost overnight.

Haryana discovered its boundaries and passing the non-existent toll plaza became next to impossible. The Delhi-Gurugram border was so heavily monitored that even swanky cars were chased away by the humble stick of the nondescript policeman. The usually unconcerned and cooperative police had finally begun policing to keep Gurugram and (Haryana by implication) safe from the Coronavirus. Unfortunately, the writer of these lines still had his medical care anchored in an institution in Delhi. It didn't matter that his regular monthly dosage of medicines would run out and his symptoms could not be attended to by random doctors who had, in any case, shut their clinics, because as one doctor pointed out: "Even the potential Corona patient doesn't tell the truth about foreign travel as there is a serious possibility of being put into quarantine." Somebody high up in the Haryana administration was spoken to. He gave a very diplomatic reply: "Sir, we will arrange for your medical care in Gurugram. But you know how it is. We make one exception for you and people will push that aperture to their advantage." So, the borders remain closed, no matter what the compulsion of those trying to cross them. At least, the country has been secured from the Coronavirus. To give everyone his due, the sceptic will ask: "Has it really?"

May 25, 2020

## Controversies and Their Resolutions: Some Reflections

The interesting thing about change is deciding its phasing and direction. While running an institution, a conglomerate, or a nation, a good deal of planning has to be executed in preparing for a change.

The considerations are obvious. No direction of change will be universally acclaimed. This is so because whatever the direction of change, some vested interests would have been negatively affected, and some vested interests will stand to gain. Be that as it may, it's obvious that for the full impact of change to take place, even if one disagrees, those who disagree will have to allow change to happen.

If a determined group of people take it on their heads, to prevent the change from happening, there can be much trouble and, indeed, chaos. Usually, in such cases, even what is reasonable itself becomes open to debate.

Hence, a certain level of maturity, reasonableness, and tolerance is the bottom line of all group activity. A society gets indexed in this manner. The English society has several centuries of evolution and nearly two centuries of global rule, has shown this resilience in managing their internal differences.

Consider the coronation of King Charles III. His personal life was riddled with a lot of controversies, and some consider it even against the kind of conservative dignity that the British Royalty was meant to observe. When such a man is declared King and supposed to undergo a ceremonial coronation, obviously emotions will be raised. It is a compliment to the maturity of English society that the whole episode was handled with dignity and grace.

Those people of British populace who were in groups large enough to be recognised (i.e., more than a given number) made their point with quite dignity. They did not attempt to disrupt the coronation. Some of them held placards reading "Not My King." A few of them did get rowdy and were appropriately handled. Their numbers were small and handled with dignity. They were quarantined and contained. Their protest was registered, and the ceremonies of coronation, went unimpeded. The roles and relationships of the English society while registering their differences agreed to co-exist. Those who did not believe in the royals could say what they wanted, but not in a disruptive manner. The method of protest and their containment seem typical in a large part.

In another context, it could have become ugly and put the community in a bad light. India, as a society much larger than the English, has handled its affairs mostly, with dignity. It is obvious that our numbers are running into the hundreds of crores. Size becomes important. The media also plays a role. The tremors can be felt, but it is important that they are not excessively disruptive or indiscreet.

Similarly, India seems to have handled its foreign affairs with a fair degree of dignity and imagination. Whether it was Party 'X' in power or Party 'Y', the foreign policies were largely similar. This was largely because India believes that in dealing with external powers, the people involved may change, but the goals remain the same.

Typically, India, being a powerful country, is still not among the five, top industrial countries. Nevertheless, it has managed to stay, almost consistently, equidistant from the global power centres. This has served the interests of the nation well and has prevented ugly jerks and ugly jolts when power changes hands.

Unfortunately, the handling of some of the domestic issues by some of the people of India has not shown the same aplomb. Language issues are characteristically vexatious. However, one must add that, by and large, in the last few months, the processes have shown a fair degree of maturity both in their manifestation and attempts at resolution. The timings of the various efforts have, often, been the same as a point needs a counter point. Even the location could have been related to getting some political mileage. The so-called language controversy, is a case in point. It is for this reason that one gives thought to these concerns for maturity and sagacity. It is an index of collective thinking.

Typically, the timing of the 'India-Bharat' name issue seems to have been made more for political gains than anything else. It is clearly not a substantive issue, as would be the case with handling communal confrontations. As a people, one need to think about this issue, as much as of any other, with maturity and sagacity. Fishing in choppy waters is not always sensible, and the risks may be so high that the gains become dubious.

India that is Bharat, with its sanctity, depth and experience, needs to find solutions to its problems in a manner worthy of its heritage, reach and depth.

October 01, 2023

## Fiddling with Wires in the Dark

COVID-19 was declared the top news through mid-March to April in India. The conventional phrase in the media for such themes is 'flavour'. (The 'flavour' of these few weeks was Covid). Like all flavours, it was expected to grab attention and pass away yielding place to new ones. No such thing happened. A top political authority in the land with his usual penchant referred to the 18 days needed to conclude *Mahabharat* and instead asked for a higher quota of 21 days to defeat COVID-19.

The people believed him because they believe him. His deep political sense has evoked global acclaim. He has underscored it in his speeches in the Parliament. Add to it the advantage that he has an absolute choice to pick his advisors.

Presumably, they are the best of the breed (at least that is what is assumed!). He, like many people of his position, has a personal staff to do all his referencing.

Hence he cannot be taken as a victim to an error of judgement of which normal mortals can be prone to. Be that as it may, the 21 days came and went and the problem became bigger.

There is never an 'error' in a forecast. It arises out certain assumptions and certain calculations The error is forever in the confidence reposed in the forecast. A forecast is not just a statistical essay—it doesn't matter whether it is done in Cambridge University or in the proverbial Timbuktu. There are forecasts and forecasts. Any output is as good as the input. Some day, some statistician will do an analysis of the different routes of calculation and explain the fallacy of errors and assumptions. That day is still far off.

As of now the bottom line is, there is very little known about COVID-19 with certitude. Yes, it is known that ultimately the disease has pulmonary overtones and that's where the casualties happen. The route to that has nearly as many options as the specialisations of the people forecasting.

After having recommended observation of coughing patterns and everything from there to the change of the colour of the toe of the foot, somehow, one doesn't hear too much of these symptoms now. There is talk of suspended particles in moist air and masks have become the new 'flavour' of prevention. It is not surprising that savvy media brands have picked up this slogan and for them wearing a mask is the same category of campaign as saving a Tiger. Amen!

Thus it is that a chain of lockdowns followed. They followed with the gush of crusading administrators, till it was realised that effectively, all economic activity had ground to stop. Everything from banging of 'thalis' to closing of borders had been tried. The sick could not cross the NOIDA border from one side to the other and Haryana was not to be left behind. A public figure with immense power on health matters, banged the table (and everything else in Haryana) to a point where even the President's nominee on a committee was not given permission to cross the border in the first instance. Huge energies which would have moved mountains in another land (with due apologies to Brecht) went into pleading permissions to cross borders. On a certain occasion when Haryana Government relented, Delhi government sought its chance to do the sabre-rattling on permission to cross the border.

While all this was happening at the so-called border and elsewhere, Covid was silently spreading. First the asymptomatic patient was declared a risk and some according to reports were whisked from their homes to quarantine centres to be put in rooms where even the toilets could cause more infection—in a manner of speaking—than COVID-19. Then of a sudden, a powerful politician in Delhi started regularly gracing the screen, stating, that people with early symptoms need not necessarily go to quarantine centres. The official view of many states on this is yet to come in the form of a circular.

The number of circulars from competent authorities of the Government and elsewhere got so large that a Maharatna company assigned the charge of reading all the circulars and doing a summary, to an exalted official like an Executive Director.

In the meanwhile, COVID-19 found its way to individual's households and offices. Some well-known office buildings of

Delhi took turns to close down. Then it was felt that this was not necessary. So much so that even in the quarantine zones full streets were not to be quarantined. They ultimately quarantined the inhabited building of the ill, and some thought that quarantining the flat was good enough.

The sub-plot of political tug-of-war had its play-out in the media.

What followed was the unlocking phase 1.0. Concurrently, Tamil Nadu, Maharashtra, Delhi were fanning shrieking headlines about the numbers rising every day. At least one state, finally, on 14 June discovered it needed more hospital beds! (Didn't somebody also, claim that the lockdown period also had the objective of preparing for a bad COVID-19, break?)

It will be cruel to ask the commonsensical question—it does not need an official circular signed by a high powered authority to tell the public that washing hands with soap for 20 seconds is the best instrument of hygiene!

They are finally discovering that person's personal immunity, healthy hygiene and 'commonsensical elimination measures of infection are the best way forward.'

But the cynic will not be left behind. Every serious step of health, hygiene and common sense he terms a 'fad'! Jai Ho!!

July 01, 2020

# 5

# Organisational Design

## National Events and Symbols

There was a time when elections to Parliament and State assemblies used to be held together. Hence, the election season used to come once in five years and the whole country was in an election mood. Gradually for various reasons, one State assembly or another got dissolved and for that State a mid-term election became necessary. With the states reorganisation becoming an oft practised intervention, some assemblies had to be reconstituted into more than one.

The results were simple. The election season was no longer a five-yearly affair. Ever so often, an election had to be called in some state. There have been instances where for one reason or another, the Lok Sabha term got curtailed and fresh elections to the Lok Sabha became a necessity. As a consequence, therefore, the frequency of elections increased and the Election Commission had to be almost continually at work.

The constancy of the election season created its own syndrome. Occasionally there has been talk of restoring the election schedule to its old cadence. The consensus on this is still to emerge.

One thing which, however, comes out from all this is that change is the order in anything alive.

This applies to rituals also. Rituals include say, the Republic Day-related celebrations and the symbolic events which accompany it. They are also national symbols of joy or solidarity. The canopy which stands today at Rajpath, New Delhi sans the Statue of the British Emperor, which was installed there to begin with, would be an example. Examples such as this have their contradictions. Many agreed that the Statue needed to be removed from the canopy in free India and so it was. There were some suggestions on whose statue should be installed there instead. Now finally the Government has decided that the statue of Netaji Subash Chandra Bose will be installed there. However, the major landmark in Kolkata continues to be the Victoria Memorial. With its exquisite marble and architecture, it is an eyeful. No one seems to particularly bother that it is a relic of a colonial past where enslavement was celebrated with grand monuments. Such are the contradictions of life!

To get back to the Republic Day story, not many recall that the initial Republic Day celebrations were in what is now the Dhyanchand Stadium. Gradually, Republic Day Parade became a display of India's cultural richness and military preparedness, so the Rajpath was chosen. No one particularly bothered about the India Gate relic, perhaps because it was such a grand landmark. Not many noticed that literally thousands upon thousands of Indian soldiers who lost their lives in World War I did so, under orders, essentially in defence of an imperial power under whose yoke Indian was groaning. That too is another story.

In a strange fusion of history, the relic of imperial wars got fused with celebration of the 1971 event and an Amar Jawan Jyoti was installed near Indian Gate in memory of 'The unknown soldier'. The then Prime Minister 'stole' as it were, the Republic Day opening focus, from the Head of the State by beginning the celebrations by a drive to the Amar Jawan Jyoti.

In the meanwhile, the political climate changed and many latent urges which had been quasi-dormant came to life. A National

War Memorial was built near India Gate and the Amar Jawan Jyoti was merged with the National War Memorial. There followed the announcement of dropping of the hymn 'Abide with me' from the Beating of the Retreat ceremony of January 29th. A natural expression of Indian identity with 'Indianness' at its core needs, to be accepted with joy and satisfaction.

February 07, 2022

## Time to Scale up Local Development

Records are an essential part of civil administration. The problem comes in seeking an all-India frame of reference, say for land measurement. This happens because the unit of measurement—acre, bigha, etc.—is known by different names in different parts of the country. There is not much problem when the unit of reference is limited and localised.

The problem exacerbates itself when different regional comparisons become necessary.

That is not the end of the story. In certain parts of India, say Goa, the ownership title itself is still a continuation of the Portuguese pattern of reference. This makes the tracing of the ownership complicated and the authentication tricky. Business, therefore, has to contend with situations to resolve which no informed reference work is available.

This makes an all-India pattern of handling land development issues complex and at times complicated. If the nomenclature of the unit of reference in use is not uniform, for planning purposes, inaccurate and locally unfamiliar yardsticks may have to be applied.

This would lead to a situation of approximation of the realities on the ground to the measurements for planning purposes. Accordingly, where precision be needed there would be a need to feel one's way through. Sometimes, it would work, on other occasions, there would be an element of tentativeness. Significantly, however, no dictionary on the conversion of land units from one to another exists. There are difficulties in envisaging it.

If that be so, it may be useful to do only a certain type of planning at a national level and leave certain other types of planning, (say in terms of frameworks reference of minor irrigation) to the local level. In effect, this is what is happening in many areas. However, these complexities can make for gaps in the formal skill formation of a civil servant before he is put on the job to start operating the system. The average Indian civil servant is smart, shrewd and has a keen eye for reality perception. These attributes can work both constructively and the other way round.

Since one of the aspirations of developmental planning is to standardise the frameworks of reference, this issue of land units and their diversity needs to be reduced to more manageable proportions. A beginning can be made to bringing in some kind of uniformity of units of measurement, to begin with, at the district level. Fortunately, this has already been happening in practical terms in the recent past.

This is the great strength of Indian administration, where solutions are devised at a local level and the basic Indian ingenuity comes to play where formal yardsticks may fail. The need, therefore, is to have norms with resilience. If the norms can tolerate deviations of a certain percentage or magnitude, the system will work. Excessive rigidity has its problems.

Interestingly, the more economically successful states like Gujarat, Kerala or Karnataka have been able to feel their way through this problem more effectively. States which emerged out of direct British rule (where there was an excessive effort to work with externally imposed units of measurement and yardsticks) have had difficulties in making administration a social reality.

As one begins the 75th year of Independence, there is time for celebration and there is also time for reflection on what are the areas of national development which require some tweaking of the parameters of analysis, investment and more.

There is a need to think on the significance to be attached to local and regional developmental processes. More than language or ethnicity need to be factored into the situation, requiring greater insight and analysis.

September 25, 2021

## Some Pertinent Questions

The world of education is huge. It is one of those few areas where one can enter almost without credentials and claim to be an expert. People still listen to such individuals not because they have any great credentials but because they hold positions of influence and patronage. With these qualifications, it is easy to find admirers. There are always hopes of pay-offs by ingratiating the powerful. It is also equally true that the route adopted by people to gain the attention of icons is sometimes quite the opposite and that is one of denigration. By throwing stones at the powerful one can also gain prominence. In essence, the choice of the route to gaining attention of the powerful is a personal one.

For the sake of a feasible, focussed discussion on the learning-teaching process, which is the foundation of education, it may be useful to focus on one segment. The choice of higher education as the segment of attention may be useful. It is also attractive because that is where the so-called intellectuals are. Plus, in the field of higher education, there is a great parade of credentials and sometimes standards. These two dimensions are fit enough topics of discussion in their own right. For the present, suffice it to say that the track record of Indian higher education institutions (HEIs) is at best, modest, be it in the track records of people who have made the grade in Indian academia or of acclaimed students who came out of these institutions that have had a huge resonance of acceptability abroad.

In one of the most widely-acclaimed institutions of the IIT chain, about ten years ago, a back-of-the envelope analysis of successful alumni award winners showed that more than 70 per cent were those who had obtained residency in the US, Canada, UK or other English-speaking communities. The yardsticks of excellence were clear. The only recognition worth flaunting was recognition in a post-industrial English-speaking country. If these are the role models who are projected to the impressionable teenagers in such institutions of national importance, the results can easily be imagined and seen. But it didn't seem to bother anyone too much.

Another analysis of the results of campus placements in IITs, IIMs and similar institutions would establish that the most sought-after placements are in multinational organisations, private companies and other institutions of the ilk. Public sector undertakings are a lower-ranked choice, if at all.

A legitimate question can be asked: Why should the taxpayer subsidise these institutions when there is no ostensible correlation between his investment and the efforts of the outcome of his investments in terms of the welfare of the average Indian?

These are hard questions, frequently asked, but never honestly or for that matter meaningfully tackled. Such lack of correlation is unique to India. And it is not as if there is shortage of money with those aspiring for the portals of premier HEIs. Consider the fancy sums of money people pay to go abroad and get a degree. Like many contradictions, these are common characteristics of higher education in India. It is truly remarkable that in the spate of webinars that mark the COVID-19 era, not one has been organised to address these themes. There almost seems to be a collective consent to let things continue the way they are. There is nothing wrong with that. These defining characteristics—so far as public information is concerned—have not even been debated with adequate sincerity in the several fora which determine the nature of higher education in India.

A common loss seems to be nobody's loss. There are also so called autonomous pan-Indian bodies of these institutions where people struggle, jostle and manoeuvre to become secretaries and presidents. It gives them influence, range and visibility. There is nothing wrong with that, yet, alas, a question on the purpose of such associations cannot be endlessly evaded. There are associations of heads of management institutions, societies of technical institutions, education fora in chambers of industry, whether in a confederation mode or in an associated mode. Most of them are huge draws to those seeking a "space under the sun."

However, an Indian citizen is entitled to ask what these associations achieve? A radical departure from some of these unusual patterns of collective behaviour is long overdue. When a few articulate ones do point it out, they are asked to keep quiet in the name of being positive. They are exhorted not to "rock the boat" and at least appreciate what has been achieved. These are unexceptionable arguments.

However, ask an Indian mother from which Indian educational institution as compared to a western one, would she like her son-in-law or daughter-in-law to come from. The answer is the answer to the relative ranking of Indian HEIs in an international frame.

July 20, 2020

## Designing and Re-designing

Some days ago, a news item was allowed to creep into the newspapers about how shortage of funds has affected recruitment even in better branded Government educational institutions. As always, funds are a matter of priority and allocations. In the last few years, the number of governmental entertainments in high-flying and super-expensive outlets has gone up by leaps and bound. There is little shortage of fund there. There are other examples, including expenses on 'goodwill visits' and 'study tours' of the high and mighty. There is plenty of money floating around—the question is of acceptability of the expenditure head.

It is one of the unfortunate facts of life that irrespective of rhetoric, funds for education are almost always at the bottom of the pyramid of priorities. This is understandable because the damage, which paucity of funds does to the social and national fabric, is not immediately or dramatically visible. Management is the art of playing the ball where it is. Hence, without regrets, one needs to get on with the act of how to find more funds for education. It is here where contradictions, enigmas and seemingly irreconcilable positions emerge.

There are parts of education system where there is clearly no paucity of funds. Consider the fees that people are willing to find and pay to send their children to private schools. Even with this kind of a bill, there is no school which is running short of candidates or applicants. In a way, this is a good thing because it shows that India is a education conscious society. The other truth is that private schools are seen as gateways to influence and power. Hence, the perception that they aid social mobility and, therefore, people are rushing to it.

Similarly, for the post school sector, there is no dearth of people vying to send their children abroad to institutions who charge fancy fees from immigrant students and provide subsidy to their own.

Similarly, there are some fancy institutions in the country, especially in the domain of medicine, management, engineering, where there is no paucity of aspirants vying with richly endowed pockets. Thus, there is no obvious paucity of funds for education. The so-called shortage is for the higher education segment dealing with governmental funding and amenable in Government regulations. For them, being in the domain of public systems is both a challenge and a situation with limited common sense options, including rise of fees. It may not be completely possible in the limitations of space here to explore this proposition fully.

However, one thing is clear: The system provides no succour to the nagging thought that one can barely raise adequate money within the broad regulatory features that prevail. Regulators themselves need to recognise what it takes to reach the breakeven of education, which could earn a reasonable accreditation of, say, the National Assessment and Accreditation Council.

The system needs to be geared to answer the questions. Last few years have seen several attempts to draft an education policy. They are all clearly well-intentioned, even though one is not quite sure how well informed the decisions systems have been in constituting these bodies. Very senior bureaucrats and even space scientists have been roped in at the effort.

Whereas other reports come in very quickly, the one on education policy consumes so much time that they almost get lost in the memory lane. From 1985 to today, these countless committees, headed by venerable gentlemen, are really a fit subject for a PhD dissertation. That will, at least, help one to understand what led them to be composed the way they were. How long did they take and how did they go about their work and indeed, what happened to their final report? There were indeed other committees on matters related to education, besides those meant to deal with 'policy'.

Be it funding, admissions, regulatory system of education, or the education policy, one is entitled to ask what are the thoughts on education funding at every level. Else, the so-called ideological wars will keep taking up the limelight and the actual process of education will only cost along.

August 28, 2017

## Male Child Deserves Our Attention Too

India is passing through an extraordinary time. It is good that women's problems are being addressed and worked upon. Women's security is now, quite rightly, seen as the responsibility of everyone. Women's confinement for child-bearing is a noble and exclusive feminine contribution to human race. Most of them have a natural inclination to be supportive as a part of this natural motherly instinct.

This is not to deny the possibility of exception. Equally, women are human and, therefore, susceptible to all the frailties of human beings. They have also all the strengths which go with being human.

Men have the same story. The crucial difference is biological that comes from motherhood. Men also have all the frailties and strengths of being human. Both men and women cohabitate in a society. Hence, the context of the society becomes crucial. The Society consists of certain values, resources, methods of work and more.

There is such a thing as the psychology of being a male. A man has, perhaps, to contend with numbers and groups far more often than the women. The concern is that, whereas womanhood requires a certain type of an infrastructure, so does manhood.

There is a common case for taking care of men and women, as much as the girl and the boy child. Just as the girl child needs to be protected against certain types of vagaries, so does the boy child. In the present scenario, where there is increasing recognition of the needs of the girl child, there is sometimes not the same kind of recognition for the needs of boy child. In the interest of a balanced child growth, this situation needs urgent attention.

The malformation of a male child needs as much care as any malformation. There is no case for a gender bias. The architecture of child rearing needs this correction. If not corrected, it spills into the workplace.

All organisations—manufacturing, service, education, health and whatever else—require fully functioning, healthy bodied and emotionally sound personnel. The damage which a malformed employee can inflict on an organisation has not even been begun to be assessed.

A malformed employee will be a bad subordinate, a bad boss, a bad team player and one can take it as far as ones wishes. The disruption which such a person causes hasn't even begun to be recognised, let alone be measured and analysed. It is little wonder then that so many organisations have so many human problems.

Further, all work organisations are embedded in a social context. Just as one cannot run faster than the train one is in, so also one cannot be more productive than the society in one which is embedded.

Much of the character of the society will influence the functioning of the organisation. It will influence the supply chain dimension, it will influence the marketing and distribution dimensions, and above all, it will strongly influence the culture of the job by bringing into the workplace the culture of the society.

This is a recognised truth of organisational life. This view is subscribed to by those who know that there is a need to have organisations designed to be in sync with society. Management institutions and consultants who do not appreciate this context will find it difficult either to make an impact or to be effective.

If the society is by and large rooted around family networks of obligations, it is difficult to conceive of an employee in a work situation, as if he has no collective obligations. Illustratively in a society where they are severely moth-eaten health care systems, the responsibility of all the elderly in the family will devolve upon the earning and more youthful members of the family.

Pretending that this problem does not exist or does not need to be accounted for or is not in keeping with modern culture of work organisation, is bound to create severely convoluted situations.

Put simply, organisations have to be designed in a manner that allows for work ethics to factor in social norms and realities. Interestingly, this will also impact the organisational models of decision-making as well.

February 06, 2015

## Re-visiting Ancient Civilisational Wisdom

The scientific temper and managerial culture of traditional India is largely gone, by default, in its projection on the global map of knowledge and learning. This is not because of any internal weakness but due to a failure to come to grips with facts and the inability to use them for generating models for current Indian growth processes.

Modern educational institutions patterned not only their method of working after the West but, more dangerously, the content too was patterned after some dated contents of Western institutions. The results are there for all to see.

Successful consultancy organisations, of which several had originated in the West, and remained anchored in the West, could not be expected to go beyond their financial interests. As a result, only a few of them could help fully Indian organisations to grow. The message was simple: The route to growth was through patterns of Western institutions.

On the face of it, there is nothing wrong with this. Only, it will not work on a large enough scale to cause mass transformation in India. Most parts of India have institutions rooted in the Indian ethos and these are not amenable to Western instruments.

Indian models of urbanisation, as represented in the Harappan culture, or navigation as evident from the exploits of the Pandyas, Pallavas, Cholas and the Cheras, simply got slurred over. Instead of studying the exploits of Kanhoji Angre, we were studying how 'sea power came to India'.

Even in the emphasis of domestic history, the lionisation of icons had to do with what political purpose it fulfilled.

Akbar was proclaimed as 'great', who worked miracles with the revenue system—even though he was illiterate. It was forgotten that he really did nothing more than continue with the revenue system which Sher Shah Suri had devised. Akbar served a political purpose, Sher Shah did not.

Time is not only a great healer but a great leveller. It straightens out many contrived curves. To get back to the intellectual inheritance, one may refer to waterways-related skills. World navigation was born in the river Sindhu 6,000 years ago. It is derived from the Sanskrit word *navgatih*. The word, 'navy' is derived from the Sanskrit word *nou*. According to the Gemological Institute of America, up until the last decade of the 19th century, India was the only source for diamonds to the world.

Sushruta practiced surgery in India 2,600 years ago. He could do caesarean and cataract operations as well as extract urinary stones. He is reported to have done a brain surgery and plastic surgery as well. Obviously, he was using anesthesia. The surgical equipment used then have been discovered. They showed deep knowledge of anatomy, physiology, etiology, embryology and genetics.

Moreover, some of the earliest reservoirs and dams for irrigation were built in Saurashtra. Indian exports in the centuries before Christ included palm oil, cast iron, tin sheets, copper vessels, perfumes and camphor.

India's knowledge of astronomy was phenomenal. Apollonius Tyanaeus, the Greek thinker of the first century AD, had commented on this. Indians knew the calculation of the eclipses and of the earth's circumferences. The heliocentric theory of gravitation was taught in the learning centres.

*Pancha Siddhantika* is testimony to this.

Indian physics and chemistry had recognised *anu* and *parmanu*. The five basic physical elements (*panchtatva*) were being used for better healthcare. Chess, polo and the martial arts were known to India. All this was apart and beyond the excellence of Indian philosophy and literature.

Such an environment is not possible without good governance and stable socio-economic conditions. There is obviously disconnect between what we see as the traits of Indians and what India actually stood for and was recognised to stand for.

China has re-acquired greatness, amongst other things, by respecting its past. No civil society can survive without some sound managerial principles and practices. We need to know what sustained us.

Our tragedy is not just the disconnect. Enough effort needs to be put in to understand what sustained Indian modes of productivity and their distribution. The managerial process, means of livelihood and ways of enabling talent, need to be rediscovered.

December 26, 2014

## Reflections on the Nature of Parliamentary System-making Frameworks

The important thing in any organisation is to be conscious of what it is about. This consciousness has to be positive and well understood at all levels. The articulation of what it is about? How it got where it is? and where it will go from there? are important. To create an organisation-wide census purpose, this has to be documented in its fundamentals, lucid in its enunciation, and actionable in its expression. Comparatively, few organisations have been able to achieve this, and it is often left to key figures to initiate and expound on it. The trouble with this kind of approach is that it may vary from one organisation to another in the same position. Handing over and taking over is not always a systematic process, and even in organisations where it is observed, very often the expression is on a small sheet of paper that simply states that somebody has taken over from somebody else and taken charge of the position. This may be a necessary component of handing over and taking over. But it is not necessarily enough. The process of transition is always delicate, and many incumbents are known to superimpose their so-called insights and understanding of the situation.

In organisational management, this is a danger that very often causes grief in the functioning of processes.

What is true at the organisational level is also true at the governance level. The legislature in any system of governance is power centre, in a country such as India this institution is under formation in some part of the country or another, throughout the year. It takes away the necessary attention from certain as aspects of governance and election related 'events' take a disproportionate share of attention and time. A lot of energy is spent in figuring out who is going into power and who is coming out. This occupies so much attention that the content of what the one who has got power, is actually doing, almost gets relegated to a relatively inconspicuous position.

Because of celebrity media attention, attention is focused on major personality shifts in the power syndrome of parties, allegations of wrongdoing, or more. The list can be updated. There seems to be little difference between what 'Party A' seeks to do and what 'Party B' seeks to do. Names may change but the broad format and trends of happening remains the same. This cannot be considered healthy.

The entire assumption that political parties have a system of fully verifiable, financing of electoral activities and that their functioning/positioning in the legislature or the parliament would be based on ideological considerations is yet to fully concretise. If there are no differences between the parties A, B, and C on issues of how to manage investment, taxation, social welfare, education, or local self-government, etc. electoral battles lose their raison d'être. In a manner of speaking, it should be possible to do a simple Metrix with 'Y' axis having the name of Political Parties and the 'X' axis having various activities a government would be planning and make a comparative statement.

Take the case of the current elections conducted in Karnataka and Manipur. It should have been possible to create a metric showing what one political party had to say about being ideologically healthy as distinguished from another political party. On the basis of the data available this would be a very difficult exercise to complete. It will be still more difficult for the elections in states such as Rajasthan, Madhya Pradesh, and elsewhere where electoral processes are to ensue. There is competitive wooing in terms of freebies and surcharges, talk about equity, and more but the ideological divide is in-conspicuous. If there is very little to ideologically distinguish one party from another in terms of its 'conceptual' basis, then even the very purpose of 'party politics' stands open to re-thinking. The electoral results would have to be understood and explained in terms of 'power' and 'patronage'. This leads to the situation one is currently facing.

The current situation is one group of parties taking care of themselves and their own versus another group of parties wanting to take care of themselves and their own. There was a time in this country's electoral policy where certain parties took a position well to the left of a given political ideology and talked of state control.

There was another set of political parties that talked about economics and encouraged private investment for national growth. That ideology device is no longer apparent. Political parties exist with such ideologies, but they stand marginalised and try to justify their existence through alliances and coalitions. This is a national loss because they put a thrust on the parties and governance in a manner that needs thought.

Ideological fuzziness between political parties encourages personality-based electoral politics and thoughts. Such personalization of the decision-making process creates corrosive clashes. On other times it results in the shifting of one group of people from one political party to another, which makes very little sense in terms of ideology.

This process itself is worth serious thought. It takes away from the basic purpose of a people's representation system, which should work on ideologies and produce their appeal based on certain ideological parameters.

Personalities are one of the basic dimension of politicking. However, personalities need to subsume their role to certain ideological thrust if the whole process of party operated democracy is to move from strength to strength.

August 01, 2023

## The 75th Year of Independence: Some Institutional Reflections

The Diamond Jubilee of a nation's independence is not a huge span of time, given a nation's existence, in terms of years. It becomes a huge span of time if one thinks in generational terms.

75 years of active life for an individual is a rarity at its best; it could encapsulate two generations. By itself, it becomes a significant span of time for evaluation and assessment even for an institution or a nation. In India, the occasion has been rightly taken as an opportunity for self-evaluation.

We have done well on many dimensions. The Indian governance structures of *panchayat*, legislative assembly, and parliament have endured the test of time. Given the inherent diversity of sub-cultures in a unifying culture that is India, it is amazing how the framework has stood the test of time.

Illustratively, the Legislative Assembly of Meghalaya or Mizoram has a composition so uniquely representative of the place that there is little to compare them with the operations of the Legislative Assembly of Maharashtra or Madhya Pradesh. Yet the institutional framework of these places has shown an equal maturity of administration and smoothness of transition from one concern to another. It is a living example of a people's maturity.

The Indian Election Commission is known for its fairness and vigour. The courts are, by and large, respected. Our major chains of academic institutions like IIMs, IITs, AIIMs, agricultural universities, central universities, and many state universities are known for their standards and integrity. Aberrations have been there, but they are quickly set right. The corrections effectively stand out. This defines an approach to development that is unique to India.

The above elaboration is not to say that everything is hunky-dory. Nothing is ever perfect. Extremism of one variety or another in a domain or another remains a demand to respond it. Consider this threat of bigotry. It does not strengthen faith in a system in which decision-making is overtaken by religious considerations. Every religion has a right to exist, but manoeuvring for expansion of its dominion on the basis of religious compactness poses a risk. It could break many institutional safeguards. India has, so far, successfully handled this threat.

Similarly, probity and fairness in decision-making cannot be a matter of debate. If there are financial transactions going on covering the decisions, so-called administrative legitimisation does not hide the fact that, in actual operational terms, there should be fair play and no bias. Clearly, India as a community has many areas to work on, to sustain and enhance its maturity.

The 75th year of independence, amongst other things, needs to be an occasion to look forward, go from strength to strength, and eliminate weakness that may exist.

From this point of view, perhaps an area that merits far greater attention than what it has received so far is the maturity of our institutional framework.

A country as diverse as India has a bewilderingly large number of institutions. In popular parlance, there is reference to central government institutions, state government institutions, local institutions, public institutions, private institutions, corporations, and of course other institutional typologies depending upon the nature of the holdings. Anyone familiar with organisation studies will know that institutions are brought into existence formally for a given purpose. Moreover, more often than not, they have to be recognised in the framework of governance.

The above is not to say that all institutions are necessarily formal institutions. There are informal institutions, especially in a social sense, that have become institutionalised through practise. These institutions govern many set-ups, including social structures that manage institutions of birth and death, not to mention institutions relating to rituals. This would be subject matter in its own right and require a detailed discussion. However, given the limitations of space, a limited focus on formal institutions may serve as the starting point for more thought and reflection. The attempt will be to talk of institutions that are formally recognised by law or are operating in a given structured form.

In this category would come societies, federations, foundations, and self-governing institutions. Indeed, any institution formed by people for a given objective. The health of such institutions is a must for the overall health of bigger institutions of governance like local self-government, state legislative bodies, and central operational institutions.

A lot of them are doing good work and this shows the resilience in a given society. Danger is apparent when a large number of such institutions become places of comfort, as it were, for personal advancement and glory. To take over these institutions, the modus operandi of the argument is that majority must rule. Majority rule, when backed by an approximation of arguments, can be used to do away with things that may be necessary to an institution's interest. This is the risk that needs to be addressed.

Institutions, big or small, cannot be allowed to become havens of self-aggrandisement, self-perpetrators, and more. This aspiration can be a challenge to meet. This would be necessary to meet, because to keep such institutions on the righteous path of probity and institutional welfare will have to be ensured.

This will have to be done at the level of creating a larger culture where institutional conscience is sensitive and norms are established to walk the narrow path to correctness and propriety. It takes time, but it can be done.

Institutional effort at self-correction is to be made an essential part of organisational operations. A possible way could be to make it a part of the Governing Body meetings and the General Body agenda to discuss the challenges that is well worth meeting.

June 01, 2023

## Culture Ethics and Audit

Culture and ethics are among the words which are often misused. Among the social sciences words which define themselves in ambiguity, culture would be among the top ones. For many, anything which one does not fully understand, it becomes a 'cultural' issue.

'Culture' is seen sometimes as the grey area between truth and falsehood. Truth is the truth because it can be annotated, it has evidence, it has its footnotes, and it is self-evident.

The opposite of it is falsehood. But between truth and falsehood is a huge grey area where interpretations come in, where postures come in, where styles come in and above all, given the human nature, 'convenience' comes in. Nobody wants to be on the losing side.

So, one has phrases like "No, what I really meant was", or "I'm being quoted out of context", or "That is not my intention, let me restate it" and then one goes ahead to say exactly the opposite of what one said the first instance. So, culture is a defining perspective of one's thought process and approach, and mental attitudes.

It can be argued that audit is as much an art as a science. It is a science when it is toolbox oriented. There, one has people swearing on it, and on technology and how much of technology can be used to replace the human element of correlations.

Finding the fault lines is also seen as an advantage. However, the more important part is that in the ultimate analysis, it is one's ability to sense a problem which becomes the hallmark of a good auditor. Indeed, internal audit and statutory audit are not all that different other than the legal weightage which is assigned to their roles.

So, there is a huge need for auditors to have a clinical sense in understanding what is it at fault, simultaneously, what is the strength of the organization. An audit report need not be just a drain master's report. It is not there for fault finding. It is there for assessing and defining organizational health. So, culture is that subtle approach between the technicalities of the audit profession and the sensitivities of the audit professional of how one goes about it.

It is not a question of how one dresses. Or how one parts ones hair or how one postures or how one chooses ones words or one walks through truths and falsehoods.

There are other ways of defining culture. It's easy to get tripped up when one is talking of things like culture, and it is even more so when you talk of ethics.

Ethics is a very slippery ground. Reflections on the word ethics can be easy if one does not mystify it. This is so because no matter what one does, whether it is as per the statute book, or it is not as per the statute book, whether it is through the 10 commandments or the directives of the holy books of different religions or not, each one does what he does because he, at that point of time, considers it the right option to exercise. Otherwise, one wouldn't do it. That person sees that behaviour as the best choice. Therefore, to oneself, one is right.

It is only the collective judgment on one's action which makes it right or wrong. Therefore, ethics walks on two legs. One is a personal orientation and the other is the collective response to that orientation. In fact, even collectives have their own ethics.

Ethics is part of self-image. Ethics is also a part of a definition, whether it be individual's definition or a collective's definition. When it comes to audit, one has to make sure whether action is as per the statute book/is as per the highest professional standards?

What are the highest professional standards? Ethics would be that which works for the good of the organization and is correct in itself.

December 01, 2021

# 6

# Operations Management

## Pandemic and the Lay of the Land

The last two years or so have been an unprecedented experience in the chain of human evolution. The phase has not been declared formally over, yet. There are ripples of different types of experiences continuing. China for one, is going through a re-spread of a version of the pandemic in Shanghai and elsewhere. On April 11 yet another version of the virus was detected in South Africa. The extent and the nature of the spread is yet to be fully worked out. Whereas social distancing has raised fewer crescendos, masks continue to be a major focus of attention. In India, some states have removed the penalty clause on not wearing masks whereas others have retained it just as an advisory. It remains in force in a few states in the country. It is a challenge to an average citizen to keep up with the various regulatory variations. The bewildering complexity does not end there. As the ART home testing kit becomes more popular the kind of monitoring system which was in place till some months ago with the district administration seems to be somewhat on a decline.

The story has other interesting overtones. Some are reporting false positives in the ART test, the consequences of which can well be imagined. Clearly, the general verdict seems to be that if there is a variance between the ART test and the PCR test, the findings of the PCR test are deemed to prevail. Notwithstanding a general decline in the number of cases and its global virulence, the feeling of restlessness and the fallouts thereof continue. It impedes natural flow to return of normalcy. The collaterals continue to be significant.

One has to also keep in mind the anxiety which would settle into anybody's psyche in the initial or the subsequent stages of the continuing trauma. The process of transmission of the virus is not yet sufficiently established in all its modes and shades. As the number of occasions grow for the number of social groups being spontaneously or temporarily formed, one can never be sure which individual is a potential carrier of the disease. In that case one would not know to what extent one is really being exposed to the possibility of an infection. These questions can only be answered by a far greater understanding and awareness of the nature of the virus and where it can survive or for how long does it survive. In the earlier stages of the pandemic, the mutation process of the virus made an understanding of the process of infection, itself open to debate. Medicines and therapies (such as the use of the blood plasma of a formerly infected person) did the rounds. With time, medicines like Remdesivir became less fashionable and the feeling grew that even the Pulmonologist could only go so far. Today, the atmosphere is far more relaxed and many a diagnosis stops with reference to a few doses of Erythromycin and more. How long this will continue to be so, as of now, evokes very few definitive projections. All told, the exacting distress of impending consequences of infection has receded but the habits which got formed as a psychological shield in the last several months of anxiety, continues. Anybody's cough in a group of people draws attention. If people then get to learn that somebody in the group was found infected, the others begin watching themselves for symptoms. All told, the infectivity seems to have waned but anxieties continue to be the underpinning in a seemingly overwhelmingly large part of the population. So it appears, the lay of the land in the era of the pandemic.

April 16, 2022

## Some Imponderables about the Pandemic

Seeking 'understanding' is a universal need. Everyone is keen to be understood in the manner in which he believes he ought to be understood. However, understanding is by definition an outcome of a communication process. One can communicate with oneself: that helps to understand oneself. One can communicate with another person: in this dyadic relationship the urge is that one should be understood as one wants to be understood. A third kind of communication can be between self and a group. This is somewhat tricky because each group member may have one's own vocabulary, one's own ability to understand and varying spans of attention. Yet another 'understanding' can be sought between one group and another. All told, 'seeking an understanding' requires here be no gaps between the person who is seeking the understanding and the person who is supposed to respond. These issues become even more complicated in the social context that the pandemic raises. A common theme in the nearly two years of the pandemic has been to 'reduce mobility'. The pressures of restricted mobility have been so large that orientations of gregariousness on the part of many have largely got stymied. This can and has produced personality disorders. Impatience, frustration and a feeling of suffocation are some of the common manifestations. These aberrations can do more damage than an acknowledged ailment. However, when it comes to impatience, frustration, a feeling of suffocation et al., the response is often in the form of truisms. Typically, it would be, "why are you so impatient?" The truth is, if one knew one was impatient and acknowledged it, it could be handled. More often than not, the person who is being labelled as impatient does not see himself as one. This could lead to a possible communication breakdown between the two persons involved. Similar examples can be made for the feeling of 'frustration' or 'suffocation'.

This has strained relationships and often times even domestic peace. The situation is further compounded by the virus mutations and their impact. Official pandemic restrictions are enforced with the best of intentions. One is limiting the number of persons who can do door-to-door canvasing to five. The logic is difficult to comprehend. It could well have been six or four. This is where the 'judgement' of the persons who draft the regulations becomes significant. Thus, it is that ultimately, it is the competency for a robust judgement that becomes the touchstone. Regulations which touch mass lives very often have contextual overtones. All in all, these are clearly seemingly simple issues which become more complex when one starts analysing them. Consider the fatigue of sanitising anything that enters a household, ranging from daily necessities like vegetables to more structured dispatches through couriers. The couriers can bring anything from sweets to jewellery; from diaries to documents. The documents might have legal implications and cannot be thrown away. Many have wondered if they deserve to be sanitised. Sanitising them may cause smudging and more complications. Indeed, it can be asked where does sanitisation begin and where should it end? The brittle get more and more anxious and the cavalier more and more nonchalant. In simple terms, either road has its grave risks. These are questions to which a scientific application of the mind is needed. Patience, logic and above all the ability to understand the temperament of the individual becomes necessary. The trouble is the temperament of an individual, be it anxiety or impatience, cannot be helped unless the person concerned is receptive to help. Maybe the answer lies in doing it with love, care, commitment and persistence.

January 13, 2022

## Marine Spatial Planning

Not so long ago, talk of South China Sea dominated the focus of international relations. Landlocked countries were either relegated to columns of lesser attention or seen in stereotype phrases or expressions of traditional aberrations in statecraft. All the while, however, confidential negotiations were on somewhere in Doha between the US and Taliban.

Nobody exactly knew what it was all about other than how serious the US was about withdrawing from Afghanistan. There was verbal peace because the 'conventional money games' were on. Millions of dollars of US aid, reportedly, to 'secure democracy' in Afghanistan, strengthen its defences and create a so-called 'stable nation-state' were at stake. The truth was that the influential entrepreneurs of both US origin and central Asian origin were laughing all the way to the bank. Some are arguing that even the business of setting up a modernised Afghan army had been outsourced to the advantage of American businessmen. Illustratively, it appears, some of them were making battle fatigues for the soldiers of the Afghan army pointless for desert warfare. This is symbolic and important because similar processes were reportedly happening in the armament and arms industry. The left overs of the US arsenal, now being paraded by Taliban, tell a story which has yet to fully unfold. Afghanistan is a landlocked territory, always important for anyone interested in traversing from Euphrates to Indus. However, to get back to the concern in the opening sentence of this text: Oceans have not lost their importance. They are just temporarily out of media focus. Of the different oceans of the world, Indian Ocean is amongst the more strategic ones and has been the pathway of many empires which at one time originated from eastern peninsular India and on others Europe via Gibraltar, Suez, Aden, Mumbai, Colombo, Singapore. That story has many layers; much of it is still untold.

Till some months ago, Quad was the flavour. Naval exercises were being held to demonstrate source of power. The news has it that the heads of Quad are supposed to meet again a few weeks from now. In the meanwhile, the purpose of the elaboration above is to underscore that whereas media attention can and does grab its story from political, armorial goings-on, it does not alter the basic significance of some processes and domains. Such domains determine many aspects of existence and quality of human life. Ocean is one of them. Marine spatial planning, though at a relatively early stage of its evolution, is one of the prime determinants of quality of human life. It has somehow got linked up with sustainable development goals dated lined 2030. There is nothing wrong with that but marine spatial planning while being a part of global sustainability has a unique character of its own. It determines and gets influenced by littoral and coastal economy. It is difficult to control and determine because territorial boundaries of nation States are not always helpful either in understanding or developing ocean or terrestrial environments. Putting it simply, marine spaces and resources cannot be effectively managed, with varying territorial jurisdictions which are essentially meant for land geopolitical situation, in the form of a 'nation-state'. Ocean resources have their own natural zones and boundaries.

What is needed is an insightful understanding of the nature of ocean management and the resources embedded in it. For the future of Indian growth, the sooner this is recognised, operationally, lesser will be the dangers of sinking into pit-falls of social anxieties embedded in a land oriented economic theory.

September 07, 2021

## Of Concepts and Experience

It is natural for people to try to understand anything they are faced with. It can be a person, a situation or an experience. If we cannot respond to a situation in an organised fashion we tend to invent a framework for understanding or simply withdraw. Thus, it is important to recognise that concepts are necessary to understand a situation. Relationships between concepts constitute a conceptual system. In fact, information on a concept calls for a whole network of expectations on the fundamental elements of a situation. Meeting with a "nobody" on the streets cannot be equated to meeting an unknown person who is known to be socially powerful. Clearly, expectations are different in the two situations so the behaviour is modulated. The challenge most people have is that of never having learnt "how to think." It never formed a part of their curriculum and not many people are able to achieve it on their own. Concepts often acquire a value and can evoke sensory images.

February 01, 2021

## It's Only About Word Play

The world of social movements is full of clichés. Every self-proclaimed thinker (or otherwise), takes it upon himself/herself to coin a few phrases and add that to a growing stream of cacophony. Consider phrases like "caring liberalism", "mainstreaming" and "people-centric solutions" and the list can go on. Of course, these phrases can be defended and they should be. Question, however, is a matter apart. Have such phrases produced any evidence of making human life more bearable, if not liveable?

The current era is of capitalism. Hence, any movement for a minority alternative will pitch for the opposite. Consequently, it can be fashionable to posit capitalism versus whatever else, asking for space for compassion. One should pause to ask how capitalism becomes the opposite of compassion or indeed vice versa? When some thinkers from the US talk of "aggressive competitiveness", it becomes fashionable to start talking about "cooperation." The simple proposition is, in this circular planet, examples can be found for anything.

Even that can be overlooked. The tragedy is a whole template is created pleading for the opposite of what is perceived to be the dominant stream. So, if the dominant stream is of competitiveness, capitalism, globalisation and cross-border transfer of technology, the opposite template is already crafted. The "template of challenge" will talk of collaborative, holistic and contextualised geographies. Of course, both sides will claim to be "innovative". Innovation as a buzzword has become so universal that it has become common to claim it to be a prefix or suffix of any thought. A buzz phrase going around in the last few years is "social innovation."

Harvard University's Kennedy School has even instituted a Chair for that. Now, what more evidence is needed about the thought having arrived and accepted? Quickly, social innovation got hitched to the concept of sustainable development. Numerous international organisations as also research communities are busy propagating social innovations as an antidote to problems arising out of developmental interventions. Some old phrases haven't died either. There is the global north and the global south. There is the first world, the second world and the third world. Anthropologically and otherwise, the third world is the first. But each serenade has its time and life.

Since what is stated above is so, there is little virtue in arguing about it. The larger question remains where it was. The question is of involuntary deprivation to acknowledged standards of living. Whereas bottom of the pyramid continues to be an attractive topic of discussion, the usual locale of conversation is mostly sumptuous, enticingly gorgeous and usually peppered by the presence of some successful politician/tycoon/media person/whatever else. There, the international goal posts are discussed and solutions sought. It would be in such places, commonplace, to keep repeating the 17 sustainable development goals. Yes, they were adopted by the United Nations in 2015 and were supposed to be fulfilled by 2030. The slogan of SDGs is to work directly with the people and, of course, talk about social norms and cultural elements.

In this select list of about 30 odd words and phrases, the entire intellectual world is cocooned. The search is forever for the new and different. New sanctimonious phrases are chanted over and over again. To question them evokes sneers. Among them are a number of slogans such as social justice, social equity, health for all, gender parity, inclusive growth and the new kid on the block pride parade. Before one is condemned of being ancient, conservative, pig-headed and worse, this writer will hasten to add that he has nothing against any of these movements. The theme of this text is simple: To establish how the crescendo of phraseology crowds vision of clarity. Chants do not deliver results. At their best, they create an environment. That, too, can become counter-productive when the chant becomes too long, too mundane and repetitive.

A solution to be effective doesn't have to be new. It may be buried in some past practice, which somewhere got lost, burnt, destroyed or simply forgotten. Discovering that is not innovation. It is simple discovery. When the tribal collective believes that modes of production are common, nature is sacrosanct and lifestyles don't get stratified by conspicuous consumption, then they don't send emissaries to seminars to present their worldview. Tribals don't have to discover their own lifestyle. They have lived with it. In fact, it is plausible to argue that people set about evangelising in tribal areas because one wishes them to think like us and not because there is an urge to find alternatives to one's own existence. Essential is the need to recognise, how in attempting to help others, one is only trying to justify ones vantage point of perception. There is little respect for or interest in the other party. This approach needs a re-look.

July 08, 2019

## Global Warming or Coming of Ice Age?

There is something happening in the world that beats many forecasts and eludes much predictive rigour. The foremost among them is the talk about climate change. The principle of global warming and the heating up of the layers of atmosphere have been so disseminated and discussed that one has almost lost track of how the discussion started. Blames and counter-blames from different parts of the world as to who or what caused the climate change process continue to be traded. A major hypothesis has been that the armoured superior powers of the world sailed across the sea and marched over the land to gain control of the planet's raw materials and resources.

On the strength of their control over the raw materials and resources, they became industrial powers and dominated the world even more aggressively. One thing led to another and they became powerful enough to be almost left unchallenged through the 19th and 20th centuries. Britain, France, Spain, Portugal and many other nations were part of the action. The ones that were left out were countries like Germany, Italy and Japan, who were forced to fight for their own space. World wars occurred and devastations reigned supreme. The powerful gained more power and the rest, as is said, is history. Meanwhile, the industrially-strong countries, with their colonies and resources, emerged stronger and began to realise that the world's resources were not going to last forever. The earliest realisation was for the need to control access and distribution of raw material fuels like oil, coal and gas among others. The powerful began to preach conservation.

What this really meant was that after the Second World War, emerging nationalities were going to be denied the same use of raw materials even if it was their own. There was animated talk about energy conservation, which would impede progress of the newly-emerging nations to the status of industrial powers. The game was not subtle and all countries were not willing to oblige. West Asian nations obviously thought that they had the first right to their own fuel resources. Countries such as China were known to be roguish when it came to many questions on international law. In any case, the law was being drafted by the rich and the powerful nations.

The complexity of the situation was aggravated by the entry of nuclear power on the scene. The powerful drew up sanctions against countries that aspired to become nuclear powers without fulfilling the terms and conditions which the powerful nations wanted to be observed. If a country attempted to dare, carried out its experiments and tests and thereafter emerge as powerful as the members of the select club, it was incorporated.

There is this easy example of the People's Republic of China. The 'club' accepted China to its membership but rules remained unchanged. Clearly, the only international law was the will of the powerful shall prevail.

Countries such as India, with a huge practice and legacy of dubious Nehruvian tradition, were forever on the horns of a dilemma. Even today, the country is not a member of the Nuclear Suppliers Group (NSG). Entry to that group is through unanimous acceptance to a membership and the Republic of China always has a problem with the status of India. Be that as it may, the experience of others doesn't always graduate to the lessons that have to be learnt. Put simply, there is something about the prevailing world order which raises fundamental doubts about its efficacy and indeed fairness to all concerned stakeholders. In such a situation, when there is talk of climate change, one has to objectively understand the boundaries, characteristics, content and the geography of climate change patterns.

Through a little over the last 10 days, the world has been testimony to a sweeping experience of deep cold in almost all of the northern hemisphere. This sort of a situation cannot be permitted to simmer. Have the forces of nature produced a situation which makes the globe susceptible to the universal reality of climate chill which will be followed later by a repeat of global floods? Some of this may sound as speculation and extrapolation of what at one stage of the planet has been described as the Ice Age.

Irrespective of that, the time has come to at least control what the *Homo sapiens* can, the factors controlling emerging climatic trends. Whether it is global warming or chilling, one needs to be prepared for the future. The powerful nations may steadfastly refuse fair play or even share the advantages of their early start. Of the newly emerging powers, those who can crash into the charmed circles have already done so. The question is of a sustainable future for a stable and sustainable planet. For this to emerge, it is necessary to recognise the contradictions and complex interplay of powers among the nations that be. It is a no-choice situation.

February 04, 2019

## Of Green Marketing and Blue Economy

The flavour of the day is a matter of choice, amongst the essential constituent flavours, which mark life. Sometimes flavour A gets emphasis, on other occasions, flavour B and yet on other occasions, flavour C or whatever else. Fashions change and sometimes repeat. Different fashions are found to exist concurrently in different parts of the world. Hence, there is a cyclical and global element in trying to understand the current fashions of flavour.

Amongst the key flavours of the first quarter of the 21st century, environment is amongst the top runners for the most favoured status. On this platform, careers are made, new products launched and several international alliances forged. This is natural.

The greatest champions of environmental protection are those countries which went on rampage, arrogating global natural resources to bolster their productive and armorial power. Having achieved pre-eminence in industrial development they stand on their fore-feet, preaching resource abstinence to others. So be it!

History is testimony to the fact that whereas analysis of the past gives insights and may lead to newer solutions, it does not alter the prevalent power equation on the ground. One has to play the ball where it is.

Hence, if one is to understand business and society in emerging markets, one invariably ends up with the talk of green marketing. Usually, proponents of green market are diffident about the power of blue economy. Others get confused about the contents of blue economy.

It may be worth clarifying that blue economy is a systematic approach aiming to foster blue growth, of which oceans form an important component. It walks on two legs—(a) it tries to address the issue of resource scarcity, and (b) it highlights the concerns of wastivity management.

Both the streams noted above, of green marketing and blue economy, can trace their origins of global prominence to UN initiated conferences and movements of the last few decades. That may be a fascinating story but is a different one.

Consider the case of the Indian Ocean, a veritable reservoir of vast and untapped natural resources. It has been in special prominence recently because of the impending round of struggle for control of the strategic waterways of the world.

The military, strategic and technological concerns of combat and control will obviously impact trade and commerce. As military activities achieve heightened pitch in international waters, so does the control of international resources. The blue economy emphasises an ocean driven economic growth.

When food security and maritime security get intertwined, interconnectedness acquires unique overtones. Illustratively, fishing communities become significant, piracy acquires overtones and fish stock depletion begins to get the Supreme Court's attention.

Be it business or society in emerging markets or blue ocean economy, it has to do with healthy lifestyles. Old problems cannot be solved with unchanged attitudes. It is these attitudes that cause the problem, to begin with. Wisdom of traditional India had at its core, respect for all living things. lost to the capricious march of accumulating wealth, by a powerful few over the hapless ineptitude of the lethargic many, the world capitalism drew strength through the bayonet: literally and metaphorically.

The time has come to look at instrumentalities of giving the law of natural order its pride of place in the global system. The natural order demands recognition of not only preserving the greens but encouraging the blues.

The plants and the trees, the forests and the animals are to be treated with respect. The fisheries and aqua culture, marine tourism, port network, customs network, the marine plastic waste cannot be just topics of rabble rousing. They need deep scholastic insights, serious attempts to put these insights in a policy frame. The process issues will then emerge and the capability factors of delivery and sustenance would have to be assiduously nurtured.

The blue economy pushes the horizon and compliments sustainability. Conspicuous consumption is as ugly as layers of fat around the belly. Technology will have to be used to identify noxious and hazardous substances. Lifestyle issues of both the supply side and the consumption side will need to be understood and addressed. A brighter future can be a reality.

January 15, 2018

## Development Lessons from Down Under

The time has come for re-examining the national script of the social discourse. Unquestionably, secularism as a theme has been a front runner in the last seven decades of the Indian evolution. This is understandable even though a dubious commentary on what stimulates emotional energy, in India.

There also has been talk on development in various shapes and sizes. There have been periods of emphasis, from the glorification of the Soviet model to that of the capitalistic market economy. On July 7, a Nobel laureate of Indian origin was reported to be pleading for a market oriented economy with a socially oriented service sector. Irrespective of these permutations and combinations, there is an almost universal discontent with the results of such developments.

The media, whether print or electronic, still displays a high degree of emphasis on that which sensationalises. Murder, rape, embezzlement and wrong doings of those seen as powerful invite large readership and viewership. It is another matter that when action is required, few have appetite to do anything about it. It is the ritualisation of such aberrations which has dulled the sensitivity.

The present Government rode to power on hope. While receding, hope has still not faded. The time has come to put productivity on the map of social discourse. The time has come to make efficiency the core of growth. The time has come to strengthen the faith in success being the prerogative of talent.

This will not happen automatically. The parameters of social discourse will need to be redone, substantially. The content will have to be redefined. The charms of personal networking opening the doors of money, power and influence will have to be put under control. The youth will need to be re-oriented to learn on what leads to 'success'. A good beginning would be to put the talk of resource optimisations, as a center piece of social discourse.

Analogies from the oceans would help to communicate the point. Australia is a brilliant example of a country that has leveraged natural resources both for revenue generation and realistic growth. It has converted not only things like the Ayers-rock to celebration but stoked global imagination with the glamourisation of the resources of the sea. This comes by the way of 'naturalisation' of the whale, the seal, the dolphin, the penguin, the pelican and the kookaburra. People spend tonnes of money to travel to Tangalooma to watch the whale. They visit Philip Island to sight the seal. They stand on the beaches to feed the dolphins. It does not need the humongous investments in tourist infrastructure which impedes all our developments.

The skill of policy planning is obvious—with applied imagination holding the strings of the purse. India with its enormous coastal line has yet to begin talking, meaningfully, of the ocean resources.

The Ram Setu between India and Sri Lanka could be converted into a viewing spot. The Lakshadweep islands with their celestial clarity of water could be great for scuba diving. The coasts of Andaman and Nicobar could be readied for water sports. The list is long.

There is a need to realise the power of widening and deepening the focus on the development talk. It's all so tantalising to talk of fugitives, scams and more but at the end of the day, the social discourse has also to see what opportunities exist and what can be created.

To go back to Australia, a natural treasure of Great Barrier Reef has been converted into a viewing extravaganza, with floating jetties, short hop helicopters; snorkeling, scuba diving and more. This reef stretches over 2600 km. It has grown on the continental shelf of Queensland for as long as two million years in the south near Bundaberg, and as long as 18 million years in the north. The sea level has changed many times and the sea has been flooded with limestone hills, corals and reef platforms.

We in India have the deep Indian Ocean, rich in resources, to fathom. We need to begin somewhere. May be that will serve as the fulcrum to turn the social discourse around. The consultants and researchers would need to serve as the advance party for this.

July 10, 2015

## Some Emerging Trends in Business Management : Marine Spatial Planning

Till not very long ago, seas and oceans were nobody's territory. In its most evolved form, certain kilometers of the sea were considered to be under the jurisdiction of the land governance to which it was connected.

Be that as it may, even the regulatory and administrative provisions of the laws and regulations of the land were often silent on what the issues were of the sea. In few cases that the laws could be extrapolated the provisions were often weak, ambiguous or irrelevant to the concerns of the ocean in some cases it added to the complexity of interpretation and application.

Further, there were overlapping area of jurisdiction because the stretch of the sea was not broad enough to demarcate the jurisdiction. This lead to unsavory situations with avoidable conflicts emerging. The stronger nation pushed and often got away with dominance which was neither fair to common sense or equity.

The coming of courts for justice in matters related to the sea did not go very far because of many reasons. For one the legal precedents in matters of the sea were few and far between. there was not enough jurisprudence manpower, sufficiently spread out, to deliver justice let alone do it expeditiously. The investment in travelling to the location where justice was to be administered were often costly, time intensive and without local support systems. This rendered the scene bewildering beyond effective management and often beyond comprehension.

The international bodies such as they exist have neither the bandwidth nor the inclination to charter out into new areas. The International Funding bodies were not willing to take the risks involved. Hence, there was not enough order or coherent development.

With a progressive strengthening of the blue economy, awareness of the marine space has become critical. There is a competitive bid to go out deep into the oceans to harness the resources and derive not only economic but also strategic advantages from the same.

It's not only the oceans and their resources of the sea but also the resources of the seabed which have become important. Amongst the resources of the sea, there are live resources of marine life, which include everything from the various species of the sea but also the vegetations which have become significant. Additionally, the corals and all that goes with the rich accumulation of sea resources that have acquired economic work. Marine Spatial Planning is a part of this larger effort.

Specially as indicated earlier, the mineral wealth stored in deep oceans is a matter of great traction.

As always because of this attractive sea wealth, there is urge for investment, creating predictability and rules which bears scrutiny. Put simply, Marine Spatial Planning has acquired the status of specialization in its own right.

Obviously, all this going to lead to concerns of cross-border issues and jurisdiction. What follows in the trail are many of those concerns which are there in land spatial planning and more? Traditions of land spatial planning, even where relevant, in an era of independent and sovereign states are several centuries old. Times require fairly clear practices of conflict management and regulation.

When it comes to the sea, story is different, and the freedom of the navigation of the seas has its own concerns. This includes piracy which often recognizes no jurisdiction. Even where practices of jurisdiction could be applicable the sheer expanse of the sea and linkages with administrative centres create problems of scale. This is of course without factoring the changing nature of marine resource use. What is needed is a policy and institutional framework. Some tentative steps have been taken in this direction; however, much of the problems remain. This has meant, dealing with, amongst other issues, those of transboundary specificity.

Add to it climate change which has its own concerns. The changes which are then affected are humongous. There are large gaps and many concerns to address. This will not happen without some sound practices of global cooperation and an appreciation of the need for interdependency.

November 01, 2023

## Decision-Making and Growth

Decision-making is fundamental to anything living. Vegetables, plants and all living existences in that category, like in any other category, have some decision-making propensities in their very existence. At a basic level their shoots try to reach out, literally, to a space where they can meet the sun. The sun rays are critical along with water, air and other elements to the making of chlorophyl. Chlorophyl is essential to their survival. Successively, as one graduates through higher levels of life, decision-making capability has more demands on it and keeps improving both in range and sophistication. A tiny existence like amoeba has certain decision-making competencies to absorb food. That chain also keeps growing. Different levels of animals and mammals have different levels of decision-making competency and judgement. They always understand when there is eminent danger lurking. Evasion, escape and moving away physically from danger is a natural instinct.

Slowly, as one graduates up the decision tree choices in facing danger, and searching nourishment and protection increase. Progressively, more sophistication builds into the process. A conscious choice may even be to face the danger and face the risks which this confrontation would cause. Obviously, this requires sound perception, critical thinking and exercise of choices. A whole discipline has grown around decision-making and the focus is on many aspects of decision-making of which business choices are often important. Decisions require both divergent thinking and convergent thinking. The literature, research and references in such domain are large.

Basically, decision-making which touches not just individual operations but dyadic and collective situations. Dyadic, collective situations are a continuing subject matter of thinking, analysis, further data collection, categorisation and more. The methodology of decision sciences keeps improving and keeps getting enriched.

At our present level of existence, it is obvious that individual decision making is one of the key foundations of activity and the aspired objective of solutions and progress. This is a fit domain of continuing research and putting that together for action.

Unfortunately, decision sciences while developing as a discipline has not yet been accepted as the foundation of all learning and growth. From the moment a child starts recognising the environment, images are being formed in the brain. These images get processed and lead to some kind of action. Parenting would require recognition of this early stage of learning in the life of a child. Social practice and smaller units of society in their beliefs have given rise to certain time-tested patterns of child rearing. This needs to be codified further and disseminated widely. It also needs contextualisation. Greater attention needs to be paid to this kind of activity.

Going up in the various stages of the life cycle. Infancy leads to childhood and then the cycle of growth—too well known to need recount—takes over as a natural process. Decision-making capacities grow with not just physical growth but the inherent mental growth. In the spaces available here, a detailed accounting will not be possible and is perhaps not necessary.

What is to be recognised is the need for a conscious approach to enhancing more sound decision-making competencies.

This growth can be many times enhanced by deliberate intervention. This can be both formal or informal. At the root of it is the concern of perceptions. Any decision is also rooted in the capacity to understand perceptions and root the action on the basis of sound judgement thereafter. One should also be aware of the consequences of action which would be based on these perceptions. This makes decision-making more deliberate and purposeful.

This is fundamental to life and all existence. Hence, it is that a conscious universal approach to this domain, becomes a fundamental need. It cannot be confined to classrooms. It has to percolate to all levels of civil society (and action) at a continuing level. It is hoped that the elaboration made above will help in a more robust understanding of decision-making culture and the need to have a bottom line of gradually enhanced sophistication to one's approach to it, and, keeping it alive.

Business decision-making is a part of this larger domain of decision-making and ultimately will get affected by the quality of the methodology used, the inputs and the context of this operation. Business itself has many forms but what is common to all its operations is finance and growth. Each orientation in business development will be affected by the quality of mind and the decision-making competencies of the individual.

August 01, 2022

## The Mind, the Body and Operational Effectiveness

Human beings are acknowledged to be gregarious creatures. They find it very difficult, if not impossible to survive in isolation. Each individual needs some association, call it company if you will, to fulfil the basic needs of life. Food requires a producer, a supply chain and method of exchange. Shelter needs support to make an environment hospitable for living: protection from nature which includes the sun, the rain, the thunderstorm to be available to keep the body and soul together. Hence, company is essential to survival. This dealing with people and processes for survival needs a shared platform for exchange. Few would render ant services to anyone unless there was something in exchange to be received for providing the service. This in turn creates a whole web of exchange relationships which then become a key foundation for the civil society. The civil society in its turn requires rules for exchange and therefore governance. Governance itself has its ramifications and the rules of governance have to be decided and agreed upon.

A simple life of solitude is neither possible nor conceivable except in the rarest of the rare cases. A hermitage is possible but even a hermit requires feeder services, come as it may from nature itself. The hermit has to create a shelter and have some clothing to keep the body and the soul together. This itself can be a demanding fare because the more powerful may poach upon him and the hermit would need to defend himself against expropriation and dominance of the more powerful. That in turn raises the need of a civil society and an ambience of good governance.

The urge for life and living thereby keeps getting from simple to the complex and from the complex to the more complex. There are no defined limits to the requirements of a civil society. By itself this proposition is complex enough. When one adds to it the nature of a human being the complexity is compounded. A human being can feel and hence feelings become important. A human being has the capacity to be attracted and repelled, hence emotions become important. The human being also has a body to nurture hence creature comfort becomes a real factor. The list can be multiplied;

however, the basic point is simple. To function has a human being relationships become one of the driving features.

Relationships in their turn generate their own logic. There is attraction to situations and people which provide understanding and support. Even support can wait but understanding is the foundation. This is a tricky process to handle. One offers understanding only if emotionally aligned. If the needs don't enmesh, if the level of mental sophistication is at variance, if the knowledge wherewithal is not on a common shared platform, relationships won't work smoothly and without relationships there can be no understanding. Grief is a natural outcome and people's ability to handle grief varies. It can lead to not just impatience and sharp words but expressions of verbal violence with physical violence not being ruled out. The anatomy of relationships has interested the intellectually oriented humans for exploration. Many well thought through approaches have been elaborated and documented on various media from papyrus to the digital. Even with all the good work that has gone into this, the domain remains open and is as wide as the sea.

Hence, it is that scholarly exploration of these various issues becomes a subject area out of which institutions with knowledge pursuits as their objective, are born.

Learning itself has been segmented as per the life cycle of the Homo sapien. Infancy, childhood, boy/girlhood, adulthood and beyond is a chain. Some communities have achieved an integration among all this a little more seamlessly, than others, but the pursuit goes on. This is the essence of institutional learning.

Like everything else, categories and clusters enter this domain too. There are different types of learning processes. None of them can be comprehensive enough to eliminate the need for other approaches and there is enough scope to learn from each other.

Thus, it is that patience and openness become a prime attribute of not just growth but survival itself. Composure of the brain and the heart, to talk of just two organs of the human body, is central to having an optimally functioning body. This is without prejudice to the understanding of the functioning of other parts of the body such as the lungs, the stomach, the intestine, the colon and many others. This is essential for the body to remain functional. Nothing else can actually discharge the function related to these organs, for any individual. Hence, the need for composure and enabling optimality of function for the body organs. Mind control and channelising of emotions are central to this.

Like everything else, all these factors affect the management of business.

July 01, 2022

# 7

# Finance and Accounting

## Treat the Cause, not the Symptom

Any person dealing with conflict management issues would agree that treating the symptoms seldom cures the cause. The symptoms are often a manifestation of the context, the personalities at play and the immediate trigger. However, the causes continue to fester. This led to a major observation made decades ago on conflict management that if two people cannot agree on something, check the assumptions. After all, logic is often found to support what one already believes to be true. Before this write-up turns into an exploration of interpersonal dynamics, it is important to realise that the above references are just a bid to answer some of the more basic questions regarding organisations and the economy.

The private sector vs. public sector debate has been running in India for decades. Whenever there is a public outcry against privately-run firms, the oft-heard refrain is "nationalise them." When the trouble is with public sector undertakings (PSUs), the quick solution offered is "privatise them." Empirical evidence has it that neither of the two has ever solved the basic ailment. The problem remains and the misery continues, though logically there's always a solution to a problem. Given the Government's recent decision to merge ten Public Sector Banks (PSBs) into four major entities, one wonders what lies in store for them.

As an instrument, a merger is neither new nor certified as efficacious. In 1993, the New Bank of India was merged with Punjab National Bank (PNB). The merger was nearly as messy as that of Indian Airlines with Air India. If anyone analysed how the solution turned into a mess, it is still a well-kept secret. Nearly 16 years later Vijaya Bank and Dena Bank were merged with Bank of Baroda (BOB). Though there were no fatal flaws with either Vijaya Bank or Dena Bank, nor was BOB the symbol of efficiency and success. Needless to say, nothing spectacular came out of it.

Many will recall how the centenary celebrations of BOB were conspicuous by their lack of visibility. Nobody quite knows how the budgetary allocations for the centenary celebrations were really utilised. Predictably the rewards came—rewards of willingness to bat along. Some of the key figures in this invisible celebration acquired roles in visible and brand-building tasks

The fact remains that there is nothing in the instrumentality of mergers which raises hopes of a turnaround. If the big taking over the small—(read big as a synonym for perceived success and small for perceived failure)—was to become the prescription for organisational success, it's time for the management researcher and analyst to go home.

The scenario in the banking sector today is very much what it was seven or even three years ago. The Non Performing Assets (NPAs) are impressive, the recovery moves are hackneyed and the major defaulters are still snapping beneath the nose of the powers that be. Lalit Modi's name has not been heard in the media for nearly a year or so and the almost weekly Vijay Mallya-bashing seems to have lost its cadence. The less famous defaulters are still cosy but a lot of trivial defaulters are being chased with the passion of a hunter desperate for the kill as he has to show results to the people who commissioned him.

The story of mergers has almost the same template as the story of recapitalisation. The oft-used slogan is of putting the losses behind and strengthening the banking sector's lending ability. The outlay for recapitalisation is being put at around ₹ 70,000 crore. Perhaps it is rooted in the Reserve Bank of India's (RBI) largesse promised to the Government.

However, there's no recorded history of recapitalisation as an instrument of success for beleaguered PSBs. On the contrary, the willing compliance of officials with any whim of the powers-that-be seems to have its rewards. Recall how after all the talk of how a well-argued theory of demonetisation was messed up, the perpetrators of inefficient operationalisation were systematically rewarded. Understandably their modus operandi of ruining a good broth continues to run its track. But that is another story.

It is truly amazing how an equally obvious action of managerial reform, bank by bank and in every region of the bank and indeed in the working of every branch is not being tried.

Perhaps what is concurrently needed is a managerial reform to accompany what economists over decades have written as their prescription. The fallacy in this, of course, being the belief that the operation of the system is perfect; it is the economic engine which needs replacement of parts. One can only say, Jai Ho!

September 03, 2019

## Killing an Idea with Overuse

Topics get appropriated by professions. Professions give to themselves prerogatives of defining. This gets reflected in the behaviour of the professionals who get certified for the profession. It applies to audit. If one is not a qualified auditor and has served as the Senior Managing Director of a major global consulting firm devoted to niche consulting including, internal audit, (as the writer of these lines) the hiatus becomes obvious.

Auditors are known to be jealous in protecting their domain. On the other hand, audit for many, is far too important an activity to be left only to auditors.

A google search on 'audit' establishes that the definition of audit is broadly about formal examination of an organisation's or individual's accounts of financial situation. The search gives versions of the definition, quoting from various references. It further implies that the examination of financial records is done to determine if they are accurate and in accordance with specified standards. These standards have local versions and global versions. So be it. The effort at undertaking an audit process requires checking, reviewing, analysing, studying, perusing, assessing, appraising, evaluating for probity. The list of activities can be added to. The ultimate attempt is through financial disclosures and non-financial disclosures, presenting a true and fair view of the actual financial situation.

About 15 years ago, the Chairman of an audit committee of a major public sector undertaking was stumped while seeking to address a simple question: Was the audit committee a fit body of the corporate entity to undertake risk management exercises? Risk management, according to Securities and Exchange Board of India (SEBI), was an essential part of a listed company's statutory obligations. Notwithstanding the Chair's personal reservations at understanding the nuances of a discipline, i.e. risk management just becoming popular, in corporate thinking, the board of the company assigned the task of risk management to the audit committee. Predictably a foreign firm was hired to move the company forward in tidying up its house to prepare for risk management.

That was the time when more than one public sector company began intensively training different levels of the organisation on risk management, as part of the audit effort. It didn't seem to bother anyone, particularly the fact that one cannot train without a policy framework in position; in this case, on risk management. It was a fit case of masquerading the observance of a form because no one knew any better. This included the competent authorities of the parent Ministry who also sat on respective company boards. This pattern grew exponentially over time cutting across so-called varying political orientations of the Governments.

This particular audit committee, referred to above, ran into further grief when the Chairman of the audit committee, almost to avenge the task thrust on his domain, took the view that the audit committee of the company was entitled to audit whatever it deemed fit.

This included energy audit, information audit and the list threatened to get extended with every meeting.

Risk management continued to be reviewed by the people who had heard of it after they became members of the audit committee. The energy audit idea or the information audit idea was allowed to lapse. The world was again at peace; all the columns were being filled. No one felt foolish and no one was any wiser. The above narrative is symptomatic of many changes sweeping today through many portals of the corporate world and many domains of national functioning.

There is nothing like killing a good idea with overuse, ascription for administering it to the people who are innocent of its nuances and above all linking it to unrelated activities. This is happening ever so often, say, with Aadhaar. Not till long ago, it was being peddled that Aadhaar is not an address proof and it has a country-wide validity. Somewhere down the line, it became necessary to change the address on the Aadhaar card after each change of residence. The facilities for doing so are either not well-known or have shrunk in number. Where they exist, the queues were forbidding. Predictably, the response time from Bengaluru for acceptance of the change of address has become unpredictable. Those who are in a transferable job or move residence either ignore the requirement or scamper repeatedly to comply. There were certain situations which require the passport, the PAN card, the Aadhaar card—the list seems open to addition.

The answer to this kind of a situation is not far to seek if one just made a simple conceptual framework of reference before rushing to execution. If there can be a Central registry of KYC, there can be a Central registry of identification marks and residential certification. Perhaps, the simplicity of the suggestion itself would destroy so many jobs that it would be another hit on the employment figures. That the citizen keeps collecting and resubmitting his/her documents could draw 'cheer', as now he/she does it electronically.

August 06, 2018

## Untangling India's Financial Services

There are so many balls in the air today that it is increasingly becoming difficult to understand what the speed of each one is. The reference here is to the Indian financial system. It is common knowledge; and any child would know it that when different balls are moving at varying speeds, then a careful calibration of the two hands becomes necessary to drop any one ball on the ground.

The problem that arises here is that if one ball falls on the ground, to pick it up, one has to run over the risk of dropping all other balls.

However, this analogy, like every other analogy, is a limited one. Consider for example even as the dust over demonetisation campaign was yet to settle down, the Goods and Services Tax has been pushed into center-stage. The story rolls on. The National Stock Exchange is in throes of initiating India's largest initial public offering in the last seven years. The Securities and Exchange Board of India (SEBI) is an overdrive not only to systemise the working of the board, but between the Chairman, SEBI and the Chairman of the committee appointed by it to set right the multiple so-called aberrations of the company boards, are determined to improve corporate governance of listed entities. There is nothing wrong with that. Yet it is true that the public sector undertakings have their own cup of wows. Well intentioned provisions of oversight by the Comptroller and Auditor-General of India and the Central Vigilance Commission, have put them in a very different class, as compared to private enterprises. like all simultaneous soap operas, the narrative further unfolds with scripts getting mixed hearing. The norms of good governance have their own considerations of business operations. It touches many things, including concern for related party transaction norms. related party transactions norms have unique requirements which are not yet amenable to digitisation!

The banks have the problems of non-performing assets (NPA) and provisioning. The Reserve Bank of India (RBI) is rightly determined to solve the problem, once and for all. However, the public sector banks touch the lives of the all-powerful common man of India, whose power everyone recognises but the entity remains elusive. Shrill voices in the name of the common man can be heard all over, once his convenience and indeed livelihood is hurt.

The financial services of India cannot operate without due cognizance of the social realities. Be it the SEBI panel on governance; or the RBI's approach to NPAs, everyone is a stake-holder. The list of financial sector interventions can be further added to. That is not the point.

The point is of the overall coordination amongst all these interventions. The reason being: At some point it has to do with the overall economic health. None of the interventions noted above can be in isolation. They are all in an inter-actuary relationship. How can the impact of demonetisation on banks be de-linked with the efficiency of the functioning of the banks? Indeed, how can the functioning of the banks be de-linked with the cure of the NPAs? Or indeed, handling of the NPA's be de-linked from the issues of governance?

The list can go on without making the point any more obvious and cogent. But whose job is it to access and integrate—forget extrapolation—the collective impact? On top of it there are longitudinal segments of global banks, public enterprise banks, private banks, cooperatives, just to name a few. If the NSE is undergoing an experience, it cannot be in isolation with no relationship to the experiences of the Bombay Stock Exchange. After all, investors are interested in the routes and assurances of stock exchanges.

The above noted situation is characteristic of a scenario where internal combustion pressure may cause the seams of the financial welfare to come apart. This is not just a statement of an anxiety-prone mind. While the slogan of too little, too late has been hugely popularised, the time has come to consider another simple point of view. That point of view is of 'too much, too soon' without a real grasp either on the enabling conditions on the consequent fallouts. It may not be premature to sound the caution of integrative approach to financial interventions. There has to be a clear-cut line of vision on the horizon if the choppy seas of reforms are to be confidently negotiated.

July 17, 2017

## Sustainable Growth for Greater Good

Human civilisation stands at the brink of many seminal developments. Some are beginning to acquire a clearer profile, others are still in the mist. It may not be possible, here, to even list let alone explore the different unprecedented changes which await human existence.

However, two sectors are touching a large number of lives and their interface with the human population is only going to intensify. One of them is 'space'. When the mystery of the far off stars yields place to scientific exploration there are many significant collateral results. Illustratively, satellite has transformed human communication and it is a quantum leap in the integration of the planet earth. Similarly, the sea with its depths is no longer a mystery to which many postulated the 'disappearance' of a parallel civilisation. The non-living resources of the sea, animals of the sea, the vegetation of the sea, not to overlook the obvious fishery resources are set to transform the way of human life.

No longer is size the determining factor of growth. A simple concept of Small Island Developing States is a new variable in the power and resource interplay of the planet. Beyond territorial jurisdiction, the regulations of the high seas are getting increasingly into focus. The possibilities of bio-prospecting, marine transport and energy available from the principle of gravity are set to fundamentally reorder human dynamics. This will require new business models. Approach to system analysis is set for change.

Obviously, various declarations in different international fora have sought to address some of the issues. This is welcome, but clearly it needs to go farther. It may not be news to point out that sea bed is a major source of hydrocarbon. Like in the case of space, new technologies are setting lifestyles.

These technologies are changing the frontiers of marine resources development. The realisation that ocean values and ocean services will alter the assumptions of economic modelling and decision making processes are bound to determine the character of management. It may be one of the lasting gaps of the consulting universe that it has little identifiable competency for exploring these frontiers.

The sea, rich as it is in fisheries, throws up the universe of seafood processing, handling and storage. Sea food quality and safety are important. They are brought together by shipping and maritime connectivity.

They are embedded in the domain of ocean forecasting. Like in many other areas, India has made interesting forays in this field and there is the existence of a National Maritime Authority which is supposed to be an apex body aspiring to address coastal security concerns. Like in every other field the non-governmental organisation are also 'fishing in the waters'. The National Maritime Foundation is a non-Governmental, non-political maritime think tank. DK International Foundation devotes a substantial part of its research energies in exploring maritime related concerns both globally and in Indian context. However, like in any other field, the Indian contributions in developing the concept of Blue Economy is at best at an early stage. Whereas, globally, during the Rio+20 deliberations, half a decade ago threw up the concept of Blue Economy, in India we are only beginning to harness the economic prowess of the sea.

The linkages between the Blue Economy concept and sustainable development is obvious, but deficient in cheerleading. The Belgian businessman Gunter Pauli made a parallel contribution in launching the concept of the Blue Economy. The Club of Rome did its bit. This was bound to be so, given the nature of any 'open source movement' like the ocean. The realisation that not only can one creature's food be another creature's poison but also that waste of one system can be the input to another regenerative system. The entire circular nature of the sustainability chain is particularly embedded in template of Indian thought.

The breakthroughs both at the level of conceptual contribution and material operationalisation have many challenging distances to cover. There is an urgent need to apply the principles of equity to this emerging domain; handle it in a gender neutral manner and link it with livelihood and prosperity for the greater good of all stakeholders.

June 19, 2017

## Restructuring India's Financial Service Sector

The banks in their modern incarnation have been in India for well over a century. Punjab National Bank, State Bank of India, to name just two, could well spell out the economic history of parts of modern India. They have had also been periodically re-invented.

The more subtle changes came which the Government walking the path of liberalisation from the early 1990s. The changes that were ushered in that period were essentially with reference to the regulatory system, with a definitive quotient of enabling foreign investment. If there was any blueprint of the recasting of the mould of the public sector banks, it has been a well-kept secret.

The result has been like two negatives rolled in one. The rich and the powerful dominated the regulatory system before 1992 and have done so since. The result was evident in the high-jacking of banking financial resources in surrogacy of the socio-politically powerful. This is bad finance.

When this was topped up with politically convenient decision, of those in public life, wanting to make it good, with the twin instrumentality of loan *melas* and writing off of loans, the narrative of disaster was complete.

Finance Minister after finance minister were all individually brilliant enough to see the point, but decided to keep deferring, the inevitable, fundamental restructuring the financial services of this country needed.

The cause of sanity was not helped by a confused regulatory system where the financial regulator (read Reserve Bank of India) continued, as it does even today, to be the ultimate lender.

The repo rates wrote the fate of many types of interest rates. In this state of blinkered and fogged vision either expertise from outside India was imported for "solution sourcing" or those with bureaucratic background lead the hordes of financial *babus*. The results are there for all to see.

The time has come to search for truly *desi* options rooted in the potential and the logic of the economic realities of the day. Interventions like the Goods and Services Tax, even if handled with economic sagacity, will not alter the lay of the land of the monitory and fiscal working. They will only go so far as the taxation structure is concerned.

There is a parallel narrative, however, which has not merited the necessary attention. In 1994, HDFC started operations. In 2000, it acquired Times Bank. The same year it started AMC operations and acquired a stake in Gruh Finance. The fourth reason for why year 2000 would be remembered for HDFC was for its entering life Insurance in partnership with Standard life.

Roughly parallelly, following the path and visioned and chartered by Narayanan Vaghul (an ex-Bank of India person), ICICI was breaking new ground. When R.N. Malhotra, then Governor of the Reserve Bank of India, asked him to head ICICI, little did he realise the phenomena he was releasing.

HDFC had a clean slate. But ICICI lead by Vaghul turned the corner from a stoic frame to a vibrant financial set up. Not just insurance, it was interested in stock broking, creating quite a potpourri of financial services. It acquired Shipping Credit and Investment Corporation of India in 1996, ITC Classic Finance in 1997 and AAGRAN finance in 1998. The same year it tied up with ICICI Prudential AMC. In 2000, it was in the life insurance business with Prudential Plc.

HDFC and ICICI were on a parallel track. Few bothered to ask what was happening to the nationalised commercial bank or for that matter even the mutual fund (UTI) which four of them had sponsored. The disaster which this mutual fund then met nearly shook the investor confidence to its roots.

The hijacking of a significant stream of national finance is a story widely known but discreetly avoided, because many of the active players are still active.

Financial reforms need the daring of a leopard and the sagacity of a panther. There are many wise and brave in the Indian public domain with these characteristics but the confluence of their daring and sagacity with the opportunity to contribute is elusive.

In the ultimate analysis on the levers of reform are in the hands of politically powerful.

The Indian financial sector will have to await for that flash point when the three converge to deliver it from their present ambivalence.

August 19, 2016

## Towards Operational Financial Thinking

With the Budget season approaching, it is time for economic survey again. This survey is a ritual that is observed with much fanfare, accompanied with noises and has little impact, conventionally.

It is a delightful exercise wherein everyone can have a go at sounding profound; indeed, everyone acquires a halo around the head. This is also the occasion to do some flashing of figures.

Traditionally, the Reserve Bank of India and the Central Statistical Office spring into action, to record a declining trend or an accelerating trend, depending upon what the figures suggest.

Statisticians then swings into action and some percentages are calculated, some charts and graphs are made. These figures are then usually pegged to the gross domestic product. They can be under different heads such as household financial; household physical and the list can be long.

For good measure, one suspects to justify one's position/job, five years or three years data is put in a sequential chain. The more imaginative ones put it in the form of a pie chart or something equivalent. What all of this totals up to is anybody's guess.

Nevertheless, the industry of economic survey continues to flourish. It's surely an innocent exercise, but it diverts attention from the core issues.

The core issue that should really be asked is: What did the powers that be and their army of advisers/commissions do with the conclusions of the economic survey? What was the follow-up of the 'wisdom' which flowed so eloquently since last February?

I have read some newspaper columns that have discouraged people who have attempted to pose this question, with pious refrains of focussing on the present.

A survey in February 2015 had suggested the appointment of an independent re-negotiation commission with political authority and reputational integrity. The purpose was to tackle some of the big and difficult cases.

Many have worked overtime throughout the year, making sure that Parliament does not work, intolerance is denounced, taking pot shots at the so-called failings of national security, deciding who is undemocratic and indeed who is more at fault.

The so-called civil society has predictably been selective about what it chooses to be agitationist about and what it chooses to ignore. Finger-pointing and fault finding has achieved unprecedented heights, one almost said, unprecedented bottom.

Putting it simply: The banks continue to be in distress. Many chiefs have gone out of office and new ones appointed after suitable exercise and due diligence. This, notwithstanding, banks, especially in the public sector domain continue to be happily practicing more of the same. This needs to change if ordinary mortals are to have a sense of security about their savings.

The distress asset cry for better bankruptcy procedures and a revolution in financial practice has been attempted by lowering the level of transactions where pan card number is a must.

There is nothing wrong with that. These suggestions are as good as any, provided it does not end up multiplying the data, contributing to the number, crunching with more pie charts and more graphs.

Some of the core issues are still to be tackled. The statutory liquidity ratio needs to be lowered. Even the opposition party will find it difficult to find a 'saffron fundamentalism' in this suggestion or find arguments to block it.

More fundamentally, the priority sector itself needs a re-classification. One does not need an economist in an 'ayog' to reason this.

Quit simply one could begin with developing viable clusters of public sector banks with commonality of issues which will make them amenable to more coherent interventions.

Clearly, there is no such thing as one homogeneous block of public sector bank. This intervention does not even need to go to Parliament! It does not need weeks of consultation with clusters of stakeholders.

Like all rituals, these rituals (of consultation) also serve a purpose and may continue. The need is, however, for a strategic re-think of categories in public sector banks and otherwise. This will help make not only money more safe, but growth will be more amenable to policy interventions.

January 22, 2016

## Changing the Financial System in India

There was a time when finance was a dependent variable. Its circulation through any organisation was compared to blood flowing through any body, a colorful analogy, directed towards showing money's all pervasiveness and how it touched each and every part of the organisation. However, with changing times, it became all the more difficult to associate the finance stream with the blood stream. Finance assumed a character of its own.

Finance could work for finance and money could be used to make money. There was no need for fresh physical effort being added to it. Investment came on board and finance acquired a character of its own.

Being a venture capitalist became a full-fledged career. Now, to talk of capital is to talk of entrepreneurship. To talk of entrepreneurship is to talk of human enterprise. In fact, one of the leading writers on this subject compared capital to steroids. The assumption was: As there is too much of cheap capital available, not only will start-ups sprout quickly, but will also have terrible side effects and indeed have counterproductive results. Flashy names in business always have unpredictable life.

Many avid readers will recall the book: *In Search of Excellence*. This book, co-authored by Tom Peters and Robert H. Waterman, Jr was read and re-read. It was assumed that this book captured the basic truths. Five years later after the publication of this book, a survey was conducted to find out what had happened to those firms most of them had gone bankrupt. So much to be said for the so-called "best practices".

Today, the world is swearing by e-commerce companies like Flipkart, Snapdeal, Alibaba etc. For how long will these companies last will be matter of conjuncture. Be that as it may, the life of these organisations is only a part of the story.

The bigger story has to do with the understanding of trends. Today, surge and venture capital has helped companies scale quickly and definitely. Between April 2015 and October 2015, Ola cabs raised around $910 million. The number of rides rose from 1,000 a day to a million a day.

It is true that capital helps to build the supply side rather quickly and create a network effect. The interesting thing about evolution of finance as an area is that it has also acquired certain regional characteristics. A simple illustration may help to clarify this observation.

In 1956, Indian philosopher and statesman Sarvepalli Radhakrishnan, while addressing a convocation at Patna university talked of 'self-employment'. This, in an era when private sector jobs were few, compared to Government jobs that were considered to be much sought after. The concept of self-employment did not actually find much space.

A few years later when the National Small Industries Corporation was set up, nucleating entrepreneurship activities (read self-employment) became a Government objective. This was truly a strange version of a welfare state.

The first geographical center that the National Small Industries Development Corporation chose was Naini.

This was the constituency of the then serving Prime Minister Jawaharlal Nehru. Whether Nehru prompted this or the powers that be in NSIDC did this, to be pleasing to the Prime Minister is a moot question. Irrespectively, something had been launched; this was to be a force multiplier. The core concern then was not getting technology for small enterprises but capital.

Sixty years down the line, the key slogan of the Government though of a different pedigree still remains 'Make in India!' One wonders about the distance one has covered.

They were discussing self-employment and entrepreneurship then, they are doing so now. While the character of finance has changed across the world and regionally, in India, it continues like in many other sectors more of the same.

Even in entrepreneurship, regional variants are loud across the globe. Typically, Australian Prime Minister Malcolm Turnbull on December 7, 2015, announced a one billion dollar innovation and science package. Australia's $100 million is going to be available in extra finding for Commonwealth Scientific and Industrial Research Organisation and provide capital gain tax holidays for investing in startup enterprises.

The message is interesting. An Indian variant of a new component to a new package is possible, provided of course, the Reserve Bank of India et al., move beyond the obsession of interest rates!

January 08, 2016

## Bretton Woods System has Run its Course

Obviously, there is a new financial architecture emerging in the world, but it is not quite clear what the parameters are like, or for that matter, what the contents would be. However, the child of Bretton Woods has run its life. The current global financial indicators are not very rosy.

Europe is in a deep debt crisis and highly dependent on exports. Due to a rise in wages, there is a big hole in corporate profitability and evaluation in the US. Emerging economies are finding the need to re-align the relationship within themselves and also between themselves.

Of the BRICS countries, news from Brazil and Russia is not encouraging. Indeed, the Chinese economy may be slipping faster that what has been imagined.

Japan has been struggling to get inflation under control. The overall scene is mixed and that itself is an understatement.

The fact of the matter is: People are trying to debate whether a recession is round the corner. There is a good reason for the above.

On December 17, the US Federal Reserve announced a hike in interest rates. The latest rate cut in China, with its resultant ebullience, reinforces the need to negotiate with excessive financial sector debt.

The situation may really be under nobody's control. There is incomplete and asymmetrical information and institutional weakness. When this is topped with freaks and foibles of human behaviour, one can only wonder, the human mind needs to adjust. We have at hand, yet another occasion to see and appreciate why the solutions cannot be customised.

Woes of sovereign nations are many and large. Greece alone is a tell-tale example. It needs to implement structural reforms, enhanced productivity and growth potential.

When this has to go together with austerity and requirement of immediate financial assistance, the potpourri of reforms required may beat many human conceptions. The Greek story is neither unique nor unusual. It may only be more intense. Many countries like Greece need to re-invent their banking system, not to forget the need for debt relief.

Clearly, a re-born financial system is not only desirable but appears inevitable. The fact of the matter is that there is an over-dependence on the institution of central banks (called the Reserve Bank in India). This dependence is pathetic and even more so, when lead by articulation in a cow boy's style.

Financial re-structuring itself may be inherent in the situation, if for nothing else, because of the propensity of the system to break at negative normal yields.

It will be a kind deed if China were not to have a hard landing, but then, it should be kept in mind that as a system, it responds very reluctantly to any market pressure. Also, for other countries, it is difficult to be against a massive war chest. The truth of the matter is that China is passing through a middle income transition phase.

Unlike China, in India, middle income groups, in coalition with the upper income groups, are firmly in control of the political processes. Many have been talking of Brazil, Russia, India and China. Also, emerging on the scene are countries such as Turkey, not to forget the prowess of Singapore and the United Arab Emirates.

In neither of the last two named countries are economic and financial challenges compounded by political issues, the way they are in many of the other emerging economies.

Of course, the Congress can be credited for having brought the entire political process of legislation to its knees by simply holding the system to ransom in India.

There is no course in political economy that factors all this. Nor has the last word been said yet. The emergence of terrorism and the inability of the sovereign Governments, to choke the financial channels of funding speak volumes of the emerging political order.

Yet, there is hope. The UAE symbolises it like few do. Dubai alone is splendidly resplendent. It is inhabited by migrants from 200 countries and, instead of going to the market, has brought the global market to its doorsteps. It's Expo 2020 is poised to be a story like no other.

December 25, 2015

## Towards More Robust Financial Institutions

The gross non-performing assets of the Indian banking system are estimated to be at 4.5 per cent of the total loans. At the same time, the Investment Information and Credit Rating Agency of India limited has estimated that bad loans of the Government banks stand at 5.1 per cent.

On March 30, the Reserve Bank of India allowed banks to use up to 50 per cent of their counter-cyclical buffer to provide for the NPAs. This was up by 17 per cent of the prevailing practices. The counter-cyclical buffer itself was an outcome of the financial crises of 2008.

Meanwhile, the economy itself is in the grip of a strange man-made situation: On matters of acquisition of land, availability of fuel, getting environmental approval etc. When this is capped with poor credit evaluation procedures, the cup of misery overflows.

Of course, the Government has progressively infused higher capital in some of the public sector banks. Many a time this has been un-correlated to the budgetary allocation. The inefficiency of some of the public sector undertakings not to take this seriously is because of their faith that the Government will keep bailing out these banks.

This is a palpably illusory situation. Clearly, the experience of Air India has not been registered seriously enough in concerned quarters. Banks' relationships with, say, troubled energy companies, have a high potential of enhancing defaults and bankruptcy filings.

On June this year, the policymakers of Bank of England flagged the issue of interest rates. Predictably, it got hinged to the Bank of England's approach towards domestic inflation. The world was in the hope that the tail-winds of global growth would catch on.

At the end of the day, there seems to be much in common in the patterns of the forecasts made by the economists and the behaviour of the stock exchange! Added to this is the frailty and unpredictability of human behaviour.

This is well illustrated by the nominal impact that low oil prices have caused on the general price index. Of course, the faithful still believe that analytics will come to the rescue.

In this kind of an environment, which resembles the babble in the tower of Babylon, no one knows what's coming and what's going.

In his Bancon address of 2010, this writer had pleaded to make the 'choice of performance' as a conscious one. There is a difference between talking of performance in a matter of making a grand stand and adopting efforts of re-inventing one's systems and procedures to meet the requirements of time.

One may or may not be a Modiite. That's another matter. However, Prime Minister Narendra Modi certainly comes out to be a person with a clear sense of direction in many areas. This has to be seen by the corporates— especially by the financial institutions—as a possible route to the solution in tune with the demands of time.

Mission-vision is fine. Equally important is the capacity of the leaders to use the compass of his judgements to find a path out of the woods. This will make solutions context-specific.

The bank and the financial institutions provide a fit case for this kind of approach. This writer's research has established that it can be done. One needs a purposeful approach to management with a clear understanding of the structure, processes and the capabilities of the people who populate the organisation.

Sub-standard designations done in different environment of loans by regulators, clearly highlight doubts on the borrower's ability to re-pay or question the value of the assets that back a loan. Political favours have to be kept out from this domain.

Apart from the Russian banks, among the lenders in emerging markets, Indian banks have the least capacity to absorb the losses.

The International Monetary Fund had warned of this in mid-April itself. Like in Chile, Hungary and a few other places, a deterioration in loan quality can threaten capital levels. According to the Global Financial Stability report of the IMF, the loss-absorbing buffer of the Indian banking sector is 7.9 per cent of risk weighted assets, as against 7.8 per cent in Russia.

Several firms in countries like Argentina, Brazil, China, Nigeria, and Turkey have relatively constrained re-payment capacity in terms of interest-coverage ratios, and the likes of them owe significant share of the debts.

Time requires a managerial response to managerial problems. It may be fanciful to treat the managerial issues with an economic tool-box.

August 21, 2015

## Financial Institutions are Losing their Sheen

It is no news that gold is losing its glitter. However, it may be news that gold prices are likely to decline further. Strong selling of gold in China, and institutional investors and the prospect of higher interest rates from the US, will further have a negative impact on the price of gold.

Prices of gold plunged to its lowest level in five years between July 24 and July 25. The price of the precious metal was $1,090 per troy ounce. Expectations are that by the end of this year, it may be around $1,000 per troy ounce. The trend is obvious: Pull out money from gold and invest in the US Government paper.

With such fundamental seismic movements, the financial world will clearly throw up a serial turbulence. The age-old problem of lack of intermediary institutions such as banks in countries such as India will multiply. The columns of newspapers will be talking about the turbulence in banks such as the Syndicate Bank or the Union Bank of India. They are not the only banks in this category. However, just to remind ourselves that there are others too, does not mitigate the danger.

Nearly two years ago, when this writer was a part of the selection process of the chief executive officers for public sector undertakings, his colleagues on the panel were former Deputy Governors of the Reserve Bank of India; A. Ghosh and S.S. Tarapore. The Additional Secretary(s) who used to sit with him were Y. Venugopal Reddy and R.D. Gupta. The former became the Governor of the Reserve Bank of India and the latter a Deputy Governor. This writer remembers that one of the Deputy Governors of the RBI even shared his doubts when it came to four of the PSUs.

It is amazing how the state of these banks have remained constant over the last two decades. Whether it is pleasing or worrying, it is a matter of fact on which side you are. Of course, careers are being made by stating the obvious. Market expert Anil Rego has asked for an unemotional investment process based on assets allocation. He has also pleaded for a long-term horizon and regularity of investment.

This writer is sure in saying this that Mr. Rego is not staking any claims at originality. But that is another story. It may be more relevant to notice that there are organisations, who only a few months ago, when in need of capital, sold short-term bonds directly to the investors at more favourable interest rates than going to the bank. Deepak Nitrite can be a case in point here.

Similarly, the issuance of this sort of debt—commercial paper has been increasing in India. The banks by and large continue to be a trigger and their believe to seek multiple indemnifications on the same issue is high professionalism. Mutual funds threaten to sell deposits at prevailing net asset value if they find know your customer at any point of time unsatisfactory. Only nobody knows what will cause this dissatisfaction.

It does not seem to bother anybody in particular. The unthinking happily sign unreadable photocopied deposit performa and the thinkers just ignore it. The race to key positions in regulating bodies continues unabated with the booty often going to paratroopers of non-resident Indian affiliation.

Talking of all this is a taboo, because it takes away from the frozen dignity, many financial specialist who insist on looking very starchy with stiff upper lip. This is not likely to fuel solutions. Even internationally, they are rumblings.

For example, in Australia, banks have rejected the International Monetary Fund's claim that there would be little microeconomic cost in forcing lenders to de-leverage. Regulators should be asked, it is argued, to prioritise the implementation of the Murray financial systems inquiry's recommendation. It is felt that it will substantially increase bank capital levels; its advisability or otherwise was not to be seen as a problem.

If one adds to it the fact that banks, globally, are not amongst the best capitalised institutions; it is not difficult to come to the reality of Indian banks. They continue to be slow, to pass along RBI's rate cuts to the customers. Cheaper funds are available by going directly to the capital market. The Government persists with the failed interventions of recapitalisation.

It's time the banking system, especially the PSUs, get together to take a collective, professional look at its future directions of growth.

August 07, 2015

## Lessons for the RBI from the Greek Crisis

The Greek financial crises is temporarily on the hold. To believe that it has blown over, may prove to be wishful thinking. It's difficult to anticipate even the trends. Greece, however, may not be the full story. As financial journalist Alan Kohler opines, irrespective of the fate of Greece, Europe's foundations will continue to weaken. This will not be the last existential crises for the Eurozone.

Unless greater fiscal and political union goes along with the monetary union, the threats are real. Commentators believe that falling apart of the euro may be a noisy affair.

A 'yes' vote in Greece gave the people access to what is left of their euro. It further enabled German cash to start flowing in. So far so good. Unfortunately decision makers, unaware of longitudinal thinking, have almost completely overlooked how much Germany owed Greece, some decades ago and how Greece waived it away. There is no accounting method to square up this state of affair.

There are other variables in the international play of financial forces. The Chinese economy appears to be on the retreat. Countries like Australia are much more vulnerable to this than what is happening in Mediterranean Europe. It will bear repetition to note that the Australian mining sector advantage is already on the retreat. The debt market is somewhat constrained. Only a few days ago, China reportedly released five tonnes of gold on the Shanghai market. In India, gold prices have spiralled down several thousand rupees.

The basic question is: How does one manage investments—both individual and collective? Our central bank (the Reserve Bank of India) like many other national institutions either goes stoically silent or when it tweets, it is over some issues like the lowering or raising of interest rates. Such innocence is adorable, even if somewhat worrying. In contrast, financial institutions elsewhere choose to keep up with the times.

The National Australian Bank, for example, recognises its vital interest in Europe, as it prepares to offload its trouble-plagued Clydesdale Bank before the end of the year. The chief of the National Australian Bank is focussing on public offerings. The discussions can be further extended. The trouble however is reflections on monetary and fiscal situation in India need to move beyond repetition on interest rates, non-performing assets and the extent of mandatory deposits.

Irrespective ordinary life has a knack of moving ahead as if nothing has happened. It is this dualism of normalcy and turbulence which gets wires crossed.

Getting back to Greece, the reports are that the Greek Ministry for Tourism does not anticipate any disruptions in visitors' holiday experiences. This applies to both Greek islands and the mainland.

Even before the European deal, the Greek Government had assured that all debit and credit cards would be fully functional. It is the small and not-so-small experiences of maximum limits on bank withdrawals that have really effected the flow of life.

The automated teller machines still work. The trouble is more at the short-term level and at the medium-term level. As unemployment soars and economy shrinks, the public debt has swollen from 110 per cent of gross domestic product to almost 180 per cent. These, at the best, remain mystery figures to the everyday life of the average resident in Greece.

The core issue remains the role of banks in a unique social milieu. The banks must remain in front of their client. The key is to respond to existing holders, and separate the act of capital raising.

Nothing is as simple as it appears. But an act of confidence and facing in an enlightened manner the risk of business, is the key.

The leadership team of any bank needs to have a core composition. Some 40 per cent of its composition should be constantly reviewed, preferably every quarter, to look at the emerging economic scenario with the lenses of specialists. The wealth management division of the bank needs to be strengthened as does its insurance wing. Suitable linkages with stable and tested international financial systems, for a time bound period, may hold some answers.

It is important to recognise that banks don't appear to be losing the plot, so far as consumer trust is concerned.

July 24, 2015

# 8

# International Business

## India can Make Definitional Contributions at G20

A category is created by having something in common. Yet in each category, an entity can and usually may have some unique characteristics. Thus, all human beings across the globe have certain common features, physically, emotionally, and otherwise. Yet with human beings, there are different races, and each race has its distinctive features. The category can be further broken down into its conglomerates till one reaches the family, and even in the family, there are certain "streams". And then there are individuals.

It can, therefore, be argued that in definitional terms one has to look at both the conglomerates' traits and individual traits to be able to develop appropriate typologies and indeed defining characteristics. This task is simultaneously essential and tricky. A lot of sociological and anthropological categories arise out of the above exercises. It needs to be appreciated that much work on the theme has been done over the years, making the task of categorization simultaneously simple yet complex. This also applies to what is referred to as "Indians".

Politically, all human beings with citizenship rights within the political boundaries of this country are entitled to be called Indians. Yet the physical characteristics from Kanyakumari to Kashmir have a range of variations. Under such circumstances, the characteristics of the 'majority' become the defining characteristic. This is a simple deduction because anything else would make for complexities.

All nation-building efforts require the need to recognize this. In the case of India, what would have been, a simple exercise has become subject to a misplaced sense of parity between one conglomerate and another.

It is obvious that a definition cannot be put in negative terms. There has to be positive content in the definition. In any nation-building exercise, the 'majority' of the population has a prime role, and the cultural element is its "way of life". "Way of life" is defined by the rituals of life, which in turn are defined by belief. Thus, it is "the beliefs" which are important. The definition of "belief" can vary, but it cannot be evaded because of the scientific efforts it needs.

Consider the USA. The President of the USA takes an oath on the *Bible*, and nobody asks why the religious texts of other communities are not included in the oath-taking ceremony. In the UK, the Sovereign Monarch is the "Head of the Church of England". Nobody asks what about the followers of Islam, Sikhism, Hinduism and whatever other religions of the subjects.

In the case of Russia, the Greek Orthodox Church has its say, and that is how the swearing-in ceremonies take place. In other words, a definition very often gets its expression through practice and acceptability.

This is an essential part of nation-building, or, for that matter, any such definitional activity. In the case of India, so many identities have been drummed up repeatedly, that the word "diversity" has acquired almost definitional proportions. There is nothing wrong with appreciating diversity. However, a definition requires, as pointed out earlier, a positive content. Respecting each other's beliefs is normal, natural, and desirable.

However, confusion will arise if the defining characteristics of a community and a conglomerate do not recognize the beliefs and the practices of the majority.

Taking this elaboration further, each conglomerate has its own unique elements, and those too have to be recognized. For example, in India, more than nine per cent of the population is of tribal descent. Hence, it is necessary to recognise that, besides the majority traits, there may be identifiable minority characteristics that need to be registered, flagged, preserved, and developed.

As it happens in a democracy, noise can often be heard over and above a mild and a sane voice. A good example, again, comes from the tribes. Perhaps because the tribes are such that they have not yet organised into a politically powerful unified group, they are not paid the same deference as some of the local religious groups. This is a national loss.

It is a loss because it not only does not do justice to a substantial part of the population but also misses a focus on some of the characteristics of a tribe that can be put to use for nation-building. Illustration can be the method by which the tribes have maintained their identity over several millennia.

To sum up the above, creating a definition is a tricky and time-consuming exercise. This has to be handled in a deft manner, and above all, it has to be handled in a statesmanlike and knowledgeable manner.

Occasions like the G20 meet are fit occasions for sharing methods for finding definitions and sharing of local experiences for universal use. India has a good opportunity to make definitional contributions at the coming G20 summit. There will be palpable wisdom in preparing for it.

February 13, 2023

## Hope Amid Despair

Finally, the commentaries in the printed and the audio-visual media have begun to change from what it is today, to what a year it has been and how things will be in the year to come. Whereas nothing on the ground has substantially, changed (and indeed many territories of the world are still passing through very demanding times even for the Covid-era), there is a growing realisation that hope is a no choice situation. Of the many basic truths of life, the biggest is that one gets tired even of despair. Fantasy is born in many seedbeds and one of them is excessive despair.

The global havoc caused by COVID-19 will someday be assessed. As of now, some are still trying to swim underwater and there are others trying to build a fortune by fishing in troubled waters. They are doing remarkably well as they understand that people pay and pay disproportionately high (if they can afford to) when the going gets tough. This cannot be an occasion for pontificating. One can only say: To each his own! Meanwhile, strained relationships in families, misconstruction and misunderstanding of otherwise simple activities are taking a toll. This is bound to happen if there is refraction of meaning through an overstrained mental capacity. Be that as it may, one of the brighter signs on the horizon is the strong mind of some people who still make sense through their sheer capacity of mindfulness. The first defining characteristic of mindfulness is recognition that one cannot project one's insecurities on others. No matter how wonderful or strong the foundations of the relationship, no one can carry anybody else's burden endlessly.

Especially of those people who do not know how to control themselves.

This has nothing to do with the uniqueness of the Covid-era. It is a common human feeling which behavioural scientists have not offered many solutions to, perhaps because the indicators are weak and defences which people put up are formidable. Along with that comes the propensity to hold on to one's frameworks of reference and plans. The reality perception of many can be weak. An amalgamation of such propensities creates a devastating cocktail.

Perhaps, the problem could be handled by an approach which travels from outside-in rather than inside-out. Plus, we need to grant that humans are complex beings and there is real difficulty in even understanding oneself, let alone others. Any attempt at "understanding" should be the end of a process rather than the beginning. The thought of travelling the route of understanding from outside-in creates a hierarchy of efforts which helps to make it progressively more effective and capable of handling increasingly more complex situations. Applying that frame of reference to the present situation of human reaction to the pandemic (and often intractable complexity and anxiety) leads to some possible conclusions. One of them is to start understanding possible responses of the economy to material conditions and then gradually move to inner layers.

Mercifully, that process seems to have begun. The World Economic Forum (WEF) has come out with a special edition of its Global Competitiveness Report: 2020. It ostensibly talks of how countries are performing on the road to recovery. It will be read and reread over its 90 plus pages as indeed it deserves.

In the limitations of space of this column it is not possible to provide a substantive critique. In India, the partner to this effort was an institution which is not so widely-known and yet seems to have collaborated with competence. Territories from Albania to Uruguay have contributed through some institution and that itself is a commendable canvas. The partner institutes helped to administer "the executive opinion survey and advance the competitiveness agenda in their respective economies." There were other institutions which pitched in with different competencies including what goes into composing the WEF's index. From collecting the data to analysis and more, was a huge organisational exercise. That itself deserves high praise. More substantially, the contents while not being revolutionary, have helped to redefine the meaning of competitiveness in a changed world context. It was pleasing to see that disruption and resilience were treated in the same section. The concept of the pandemic has made its mark on the literature on economics.

More efforts in the genre will surely come. For the present it may suffice to mention that it is a great attempt of analysis of the past decade and of future trends. The pleasing thing in the WEF's report is the focus on the idea of the "road to recovery." Obviously, for any meaningful journey, it must begin somewhere. No revival or turnaround can take place unless some people believe that it can happen. The WEF's report is a nudge in the right direction. The scientific method would require some instruments of measurement. All that would involve a cushioning crucible of faith and belief in it being possible. This should be not only an interesting but a worthwhile journey.

December 21, 2020

## Quest for Creating Global Space

In 1985, a convention was held on Human Resource Planning and Enterprise Management by the Indian Society for Training & Development (ISTD) in collaboration with the Bureau of Public Enterprises, Government of India, at Vigyan Bhavan, New Delhi. Over 80 organisations were represented. The themes explored were: Human resource planning activities; human resource information systems; human resource accounting and auditing; human resource training; development and organisation. The one thing that the convention established was that a perspective on human resource planning activities in enterprises in India was not only feasible but doable. In corporate enterprises, the approach of business configurability was advocated.

Thirty years down the line, if there has been any significant progress in this direction, results are yet to be documented. In the meanwhile, what has happened is that the talk of skill augmentation has occupied prime attention in the domain of human resource management. Pressures for this have been so huge that there is little known serious attempt at converting it at the corporate level for optimisation and goal directed purposes.

Revenue concerns and populist pressures have thrown up some new elements on to the scene. Inter alia, they include the huge spaces that consultancy companies—especially those carrying the tag of foreign brands—occupy. Political entities with avowedly nationalist slogans lead the patronisation brigade of such organisations.

Simply put, these institutions have never witnessed such a boost to their revenue streams as they have seen in the last few years. If this combination of *desi* governance processes, leaning heavily on *bii-desi* (foreign) entities, have produced any dramatic breakthroughs, it is still to be established. Nevertheless, the tango between the two is only rising in its speed and range.

By itself, there may be nothing to regret in such a combination. If there is any regret, it is about poor returns received on per unit of investment made in lubricating the revenue streams of consultancy enterprises with apparent foreign veneer. It almost tantamounts to wasteful expenditure.

The time is not yet ripe for governance systems—be it at the Centre or the States—to buy this perspective. This may not even be an issue of any great significance in the projected national election of 2019. Chances are slim even for them to get flagged. Perhaps a core determining element would be that many of the so-called opposition parties also believe in acquired status through association with foreign brands.

Perhaps one of the significant deviations in this sorry theme would be the Van Dhan scheme of the Government of India. Even though the scheme is yet to be fully launched, its perspective is right. It talks of strengthening the market for indigenous products from tribal areas, value addition with technological intervention. This needs to be coupled with better market mechanisms. This proves, if any proof be needed, that there are options of an indigenous genre to unselective and continual introduction of non-Indian experiences.

The core issue, therefore, remains inventorising indigenous competencies, knowledge bases and upgradation thereof. More than anything else, this will require re-positioning of the vantage point of perception. An analysis of the list of dozens upon dozens of themes of doctoral dissertations and research projects of leading Indian institutions will show that selection of themes has a comparatively small percentage of space for those areas that have to do with indigenous models.

Value addition to indigenous growth processes and elimination of obstacles, that arise because of the context, needs attention.

The reason for this eschewed profile is not far to seek. Promotion graphs in institutions such as Indian Institutes of Technology, Indian Institutes of Management, Central universities and also the lesser institutions in these streams, are determined by the recognition received in foreign journals, foreign institutions and others.

Whereas, it is understandable that progressively human capital is being taken as an asset and money spent on its augmentation is taken as an investment. This approach needs a twist. Focus is needed on issues which accelerate indigenous developmental models. This alone can be the bedrock of creating an environment of pro-active ownership of the costs that development entails. This is a plausible approach, provided in terms of intellectual emotion, we are prepared for it.

May 21, 2018

## Roots of Turmoil and Living Through Them

Between 1945 and 1960, world order changed dramatically. Not only did empires crumble, following the conclusion of World War II, but unprecedented forces were released, realigning, not only empires but also conglomerate of states, which included the Chinese land mass.

During this period, Chinese military and political leader, Chiang Kai-Shek, sought refuge in the island of Taiwan and the People's Liberation Army got China on a trajectory of moving from strength to strength. In less than three years of the communist take over (1949) of mainland China, the statesmen of that country started looking at the boundaries which were open to question because of various legacies. From Japan to Tibet, even in the face of unsettled domestic situation, the Chinese leaders were pushing beyond the conventional existing maps.

A classic case was that of incorporation of Tibet as a part of China with an obliging leadership in the neighbourhood. Because of a self-styled iconoclast as the Indian Prime Minister, the agreement on Tibet was easy. Further, the permanent seat in the United Nations Security Council, which could have gone India's way, was gifted to China.

The issue, however, was of crumbling empires, redefining boundaries and contentious posturing. There is a common thread weaving through all this disintegration, reintegration, redrawing of boundaries which provide a thematic unity to the times. Indeed, it was not always armorial power which defined the day. In some cases it was just the clarity of purpose or statesmanlike, proactive, moves clinching the issue.

In this period, much of the British empire ceased to exist. French, Portuguese, Spanish, Dutch colonies got freedom. Residue and dust would take long years to settle. Much of Asia was in the throes of border disputes. However, this is not the place where these disputes can either be analysed or sorted out or explained. But one thing is obvious. Communities, which had clear thinking and little gap between aspiration and action, carried the day and held sway.

This hypothesis on overlap between aspiration and action having their way is an important one because much else then follows the suit. In an unstable world order, where there is a gap between aspiration and action, self-driven enunciation of standards and conforming the same becomes the reference point. A stable global world order requires enunciation and sharing of these standards.

Perhaps the setting up of United Nations on the ashes of the League of Nations was a step in that direction. However, the nature of conflicts, particularly in Asia, heightened the role of amoral superiority and commerce in armaments. The economists don't usually flag this but the economic world order also rode to prominence on the back of regular and irregular arms deals. Dealing in arms opened the flood gates of fight over resources. A struggle for control over energy resources, mineral wealth, resources of every conceivable order created a new world order grappling with controversies The rest, as they say, is history.

Sometimes, the gap between aspiration and action leads to battles, and on other occasions, wars. In some cases, it produces a revolution, and on others military coups. And the list can be added on.

However, in the ultimate analysis, the social fabric almost all over Asia was severely strained. The generation which was born during the 1945 to 1960 period in this part of the world, faced tumult and turmoil as few generations in history before them had faced.

This was not easy to bear because it threatened the traditional social fabric, family relations, definitions of marriage and contours of personal happiness. Immigration got flagged as an evil if it crossed a measure not to the liking of receiving communities. These issues made it inevitable that the turmoil of developing countries spilled into the mother countries of former empires.

When convulsions of this order take place, there can be no winners or losers. There can be only shared sense of disquiet, disruption with some rear guard action in the name of order and regulation. The time has come to distil from the turmoil, the underpinning causes of this turmoil. For a commonly shared approach of reasonableness, alone can mark the beginning of a road, which is bound to be long.

August 14, 2017

## Different Calendars, Same Global Issues

The year 2016 of the Gregorian calendar has just concluded. India, officially, as per the Nehruvian diktat, follows the Saka era. In my limited interface with the Government over the years, I have never received any letter from the Government even mentioning the optional Saka era.

A vast majority of the country follows the Vikram era. This era is largely lost upon the political and social elite of the country which is predominantly, anchored in the Western tradition. The corporate world is also largely dominated by this class. There too the Gregorian calendar is the popular framework of working.

The New Year is celebrated by a large part of the elite of this country as January 1. The immediate preceding week, having the celebration of Christmas, makes it largely blocked for much serious business activity. This is not a rhetorical observation. It has implications on our search for identity and quarantining one's place in the global system.

Consider the period of *Ramzan* as a factor in West Asia. The world knows that these are special days and factors in the office timings while dealing with them. Examples can be multiplied.

However, the bald truth remains that the Gregorian calendar does dominate the business cycle in India. Hence, the media in the fortnight around the New Year is replete with business forecasts.

Of course, in the British tradition, our financial year ends on March 31. Australians begin their financial year on July 1, and many other economic zones have other financial new year beginnings.

Till not so long ago, traditionally, the Union Budget was presented in the afternoon in Parliament because, ever since the Budget presentation began, it had to be in time in the UK for the country's business hours to begin. Mercifully, we have now got beyond that. This year's parliamentary Budget session is to begin early.

Identity requires a 'form'. Indians are often identified with the *dhoti*. It may be worn cross-legged or waist-tucked in front or back. A certain percentage of the population, however, does not wear the *dhoti*. Identity is the business of perception and conditioning.

The larger point is that, around January 1 is the time when business forecast are attempted by many of the Western educated elite, in India. Irrespective of the reliability and credibility, there is no dearth of people who have suggestions to give for the new year's economy. While making an inventory of the concerns raised, the front-runners as of today, in the class of international economic variables, is the US Federal Reserve and the raise in rates at a faster pace than earlier on. The theme of Organisation of Petroleum Exporting Countries (OPEC) and oil prices continues to keep economic analyst and the soothsayers busy. The GST and the demonetisation process are matters of endless speculation.

If this was not all, the political uncertainty of Europe, the likely redefining of the London economic market and, the impending swearing in of the unguided-missile called Donald Trump, continue to catch everybody's attention. India goes on endlessly with its cathartic political sloganeering, as China contributes its share to the volatility of global financial markets. Today, the flow of capital to US assets has pushed the dollar to over a decade's high and Renminbi is being subjected to downward pressure. The Chinese economy and its leveraging corporate balance sheet remains an enigma wrapped in a mystery.

Be that as it may, no narrative, like the one above, can be complete without reference to the fact that in all the wisdom that is pouring out in the media, there is no reference to the biggest and the most lucrative market of them all. It is the market of arms and armament. This unlisted market perhaps determines the state of the global economy more than any other single product or service. It is duly serviced by tax havens and by experts outside the acknowledged global system agencies or at best subterranean streams of the existing political systems.

One wonders about the calendar, form, content, price and worth of economic forecasts. What is the price of believing the forecasts of the flourishing-industry-and-trade of financial analysts?

January 09, 2017

## Economic Lessons India Must Take From China

Asian countries have many commonalities. Pan-Asia, there is great belief in the values of family system—it transcends geographies and ethnicity. The list can be long. Similarly, there are a number of common problems.

There is problem of terrorism in many parts of Asia, including China, India, the Middle East, South East Asia etc. Notwithstanding these constraints, some countries have their lenses clear while others are still groping in the dark.

One of the common problems in Asia is population. Consider the following figure. India has approximately 1,225 million people. China has approximately 1,343 million people. It is estimated that India adds 28 million people every year. On the other hand, China adds only 17 million people. Like many other things, India's population policy predates China. However, by present estimates, India will overtake China, in population, by 2045.

The crises of monsoon, irrigation and agriculture are not autonomous variables. There are other variables too. The present Government is talking much about eliminating black money and expanding revenue collection. That is how it should be.

The facts of the case are: less than three per cent of India's population actually pays taxes. It is estimated that less than six per cent of India's population are permanent account number (PAN) card holders. By another estimate, 93 per cent of the workforce in India is working in the unorganised sector.

The media, with huge alacrity, talks about Indian business. There is nothing wrong with that, but the fact of the matter is that fundamental changes which should have taken place are still awaited.

There is a good report on select implementation of technology. That is welcome, but what is required is a serious re-look at the paradigms which determine domestic priorities; lines of foreign policy and international investment.

All of these have strategic overtones. Reference to China may be in order. Indian scholarships and research has still to come to grips with the significance of China's 'One Belt One Road' policy which was initiated in March 2015.

Economically, it is a grey area. Many Chinese scholars do not expect re-payment of 80 per cent of loans to the China-Pakistan Economic Corridor projects. The repayment on other 'One Belt One Road' project loans would be between 30 per cent and 50 per cent. It is apparent that this burden is being accepted as a conscious choice. For this, the advantages that China would get are non-economic, including strategic and diplomatic.

Clearly, the 'One Belt One Road' project is based on a paradigm of the aspiration of a great power. A student of Chinese history may recall in this approach and echo of the Middle Kingdom status of the Chinese evolution. The aspiration of China to dominate Asia and its surrounding seas and oceans would be apparent to many.

A sub clause in making is that of China casting significant influence on the less-developed parts of east Europe. The recent experiences of China's reaction to Hague court of Justice on matter related to the South China Sea are a definite pointer on the aspirational contours of China.

The purpose here is not to eulogise or condemn China. The purpose is to focus on learning by observance of analogies and approaches from which some models can be drawn.

If India has such an approach well indexed, it is still to surface in the public domain. However, one must hasten to add that there is a refreshing beginning of the realisation that it cannot be 'business as usual' for India.

China's method of dealing with internal resistance movements may or may not be worth emulating but it certainly needs observation and analysis. Here one is not talking just of Tibet but also of Chinese Provinces where ethnic descent is both about armorial strength and also drawing strength from beyond.

Some scholars working on the index of power potential have come to the conclusion that China became a potential great power around 2009 when its economic power exceeded 25 per cent of what was with the US. By 2015, it had grown rapidly to an estimated 42 per cent, according to such index.

The 'One Belt One Road' doctrine and plan is the seed bed of Chinese economic worldview with strategic tentacles. India needs to be alert to developing its own *desi* model of handling growth linked with internal stability and external networking.

August 05, 2016

## Moving on with the New World Order

The media flags shrieking headlines: Death, accident, terror, rape, murder, fraud and of course, verbal slanging matches. It does not need a comment.

The world, however, in most of its evolved zones, moves forward. There is jostling for space amongst nations, and in many parts of the world, old order is crumbling and new ones are emerging. China is out in the front.

It is obvious that as it is the case, Indians will choose what captures their imagination. However, there is a need to take a look around. Few things speak as clearly as a chronological narrative. The other wheel of action, which can give insights into this chronological narrative, is finance.

If you look at the last two years, you will notice fundamental changes that have overtaken the global economic order.

In July 2014, the New Development Bank (NDB), also referred to as BRICS Bank, was born in Brazil, it took years to reach this agreement. In less than three months, China signed a Memorandum of Understanding with 24 counties in October 2014, for the formation of the Asian Infrastructure Investment Bank.

Interestingly, it was five months after the unveiling of the New Silk Road, and as noted above, three months after the agreement of NDB.

Soon, the 'One Belt One Road' project was on the roll. In fact, amazingly, a phrase which got into the lexicon was Maritime Silk Road. In reality, the play on the word apart, it was a serious economic breakthrough and had significant new security/strategic thought.

The strategic Maritime dimension of 'One Belt One Road' included developing a string of logistic bases in the India Ocean region. Clearly, the option of developing them into Naval bases was open.

It is here that the ports become important. At the intersection of the 'Maritime' Silk Road and the New Silk Road, were the new strategic centers. The origin was the Chinese landmass. The hub of not only the new market, but the new strategy was the ports.

The maritime component of the string of pearls in the India Ocean extends westwards to Europe through the Red Sea and eastwards to the South China Sea.

The economic development part assumes a huge over capacity in Chinese manufacturing and construction industries; almost ignoring the returns to domestic investment. Clearly, low cost of funds allowed low profits and high economic risk investment in foreign infrastructure.

Eye was on raw material supplies, globally, and equally, global was the search for the market of Chinese goods. Foreign exchange reserves were intelligently used for small capital outflows. Large foreign exchange assets were used to support exchange costs.

There was a unique symphony of Chinese finance, with Chinese material and, of course, Chinese labour. While in India, people were delivering talks on 'disruptive innovation' to win awards, China, as usual, was working on the real world.

Instances have come to attention where Chinese prisoners were sent to live out their rigorous imprisonment spell, by working on constructions sites in Africa.

The 'One Belt One Road' was not just dealing with vehicular traffic and movement of people and goods.

Parallel to it was rail road traffic, oil pipelines and fiber optic cables. The focus was again on ports, airports and production estates.

The territories through which these passed required the Governments of those nations, in many cases, to transfer those lands to Chinese control. The script was from Mozambique to Zaire. Here was a new concept in economics of resource highways which is yet to surface into textbooks. The world had moved on and being daring was the requirement.

The sea-change of economic theory rolled out on the land and the sea shows the deep reflection which preceded this action. In times to come, concepts of economic viability, sunken costs, not to overlook the nature of capital and investment, would need re-definition.

The world will never be the same again. Americanism, unless it reinvents itself, may well be on the road to be where Britain finds itself today.

That India has finally woken up is a good omen. However, to operate, we will have to recalibrate our focus and relook at the priority areas of national themes of discussion and action.

July 22, 2016

## Asia's Fast Changing Fundamental Values

It is no discovery that the world of business is changing globally. This is natural because everything is changing all the time. Only in this case the change is basic and, in certain ways, dramatic. An observation of the European Union and Asia flags certain interesting patterns.

The constituent states of the European Union have a range of views on their membership of the Union. Often this is driven—understandably—by their inner domestic compulsions. Germany wants to abandon the Euro but not the Union; France has been struggling to recover growth; the anti-European Union sentiments in UK have really never gone away for many people.

By the same token in Asia, there are large Unions, say China or India. There are other attempts to forge conglomerates as the Association for South-East Asian Nations or the Organization of Islamic States. Tensions, however, remain.

The changes taking place in Asia are in many ways more fundamental. The turbulent conditions of India or Indonesia are not ideal to attract investment. Military tensions and armed conflagrations, in other parts of Asia, seem to be on the rise, if the base line is taken from 1985.

In Asia, the ownership patterns are clearly biased in the favour of family combinations, and even when the ownership is not family oriented, the dominance of a given family or a group of families is obvious. The recent judgement on the Uphaar Cinema case has drawn attention.

Given the sophistication of the Asian mind, just about anything can be debated till the cows come home. In Japan, there is a dominance of what is called the Manager Kings. Even the Western multinational, in the Asian context, has become increasingly impacted by local behavioural patterns. In China, the Government's role in the economy is tell-tale.

Many stereotypes about Asia also need revisiting. Illustratively, many parts of Asia are no longer known for low labour costs. Ageing in Japan has become a significant industrial issue. The recent experiences of holding the Parliaments to ransom has made its point.

In large parts of Asia, the wealth of tycoons and their proximity to Government is a major industrial factor. This creates a special kind of business environment. Notwithstanding this situation, many Indian companies have gone multinational. Or is it that because of this condition many business magnets in India have transferred their wealth abroad to invest there? It is no secret that in many parts of Asia the powerful incumbents enjoy high privileges, if not immunity.

Strangely enough, much of this is continuously embedded in the chant of 'innovation'. Recognition in many parts of Asia takes a route through some political capital of Atlantic rim countries. It is also a fact of life that a Chinese internet entity is listed on an American stock exchange or that an Indian firm is amongst the world's biggest technology company. It is just such a mixed picture which creates the ambiguities which makes the risk of business often appear as the business of risks.

The management researcher continues to plead for professionalisation, internationalisation, creating brands. These captions have become slogans.

One is not quite clear on what are the directions and the content of professionalisation that one needs to follow. One is also not clear on what would be the directions of research investments—not to talk internalisation. It is not unusual to see the brave advances made in one domain lost out in a cognate domain.

Here in the role of educational institution and institutions of skill formation becomes more significant. We need to work consciously towards reversing a situation where there is much heat and little light.

The ideal, say of management schools in India remains imitating the syllabus and content of branded US business Schools. This when fuelled by almost silly invitations, that the initiators of such effort get from some US outfits—the baits become apparent. Notwithstanding the roots of such invitations, it is equally true that they raise the stock of the recipients in the domestic environment and, therefore, become much sought after.

To say the situation is complex is an understatement. Complexity can at times be handled but vagueness and lack of clarity is another story.

September 04, 2015

## Bhutan Shows the Way to Happiness

Bhutan's King Jigme Singye Wangchuck coined the term 'Gross National Happiness' in 1972. He brought this country into the modern age, based on a vision of Bhutan's economic development that was premised on Buddhist philosophy. The concept received momentum at the Centre of Bhutan Studies under the leadership of Karma Ura. He developed some instruments to measure people's well-being. GNH is rooted in the concept of people-centred holistic development. Materialism and spirituality were the twin issues that had to be addressed and that too in an integrated manner. Happiness was supposed to ride in on these two wheels.

The attempt to root development, prosperity and welfare in the Buddhist concept of *Dhamma* underscores the need to link development with classical principles. Since Buddhism started as a reform movement in reaction to Hinduism, it was easy to see the more evolved Hindu concept of 'Dharma' in the Buddhist elaboration of 'Dhamma'.

*Dharma* is not religion, as understood in the Greco-Roman tradition, but instead a list of doables and duties. Both concepts lend themselves easily to a developmental paradigm.

The Bhutanese contribution lies in having incorporated this into their planning framework. Moreover, they have made the GNH indicators not just tangible but also universal, without rooting them in religion. The GNH indicators serve as the guiding principles for Bhutan's national planning process. There are four building blocks of GNH—promotion of sustainable development; preservation and promotion of cultural values; conservation of the natural environment; and establishment of good governance.

It is this universality of the principle that needs to be understood and considered. It is almost as if it has nothing to do with Buddhism. Indeed, sustainable development, cultural integrity, environmental conservation and good governance are further defined into eight general contributors to happiness. These are physical, mental and spiritual health; time-balance; social and community vitality; cultural vitality; education; living standards; good governance; and ecological vitality.

Mr. Med Jones, who is best known for having predicted the financial crisis of 2007-2008, has proposed a second-generation GNH concept, treating happiness as a socio-economic development metric and measuring seven development areas. These include economic wellness, environmental wellness, physical wellness, mental wellness, workplace wellness, social wellness and political wellness. These seven matrices were incorporated into a global survey wherein on the one hand, GNH reflected a psychological state based on moral criteria while on the other hand, GNP reflected on the consumption of goods and services.

A concept such as GNH is bound to have challenges in quantitative measurement; yet, applied systems analysis methodology establishes that almost anything which is 'done' is measurable. Applied system analysis methodology has instruments which are capable of doing this as an act of approximation. There are other correlations possible. For example, low rates of infant mortality positively correlate with subjective expressions of well-being. The notion that subjective measures like well-being are more relevant than objective measures, is one of the building blocks of the GNH concept.

June 14, 2013

## Yet Another Cross Road

Every individual, every community considers itself special. It has to with self-image and a lore which goes with it. The vision of grandeur, is sometimes based in a recall of a past which was glorious. On other occasions some collective virtue is picked up and held out as an ideal where other communities should be aspiring to arrive.

The list is endless. Some country is seen as a land of the rising sun, another as having a series of imperial leaders who rushed across the world (as known then) waving the ethnic flag. Several cities in different parts of the world believe that when the sun rose for the 'first time', rays of the sun hit that city the first. These sentiments can't be grudged because aspirations are very often encapsuled in mythologies. If the mythologies were to be suitably analysed community psyches could be far better understood. Unfortunately, the history of nation building (which is essentially a post-nineteenth century phenomena) is overladen by the historical framework of reference of the leader who had a prime role in the national identity movement. In many cases, the identity has had to be modified. Central Asian state are a good example, there are others. What began as the German unification and the Italian unification about a century and half ago has had many versions especially in the Third World countries. Interestingly nationalism was in many cases was the successor to the European phase of imperialism.

Geography helped to resolve many of these identities as they did in the case of Australia and New Zealand. The unification of hundreds of islands as 'Indonesia', was an exceptional phenomena. It did however leave certain contentious issues. Philippines and China are still arguing over the sovereignty affiliations of certain islands. Border dispute takes many forms and as a Sanskrit proverb states, "it is the strong and the brave which avail the land". Ultimately, logic takes a back seat and the real world forces call the shots.

History can be evoked selectively. It's done. There are also cases of unions and federations because of centrifugal forces. Even smaller countries have split up further into smaller countries and there is a constant struggle between the ethnic centrifugal and the imperial centripetal forces.

Technology seems to bind but only up to a point. Fundamentals of technology can vary from the assumptions of the scientific insights which were used. The technology of a Boeing is not the same as the technology of an Ilyushin aircraft. The American spacecraft returns to the earth to land in water. The Russian aircraft returns to earth on hard land.

April 01, 2023

## Preparation for the G20 Summit

As the preparations for the G20 Summit pick up, there is an increasing crescendo for different topics for inclusion in the Summit agenda. This is natural because the G20 is one of the major fora for articulating global causes, among other things. In the domain of "other things", regional issues that have a global impact or are bound to have some significance are included. An illustration would help to clarify the point. Globally, countries have been classified into the 1st world, 2nd world, 3rd world categories. Interestingly, the 1st world countries are the European countries, which were probably the last to enter the community of established civilizations.

The 2nd and the 3rd world countries are the more recognised ones. But they, while being referred to as 2nd and 3rd world, are some of the oldest civilisations in the world. Much of this is an outcome of an Euro-centric mind set and way of life. Events like the G20 summit being led by India, even if it is by rotation, provide an opportunity to impact its view. It could also help in mid course correction.

Over a period of time institutions and processes such as G20 or other international groupings have acquired a growing influence in formulation of a global approach. Taken in conjunction with the fact that the United Nations as an entity has consistently proved inadequate in reflecting the realities of the emerging new world culture, such opportunities as elaborate above acquire added significance.

Some concerns surface, one is the concern of "learning from the past." This business of "learning from the past" is not just a slogan but an approach that becomes increasingly prominent with the passage of time in both big and small matters. The recent episodes of experiences in Joshi Math have shown this concern with dramatic potency. So many structures would not have collapsed with such dramatic suddenness if it hadn't been for an excessive obsession with 'modern building styles' in a terrain that was better handled with conventional building styles and conventional building materials. One shall return to this concern a little later in the text.

The 2nd concern referred is the concern of recognising indigenous aspirations. The case of tribal communities is a tell-tale story. They have survived in different geographies of the world with tremendous tenacity and contribution. They have shown an economic strength, and capacity to renew oneself that is bewildering to many 'modern' strategists.

Many of the conventional tribes have been able to live in harmony with nature and be economically productive. Many other so-called 'modern communities' have not been nearly as successful, in perpetuating themselves or their values, as the conventional tribes. The ability of these tribal communities to harvest what is needed to live in positive relationship with their own needs and nature is something quite unique. So called modern civilization(s) are only beginning to learn how to live in since with nature.

It would thus appear that the two thoughts of learning from the past and indigenous aspirations/inspirations need to be flagged during this G20 summit.

In both cases, it is necessary to project the Indian example. This would come from taking an informed approach and projecting it with conviction.

In much of this, other communities around the world may also have something to say.

The net approach could be to showcase the achievement of traditional communities in having a set of solutions to contemporary problems. The powers that be behind these organisational efforts need to reflect on these concerns to make the G20 summit a true success in international conferencing.

To sum up the above, international conferences are a reality only when they break ground, or cement some ongoing thought. Over a period of time, the number of international conferences has increased exponentially to the point where an international conference may come and go without anyone even noticing when it came and when it ended. The truth of the situation requires insight into the fundamental tenants of human growth and development. 'Thought" is essential, and an opportunity comes to hand only with forethought and foresight. The G20 summit is one such experience which needs to be used to its full potential to project the uniqueness of India not just in a civilizational sense but also in an intellectual sense. India could well provide an illustration to the world in intellectual thought and preparing better for the future through the platform of G20. The indicators seem positive.

February 01, 2023

# 9

# Information Technology

## Digitalisation: Handle with Care

Each era has its buzzwords so has the present one. The list could include 'diversity', 'inclusion', 'innovation', 'creativity', 'digitalisation' and more can be added not only as per fashion but as per region and intellectual predilection. There is nothing wrong with that. The issue, however, is, that insufficient thought in the use of words, spreads vagueness in the environment. Fashion becomes a substitute for content. As a result, thereof, the overall sense of direction gets defused.

In the list enumerated above, the word 'digitalisation' is of particular significance. The worshippers of technology have a good case with the project 'digitalisation.' It is an important component of the growing use of technological wares. The use of microchips and other interventions has altered the character of many 'engines', including telephones and other instruments which affect everyday life. Territories like Taiwan have based their economic prosperity on the specialised manufacturing of the chip. Other territories have done the same. That is another story.

Coming into India, the situation is unique. To put it simply: India is a conglomerate of practically all slices of human civilisation since the most ancient times. Beginning with ancient times to the present, there is little binding these different slices of civilisation into a unified whole. Perhaps, it's arguable that the cultural variables put together different civilisation eras into some sort of cohesion. This cohesion is visible in terms of values, ability to deal with nature, and approach to wealth and work. This is needed not only for identifying culture but also for giving people's identities to a landscape.

The coming of digitalisation would affect almost everything in the landscape. The most obvious and universal is the use of digitalisation in the handling of money. Gold was a medium of exchange. It gave way to other systems of its kind, and then tokens or paper currency came in. The token or paper currency is being progressively replaced by a symbolic transference of money from one hand to another through digital processing. For this proper availability of instruments, skill preparation to use them and the ability to understand numerals in digital form are among the many requirements. A countrywide community of literate 'digitalised 'users would perhaps be less than 50 per cent of the total population. Its use will produce hiccups. Creating media hype over the digitalisation process, will in such cases only compound the rampant confusion.

The language of communication has first to target 'literacy' both overall and in written form. If this is ignored and the digitization process is serenaded, the result is going to be great schism and confusion within society. This would not be a healthy trend. No social change process can ride the wave unless it first creates a foundation of bottom line literacy. Hence, it is logical to conclude that digitalisation assumes literacy.

This is one of the paradigms that cannot be wished away by a policy decision. It needs to be appreciated that digitalisation is the outcome of an extended process. This extended process may take much time to bridge. Hence, the precursor activities of digitalisation are a must for successful digitalisation.

Even when this is accomplished, the availability of technological gadgets is a prime instrument for the use of methods of digitalisation. Those who are not familiar with it may respond to its needs with empathy, bewilderment, or simple negation. In any of the three cases, progress is stymied.

Thus, the deduction is that digitalisation is an important follow-up step in the successful implementation of any action directed at a community. Until certain basic conditions are met, digitalisation would have to wait. As mentioned earlier, even when the basic conditions are met, modifying them for digitalisation requires certain gadgets to be physically available in given numbers. Even when those numbers are reached, maintenance may further require the vocational diversification of related professionals. People who are dealing with maintenance efforts in general, also need to be sensitised to the maintenance needs of different forms of digitalisation-related gadgets.

Take the case of a mobile: its use requires familiarisation of commands for use of the instrument. It is bewildering to recognise that electronic devices have a variety of unique vocabularies ranging from 'cookies' to 'sync.' Many of these words don't even figure in dictionaries, and one can only get used to them through time, careful mentoring and support in the practice of the commands. All these have conditions that are difficult to attain without errors. These errors can be costly when they cover not only the earth but the "clouds" (the pun is 'unintended'). The elaboration can go on and needs to go on. The purpose of this text is to focus on the simple proposition of the precondition of effective operational digitalisation. It is about time the experts in digitalisation also started focusing on this aspect of the digitalisation process. This a process that may be seemingly difficult to grasp but inevitable in the evolution of the progressive use of 'digitalisation.'

March 01, 2023

## The Media and Its Impact

Civil society is supposed to be run by an executive which implements the regulations; the legislature which drafts the regulations and the judiciary which adjudicates in matters of controversy. The structural versions of the three can vary from one form of governance to another or from one entity to another. In case of kingship, it is one form of executive; in case of the presidential form of governance, it is another form of executive; in case of parliamentary form of governance, it is yet another form of executive. In course of time, in the evolution of French history, there came the recognition that beyond the three forms of institutions of executive, legislature and judiciary there was a need to recognise a fourth set. This came to be termed as the fourth estate. It was the press. It meant that public opinion if expressed and channelised in a sufficiently identified form it could be an impact making stream. Gradually, this so-called fourth estate acquired power enough to receive sufficient attention from the executive, the legislature and judiciary. Its power gradually increased as the electronic media became popular than print. The growing influence of digitisation also extended the range and influence of the electronic media. Today, the power of the electronic media is immense. Like all situations of power manipulation, it has also become a sought-after part of the scene. The slant of news can be manipulated to create the necessary impact on governance. The manipulation takes the slant of the political orientation and at times of the political institutions. Awareness of this is necessary for the strengthening of a responsible and healthy governance system. An interesting case in point is the media representation of the movie, 'The Kashmir Files'. It would be easy to recognise that the reported treatment, experiences and fate of many Hindus in the Kashmir valley, through parts of the 1990s, was most unfortunate, and perhaps verged on the barbaric. The skill of the so-called left, which has a track record of whipping up mass sentiments in matters big and small, subject to their political convenience, is widely recognised. They have reaped the harvest of such interventions from a period going back, at least, to the Vietnam war. The so-called rightists have also attempted to do the same, but often their reach, methodology and impact have been less powerful than that of the leftists. The result is there for all to see. The purpose of elaborating the above is to show how the selection of the content, the language of the presentation and the extent of repetition is central to the extent of impact the effort makes. The issue is of matching the method with the nature of the audience being targeted. Today, the media has various incarnations, even within the print and the electronics media. In print, the language becomes critical. The English print goes a distance and so does what is printed in Indian languages. The segmentation of the English-reading public or the public which reads one or the other of Indian languages could be significant. Each constituency has to be handled in a different manner and each constituency has its own political value. In the electronic medium, the social media has acquired progressively a more impactful position. At times entire movements have been influenced. The skill formation in manipulating this as of now is insufficiently institutionalised. It appears to be handled by acts of association and personal contact. This is an understandable phase in any stream of specialisation. Schools of journalism need to develop a more strengthened research wing to look into these issues.

March 28, 2022

## Towards a Composite Tech Evolution

Throughout the recorded history of mankind there are several references to technological marvels and breakthroughs. They have come in the form of building constructions, weapons of warfare and handling of water flows and other sectors. The evidences are available from the Andes region, river valleys such as Tigris/ Euphrates or Indus/Ganga, Yangtze area in China and more. Be it the Inca civilization, the Egyptian pyramids or Indian temples, there are many technological marvels. Some of them are yet waiting to be fully deciphered and replicated. The unique thing about all these experiences is that most of them could not replicate themselves. There was no continuum, and it came to an abrupt break, illustratively, some of the features of the temple architecture of peninsular India are still fully to be explained. How pyramids came up without any current evidence of cranes remains a marvel. How these powerful intellectual traditions came to an end is not known. But come to an end they did. The unique feature of the present 'industrial revolution' is not only that it has a technological base, but that revolution is a continuing one and has gradually spread to more areas. It is not only continuous and continuing but the spread is widening and deepening. That is what makes the technological dimension of this industrial revolution a unique one in human history. Having said that, the current technological revolution needs to be understood still more thoroughly. It has often meant faster, diversified and constant upgradation. It has given rise to a whole new technological expertise. An expertise which is required not only at the operational end where more and more people are covered but at other levels also. The other levels include an almost continuous upgradation of technology. Of this the mobile phone is a good example. Ever so frequently, the technology reaches a new threshold and the commands become more complex or simple. Whichever way one looks at it, they keep changing. This simply means a technology is impacting every day lives on a continuous basis almost everywhere.

It is not possible to ignore this process because even in one of its manifestations, let us say digitalization—it has been adopted as a governance instrument almost universally. This leaves the technologically uneducated individual not just in the backwaters, but in wilderness. The person can attract clauses of legislation in areas where they may not simply have the ability or opportunity to adopt or even upgrade. It may need access to resources, of purchasing an instrument for which he may not even have the capacity. When daily living is itself a matter of doubt because of deficiency of resources available at an individual level, what can be the hope of looking at technological literacy let alone technological upgradation? Concerns like the one outlined above need to be flagged as important policy concerns which need to be built into the larger civil society debate.

Excessive admiration and observation of technological compulsions may create divisions in the society which will ultimately need a response. However, it is much better to anticipate them. The above narrative amongst other thing, intends to focus on an urgent need of policy realignment and refocussing of the protocols of progress. This has become more evident during the pandemic experience. There are several country cases from South Sudan to Singapore which needed to understood to ensure that the evolutionary growth of the human race continues to be more uniform and manageable. The way to do it would be by creating a holistic vision of a composite technological future.

March 12, 2022

## Moving Towards a Tech Evolution

It is this continuity which puts it apart from other previous similar revolutions.

The current technological revolution has often meant faster, diversified and constant upgradation. It has given rise to a whole new technological expertise. An expertise which is required not only at the operational end where more and more people are covered but at other levels also. The other levels include an almost continuous upgradation of technology. Of this the mobile phone is a good example. Ever so frequently the technology reaches a new threshold and the commands become more complex or simple. Whichever way one looks at it, they keep changing. This simply means a technology is impacting every day lives on a continuous basis almost everywhere. Its not possible to ignore this process because even in one of its manifestations, let us say digitalization—it has been adopted as a governance instrument almost universally. This leaves the technologically uneducated individual—not just in the backwaters, but in wilderness. The person can attract clauses of legislation in areas where they may not simply have the ability or opportunity to adopt or even upgrade. It may need access to resources, of purchasing an instrument for which he may not even have the capacity. When daily living is itself a matter of doubt because of deficiency of resources available at an individual level, what can be the hope of looking at technological literacy let alone technological upgradation? Concerns like the one outlined above need to be flagged as important policy concerns which need to be built into the larger civil society debate. Excessive admiration and observation of technological compulsions may create divisions in the society which will ultimately need a response.

However, it is much better to anticipate them. The above narrative amongst other thing, intends to focus on an urgent need of policy realignment and refocussing of the protocols of progress. This has become more evident during the pandemic. There are several country cases from South Sudan to Singapore which needed to be addressed, analyzed and understood to ensure that the evolutionary growth of the human race continues to be more uniform and manageable. That is a much-needed requirement of the future for which action must begin now.

February 24, 2022

## The Quotient of Credibility

Nobody quite knows when and where audit became an important legal obligation for a certain level of enterprise in general, and business enterprise in particular. Before one knew, it had almost spontaneously got into this role. This was understandable because everyone wants to know where one's money is going. The issue of standards became all-pervasive in the audit process. A predictable institutionalisation was one of the outcomes. In India, a fall out was the coming into existence of an 'institute'. As money began to travel with greater speed and wider range, contours of international financial reporting standards became more pressing. Slowly, what happened to cricket, hockey or the invention of United Nations happened to audit. The powerful flexed their muscles, got together and wrote the rules. While all this was happening, technology from being a faceless entity acquired a character. From a supporting function, it became an integral function of the financial reporting system. Machine learning became not just a fad but a necessity. Technology brought with it a need to be familiar with devices. Reporting transactions in domains such as income, expense, assets and liabilities raised issues of policy frames and rules. The last two decades and more have always had a talk of some financial crisis in some part of the world, in some sector. The celebrated 'global village' was faced with far too many reverberations. The amazing thing is that the globalisation of this process has not blurred the defining characteristics of regional economies. India is a savings-driven economy. Gold bullion and landholdings are indicators of prosperity. Such a set-up requires an ethical platform, workable governance practices and quality of reporting. The audit process today has pressures of responding to increasingly complex demands of credibility quotient. But practised systematically and regularly, audit becomes an invaluable tool of exuding confidence. The investment climate and the investor's confidence are deeply affected by this. If market efficiencies are to increase, the quality of both the quantifiable aspects and the non-quantifiable aspects of transactions must keep improving incrementally. This requires rules. Mature communities appreciate the worth of stable practices. Reliable processes of corporate governance yield results. This by itself does not always prevent abuse of power or arrest high risk. By itself it would not even eliminate all imprudent behaviour. However, systems of work well thought through, do encourage shareholders and depositor's confidence. Unfortunately, technology has its own banes. Sudden, sharp and often misplaced policy initiatives cause more exasperation than delight. A bigoted approach to technology allows little change of track, mid-way. This causes its own grief. Data protection often at tandem with unpredictable data predatory practices generates its own business. This very often becomes a business in its own right, diverting attention from the focus of investment. Indeed, the process detection of processes is on the verge of becoming a discipline. The way forward is to reduce the pressures on the depositor. He is at the heart of the whole activity yet largely neglected, often because, he has no forum. All this perhaps requires a package of solutions. Teaching of banking in an economics curriculum may mark a beginning. Simulation-based training could help contain stealthy demeanour. Maybe the individual investor and his plight when recognised will help all other stakeholders in financial operations to be more effective.

All this may take time, but the wise man does not always expect to see the distant scene. One step at a time, could help.

October 02, 2021

## A New Medium of Expression

The most common topics on which training programmes are held are leadership, communication, management of self and so on. In a programme on communication one of the essential topics is to explore the relationship between the message and the medium.

One of the commonest statements is: "The message is the medium and the medium is the message." Typically, if a notice board is a medium and the message conveys affection or is proposing a marriage, no one uses a notice board for such a communication. The softer messages are usually more appropriate to convey with a flourish or a card, note, in person and in today's world on a personal chat. This would add a certain degree of gentility.

In the choice of the medium, too, there are at times flourishes that are used. Typically the use of calligraphy with a thick nib goes well with certain sentiments. There was a time in courts where after writing a death sentence, the judge would break the nib to underscore that he considered the task distasteful and did not want to write another such verdict.

However, the COVID-19 pandemic has taken a toll on such approaches or sentiments. Messaging online has become a universal medium demanding some appreciation of technology and some familiarity with the computer keyboard and smartphone keypads. Those with a receding vision or limited understanding of the workings of the keyboard and smartphone increasingly face less tolerance.

Technology itself is a recent phenomenon in public spaces in India. In the early 70's even a photocopier was unknown in most public spaces of learning institutions. A microfilm reader was the acme of technology in an archival space which couldn't cope with heavy binding or with pages that were getting too brittle for regular use. Five decades down the line, even the storage disc has undergone multiple changes in size, density and machine.

Similarly, recording instruments have evolved, too. Those who could not detect how totally extinct an extant technology of storage could become, lost much data. That is a story which has often unravelled silently, with very little to evoke even a small interest in the theme of a technology which gets outdated with time. Indeed there were disc manufacturing enterprises enjoying a flourishing business, that were almost wiped out before they realised what hit them. New chapters on return on investment had to be written and the short, half-life of technology was difficult to keep pace with for most businesses. As a result, the impact was huge on Information Technology-related businesses and many suffered losses.

When the Covid pandemic struck the world, it took several months to realise how dramatically the nature of communication would change. There was something rolling out which had no space in conventional learning, skilling or training. There was a mass exodus to online processes. Those who got left out belonged to a bygone era or were on the fringes of society.

Online learning, skilling, training were not all that new but never was it such a "no-choice" situation. I was a member of a policy group of educational governance dealing with management education, about 30 years ago. The role demanded me to become the chairman of a sub-committee on technology in management education. One of the recommendations was that online technology in management education would be a matter of bandwidth availability. Nearly 30 years later, many of the semi-baked management professionals were discovering that "online teaching is quickly becoming bandwidth intensive." It was also being discovered that reliable connectivity to the internet and multiplicity of web servers would be needed for prompt "net response and reliable service." The message was simple: The lack of a clear sense of direction when it could have happened led to a crash crescendo. Responding to this crash crescendo became fanciful and avant-garde. The truth was, it was a response to a miserable learning situation which no one was expecting or was prepared for.

Hence, what was often projected as a modernisation of the learning process had strong possibilities of becoming a learning disaster. Skilling was equally affected. What can be shared in skilling on the online medium would not be adequate for "operational skilling", simply because of the need to focus on competencies.

Similarly, the process of training landed in the deep end. Any person in the profession of training would know that there is very little substitute to personalised interaction, particularly in a short learning event like training. More problematic fallouts of such a situation can be flagged. For the present, suffice it to say that even the need to limit the losses in such sudden shifts—voluntary or otherwise—is slow to be registered or be acted upon. Hopefully some in the profession will awaken to this need, sooner than others.

January 18, 2021

## Technological Intervention

Triumphs are easy to recognise. Failures speak for themselves. Somewhere between triumphs and failures is the grey area where intellectual termites eat into the structures of reality corrosively. It happens because of distorted perceptions. This is a tragedy in which victims can often fight with great tenacity. Victims from their comfort zone do not realise the tenuousness of their position.

This analogy is apt for our public institutions too. The triumph of an Indian Space Research Organisation (ISRO) launch, the effective working of the Election Commission and the sheer intellectual range of places such as the India International Centre are worth celebrating.

Insanity and crassness of using religious or caste planks to garner votes are obvious. Inadequate focus of celebrated Indian institutions on Indian issues of development evokes few tears. Their research orientation and end product of skill formation is very often for environments other than India.

Herein comes the catch. What are the intellectual and research resources available to handle Indian developmental issues?

Moving the discussion one step further, a specific elaboration of ground realities may help to show what the problem is. Take technology, for example. The media is full of issues of digitisation but surely there are other facets to the use of technology for national development.

Ever since Prime Minister Narendra Modi went to Bastar and talked of Van Dhan, there has been ceaseless talk of self-help groups and Vikas Kendras. The process of funding literally thousands of such kendras across selected districts is still in the works. At the time of going to Press, a Secretary of the concerned Ministry retired and another Secretary would have just taken over. When the issues roll, it can only be speculatively answered.

The core concept of Van Dhan is assuring the harvester-cum-owner of these products, a minimum fair price. That does not require any technological intervention. What does require a technological intervention is the issue of value addition to these forest products.

Reliable statistics are not available but it seems reasonable to assume that there are not even 50 institutions across the length and breadth of this country which have the capacity to add value to Van Dhan products at an operational level.

Much has been made of the value addition to tamarind, if only the seeds were to be taken out and the rest of the pulp cleaned up. This can be done with bare hands. There is nothing wrong with that. If anything, a technological intervention will expand the mass and value of the product. Such gadgets, if they exist, are still to be brought into the popular domain in adequate measure.

Time has come to take the narrative beyond tamarind. A listing of some products may help. There are Gum Karaya, Myrobalan, *Sal* seeds and the list can be added by recalling *chironji*, *mahua* flower, *karanj* seeds and more. Beginning from the bottom, one could consider *karanj* seeds. It begins with the dehusking of *karanj* seeds.

Kernels are crushed with the help of a hammer mill, dried in an oven at a given temperature and moisture, conducting the transesterification, going on to produce KME from the kernel.

Then, distilled water on KME through water treatment leads to bio-diesel. It is a perfect case for developing indigenous technology, equipment and product to support this process. Barring sporadic and unrelated efforts, there is much more scope to work in this direction.

We need our technology institutes to focus on such issue. As it stands, such thoughts are not even a subject of political debate.

More examples can be cited. The message is simple: There is a missing link in the chain. Sooner or later, the public psyche is going to catch up with this and what turn it will give to the political processes when that happens on a sufficiently large scale, is anybody's guess.

However, if one thing is clear it is that it will lead to a paradigm shift of the electioneering process, at least at the local level. The road to that may have possibilities of huge overtones of unpleasantness.

Wisdom lies in visualising a future possibility and imaginatively causing course correction.

July 07, 2018

## Age of Superficial Fact-finding

Business effectiveness usually emphasises operations and evaluation by results. This approach cannot be grudged too much.

If people want to see results on the ground, that raises its own questions. However, the approach has its own logic. For example, in an academic institution evaluation is increasingly requiring citations for research done. In other words, the question being asked is if research is being done, what is the impact it is making. The impact fortunately or unfortunately has to tangible. It is possible to squirm at this approach, because research, when it is fundamental in character does not necessarily has any immediate and noticeable impact.

In a corporate entity or a consulting firm, people want rising sales figures or increasing revenues. Often the expectation is of a double figure rise every year. This is difficult. The result is a totally undesirable pressure on everyone concerned which destroys not only health and mental peace but at times also relationships. One cannot be a performer 365 days a year. Indeed, with the coming in of the electronic media, social media included, the pressures have grown many fold. The public exposure and scrutiny has taken on many more forms. Facebook, Twitter, LinkedIn have widened the scope of vulnerability.

Blogs, SlideShare, YouTube have brought in unusual methods of sharing content. There was a time when no research was taken as serious research unless it was duly footnoted and the evidence was actually verifiable. We are now living in an era where contents ride on blogs. Ideas are presented in form of slides and power point presentations. They are supposed to be brief—not more than, perhaps, 30 words per slide, if even that. They are supposed to be colorful with graphics and flowcharts. Of course, this is useful. What has not been explored is how far this is useful and to what extent are the contents verifiable.

It is amazing that there is little serious study available exploring the value of such medium and its proven utilisation.

Nobody doubts the utility of social media in opinion formation. However, opinion formation is a limited dimension of serious research.

The proposition is simple. These are times of huge journey. One is not quite sure in which direction this churning is headed and where it will turn. In such a situation, not only do jams take place in flows but also documentation suffers. Random searches through Google, Wikipedia, and more; all these sites get business prone.

A cursory look at the contents of Wikipedia will show the possibilities of uneven frameworks of content in areas that are alike. Entries in the name of X and similar entries in the name of Y may have been found; through uneven understanding of inadequately framed policy documents. These policy document many not even be culture sensitive.

Be that as it may, theses are privately sponsored efforts and should be seen as such. Typically, Wikipedia runs on voluntary contributions of time. To expect from it, the rigour of standards and universality of applications like a standard encyclopedia may be expecting a bit much.

One can put up with that in an informed manner.

The dangerous bit is that a whole generation or more is confusing Google search, Wikipedia search and electronic reference as the only thing they need to know of. They are willing to swear by it.

Visiting the stacks of the library, especially the reference section, is considered old-fashioned and has few takers. In environments like South Asia, library purchase grants have been severely cut.

One is entitled to ask what kind of informed generation is being created. The problem does not stop there but spills into impacting the road to creating proper operational channels for business and indeed skipping steps in policy implementation. Say, typically, if one needs to ask how much liquidity under the Goods and Services Tax will be available for use when taxes have to be remitted every month but the trade credit remains for 90 days? A Google search will not answer this question. It needs a trained mind that is on top of thoroughly put processes.

Business, like any other profession, also, rolls on the strength of strong wheels of applied research.

July 31, 2017

## Coming to Terms with India's Digital Dream

The idea of a cashless society is great. But it may not be too much to expect a delivery infrastructure in place

There is now even a greater push for the digital era. This is perfectly understandable, given the lure of a technology-driven ambience. It fuels an understandable scramble for modernity. A look at the lay of the land in general and going-ons in the electronic world may be in order.

Technology in the consumer electronics domain has its roots in the American/Japanese/English/German experience. The economy of these countries is in-a-manner-of-speaking a 'replacement economy'. The life of the gadget is over not by a natural wear and tear, but when the corporate manufacturing brand decides to phase out one set of equipment with the invariable claim of an up-scaled version.

Very often up-scaling is token, if at all. However, the specification of the part is suitably altered to make sure that maintenance/replacement of parts becomes an outdated concept. This obviously lubricates the wheels of the producer's investment and a feeling of well-being is generated amongst investors.

The backup of this economy has certain financial assumptions. Poverty is not seen as a factor. For another, these countries do not rank 98th in the human hunger index of a survey of 113 countries, as does India. There is no premium on fixed deposits in banks because the interest rates are low.

Compare that to what is happening in India. About nine-tenth of the population in the so-called retired category in India survives on income of fixed deposits. The remaining one per cent keeps moving, through re-employment or survives on assets accumulated over the working period.

This variation alone is enough to show that the nature of consumer electronics in India cannot be viewed parallely with the nature of consumer electronics in countries named earlier.

The results are for all to see. In April 2014, Microsoft stopped offering security updates patches and technical support for a very large number (72%) of the 2,02,000 ATM machines in India, run on windows XP.

Today, they are all a hackers' delight. The news surfaces in business repeatedly. The argument forwarded is that it is for the banks to upgrade the software of the ATM's. Globally, Windows XP in ATM's have graduated to Windows 7. India has yet to find its way.

Is it possible that the initial contracts were signed without reading the fine print? The writer of these lines in the last few weeks has had two experiences of going through contracts with reputed organisations.

In one case, because of certain office exigencies, he had to look into the possibility of opening an account with a multinational bank. The multinational bank representative produced a contract where in a font of size six pts said everything which totalled up to protecting the so-called interest of the bank, giving to the applicant practically no protection.

Indeed, it went on to say that all subsequent changes in the rules and regulations of the said bank would apply to the customer even if he was not so informed.

This would stretch the imagination of the most gullible and cooperative ones. The story doesn't end there. To download the software of a taxi provider you are asked to sign electronically on a statement that you have read all the rules and regulations!

The present writer again, wanting to be careful, had to spend time finding out where he could get these rules and regulations. The source of information was difficult to get and when reached the website refused to download! Clearly if you care, you do not proceed.

The above is not the approach of a fevered mind. Several newspapers have reported that suspected outages have become a menace across points of sale terminals at key Gurgaon outlets.

The story rolls on and small vendors say that many customers are technologically simply not savvy enough to even use card swiping machines. The argument is for small changes. Obviously this will effect business. The cabbies refuse e-cash and want notes; machines which hang and you can't operate it when you want to.

We would all love to go cashless. But perhaps it may not be too much to expect to put a delivery infrastructure in place.

December 23, 2016

## India's Independence in the 21st Century

The 1960s saw various services emerging, notably data in many forms. This included video-text, telex and facsimile. Carried over telephony and telegraph networks, infrastructure became the focus. Gradually telex and video-text waned while telephony, data, data-derived services and facsimile thrived.

Now, email is well-established as a derivative of data services and numerous other variants have been developed. Email is an important factor because, for some time now, it firmly marks the convergence of communication and computing. Telecom-derived data networks are used, and so also are computer-based networks.

Computer-based networks use local and wide area networks to the stage at which their information flows can be readily handled by the same switching technique that handles telephony information flows. The emergence of multimedia services has followed.

The emergence of mobile telephony has made portability both a 'weapon' of action and social incoherence.

Access to networks is an important component of this transformation.

Convergence with the entertainment industry has caused further decline of some professions and industries and the rise of new forms. These continually demand fresh purchasing and upgradation of capabilities. The rules of investment have had to be rewritten as technologies have to be phased out sometimes even before the break-even period is completed!

In many ways, transition of telecommunications from a service ethic to business ethic has altered the work desk situation. Ownership and control also seems to be migrating from Government agencies to business interests.

This is an important dimension in management of governance. Good governance requires a perceptive understanding of shifting issues. These shifting issues operate in the framework of international manoeuvring, and grow in the context of contextual, traditional capability. Happy times, when slogans like "greatest good of the greatest number" could carry acclaim because of ambiguous formulation, no longer give guidelines of sustaining public euphoria.

Not long ago, debates on trans-national enterprises focussed on their capital contributions, their impact on balance of payments and employment of home and host countries. Today, one has to factor in the effects of technology on national industrial structures, competitive abilities and income distribution.

Striving for technological independence is as important an element of the national axiom as the need of recognising the imperatives of technological interdependence. Those who sloganeer the wastefulness of 'rediscovering the wheel', need to be reminded that R&D is necessary even for absorbing technology.

As the technological contribution of some TNEs become increasingly questioned, the need for emancipated regulation has become more insistent. There is a great need to have methods of examining alternatives of regulating the transfer of commercial technology. The prospects of such methods need to be examined in a scholastic mode.

The future of effective governance may be determined by the deftness of the ways in which this issue is handled. The ambit of technology transfer has to be widened from the broad sense of industrial design, product design, and process design to include other factors. These would inter alia cover managerial systems; technical skills required to establish and efficiently operate industrial facility. With the permeation of information technology, the dangers of trespassing have grown and become real.

There are no new issues of technology transfer. There are only new possibilities of technology breaching many traditional defences of Government systems. Clearly, there is a need to have a framework of governance suitable to the high tech era without necessarily forsaking some of the moorings of the past. There is an urgent need to re-understand the concerns of technology transfer.

The journey which began with the United Nations Conference on Trade and Development-1(1964) needs to be revisited. The focus on capital goods, intermediate goods, human labour and information remains. What is new, is the need to study the cusp of IT and human skills which is a no-man's zone. Decoding traditional decision making patterns may give the key to the inscrutable problem.

A nation's skill formation on technology handling cannot be mortgaged to another nation's need for technology transfer and their need for technological growth.

August 08, 2014

# 10

# Human Resource Management

## Both Freedom and Discipline are Needed

Anything living needs some ground rules. A living creature, be it a single-cell organism or a conglomerate of millions of cells, will need to nourish oneself and expel the waste from the body. This itself requires a routine. The ground rules of each species of a living entity define how long it will live. The same applies to human beings. To move away from the gross level of activity—rest, sleeping, awaking, breathing, eating, whatever else—one has to fall into a pattern. If there is no routine, the organs of the body start malfunctioning and some form of illness takes over. Illness has its own issues and has spawned multiple breeds of doctors, variously known as allopaths, homeopaths, Unani specialists, Ayurveda acharyas, naturopaths, etc. None of these schools of medicine claim to be complete or have all the answers. Very often their assumptions are so widely different that they seem to be at war with each other. The basic need is to have a system and a logic, an experiential guideline as the basis for action. This is needed for life itself, social existence, mutual interaction and indeed is the basis of civil society. A basic act like walking on the road requires observance of certain well-understood protocols. It is important to emphasise this because there is a growing crescendo in favour of 'do what you want, when you want without a care and concern.' The principle is interesting and perhaps even enticing. Whereas such 'letting down of the hair' is desirable at times, even the location for doing so and certainly the time for doing so has to be carefully thought through. So, there is a case for freedom with thought. Taking the discussion at a higher level of thought and action, it is obvious that all group living requires some 'discipline.' 'Discipline' is resented by some and many advocate 'Bohemian freedom.' This can be dangerous if freedom is exercised by people of poor judgment. In short, the matter also becomes the orientation and maturity of individuals. It is at the level of dyadic relationships in groups and larger conglomerates of organised existence like the state or a nation.

The matter is also of the threshold where freedom can become excessive and discipline, an overbearing phenomenon. The relationship between freedom and discipline can be subtle and yet critical for organised life. A comparable example can be when to persuade with judgment and gentleness, and when to use emphasis and assertiveness. There are no easy answers. In all this, the role of leadership becomes critical. How a leader marshals his argument, organises his data, and makes a presentation becomes an essential part of not only creating norms but the functioning of a civil society. Those who had the occasion to listen to the Prime Minister Narendra Modi's address of May 2 to an Indian audience in Berlin would have seen an example of selection of facts, piecing together an argument, and backing it up with appropriate intonation and emphasis. All put together, it creates impact and could produce results. Most of us would not have that podium in one way or another for making that presentation. However, all of us will have occasion, in one way or another, to marshal facts, organise our thoughts in a disciplined manner, and communicate to someone in an acceptable idiom. This is also what life is about. Freedom and discipline have to walk hand in hand. They touch all aspects of life just as they touch all aspects of existence. In every case, judgment is the key and constant practice, and awareness is the path.

June 08, 2022

## Time to make a Fresh Start

There is often talk of history of the planet and history as a discipline. The bald truth is that most histories are actually recalls of experiences of a limited part of the planet over some limited geography with a given vantage point of perception. There is nothing wrong with that. The problem is when it gets mistaken as something which applies globally or has significance beyond its boundaries of focus. This is a common error. It is akin to a half-educated person who begins believing that his/her experience and perception has universal validity. It can never be the case. This is matched by another cardinal error namely, that of expecting others to respond to our expectations. An index of fair relationships requires recognising varying expectations. But varying expectations cause conflict, confusion and heartbreak. The attempts at resolution of varying perceptions and outcomes are often half-baked, if not irrelevant. The fundamental laws of life require an understanding of the aggregate power of human civilisation and the Earth's ecosystem. As distances shrink and time expands because of technology, the fundamental constructs of "how to think" need serious thought. This is apparently yet to be tabled as a major global agenda for reflection and action. The proposition would be clearer if what is said in the above paragraphs is focussed on "energy studies".

That life itself needs energy is fairly well-recognised. Where that energy comes from has many schools of thought. Those who find the cartoon character of Mandrake interesting, obviously, will believe in the power of the brain. There are claims in ancient texts of interplanetary travel of mental visualisation through brain power. Hence, the ability to recognise inner power and experience wholeness of external energy should be a legitimate goal of a person claiming to be educated. At a personal level entropy is a formidable reality. Expression of entropy is in the form of aging. Organisation of self is a major challenge and a realistic hierarchy of personal values is essential to make relationships work. This is again one of those areas where a lot more attention needs to be paid than has been possible so far. At the global and the external level, like in the case of the inner world, it is important to realise more evolved postulates. That energy flows from the Earth back into the universe surrounding it as heat energy in the form of infrared radiation needs to be seen as one of the basics of all energy studies.

Putting it all together, the COVID-19 experience should be helping the planet to revisit its assumptions of learning, be it internal or external. If that were one of the outcomes of the shake-up the planet is going through it would be a civilisational gain. As of now, individuals have suffered, groups have been shaken and assumptions of productivity and progress look greatly challenged. Whether it has caused any new constructs to emerge remains to be seen. This is totally understandable because the Covid experience is still an unfolding reality. Perhaps one of the biggest results of this extended experience is the general fatigue the whole experience has caused. Being alert in one's own defence requires a general environment of good sense, and as any thinking person knows, good sense is rare. People risk suffering and even death when their balance of energy has been exhausted in taking extended precautions. Time not only heals, it also exhausts.

The important question remains, are there limits to human response to feelings of agony and testing times? As attempts to restore past lives gain strength, the approach seems to be to bring it back to where it was to pre-pandemic experiences. That is understandable, but there should be an attempt to create something different, incorporating the learning of underlying behaviour of the human species. It is time to hold up the process of regression. It's time to make a fresh start. One needs to look at new assumptions and approaches to create a world order for the future of the planet and its inhabitants.

March 01, 2021

## Picking up the Pieces

The last 13 weeks or so have been exceptional and unprecedented in experience, reflection and all that goes with it. The dominant theme has been of worry, anxiety and the strange feeling of helplessness, should one be unfortunate enough to be infected with the Coronavirus. The fear of the unknown, coupled with the pressure of several confusing containment operations, cushioned marginally by some precautions, can be a very difficult process to go through. That may be another story for a different day.

The coping experience is yet to be clearly comprehended to be articulated here. A reflection on the time frame mentioned above triggers some thoughts which are a potpourri of notions and emotions, sometimes verging on exasperation. There have been a spate of webinars and obviously this has lubricated the business of communication platforms. They have seldom had it so good. The disinfectant and the medical palliatives industry is booming, the latter particularly on the promises of increasing immunity and giving reserves to combat the dreaded disease. Both the narratives are inductive and in the absence of anything better, rule the roost.

The pharmaceutical industry is much in demand and reportedly the top bosses of the Ministry concerned were working 24×7 to keep the supply chain moving, specially for the export of some formulations. News channels and various media reports have it that the US had mopped up the entire batch of the current global production of Remdesivir. There was a concurrent protest on such matters, because the fear was that other formulations, when perfected for use, may have a similar fate. During this pandemic, one is truly trying to find a response for the unknown and the unpredictable lay of the land. One can only hope for luck.

It is no secret that the global economy has taken one of its worst beatings on all the conventional parameters of economic worth: Output, income and employment. However, the International Monetary Fund (IMF) and its sister institutions are not yet out of a job. The World Bank still has its pretensions. This is one area where the Chinese are still to catch up. The parallel institutions they tried to set up as alternatives don't seem to be firing even on two cylinders. Perhaps the Chinese obsession with creating its 21st century version of the Silk Route, with the Chinese economy being the hub of world economic operations, seems to be the undermining of their efforts.

The Indian economy still seems to be faithful to the traditional platform of sticking to bailouts, doles and largesse. For the economic strategic thinkers, who control this country's State-oriented growth processes, 2020 could just as well be 2008. The comfort of such thoughts is almost incredibly unreal and yet it can create the happy feeling of "something is being done."

For those who can see, the writing on the wall is clear. The paradigms of not only growth and welfare but of survival and safety have to be rewritten. Doing a cadence count with rising tariffs and surcharges alternately (and sometimes together) on petrol and diesel does seem to have exhausted its potential.

Yet the conventional economist knows that to be in business he must always tell a story of growth. The present one is that the recovery for 2021 will be 5.8 per cent. The repetitive accuracy of decimal precision these calculations always achieve is amazing. The unhappy sequence that some economists talk of, namely, the cycle of contraction, recession and depression, is taken up only by the fringe elements. It's not even fashionable to debate it anymore. Confidence is rarely sighted. And not enough thought is being given to structural shifts the firms need to be considering.

For that matter, even household behaviour does not seem to have change enough with the times. Many in the household set-up are practicing decontamination and hope to protect themselves from the virus. It is not quite registering that this may need to become the new algorithm. There is a good case for doing so.

The kind of vegetable shopping which takes place, even in normal times, in the filthy cradles near drains in parts of some cities like Mumbai, needs to be stopped once and for all. Hygiene cannot be only a contagion-specific behaviour. A more hygienic and enduring supply chain of daily goods needs to be put in place for households and this cannot be a COVID-19-based effort alone.

With the disruption of aggregate demands and weaknesses in conventional sources of supply, there was never a better time to recast the survival safety net of human efforts in many parts of India. Deliberately, no claims are being made to an all-India model. That's because the Indian economy is far too variegated for a one-size-fits-all model. If the current health emergency leavened by economic disruption can impact the structure of demand, reform of capital flow would follow. Commodity prices could be redesigned and an overall more stable platform of everyday operations—both corporate and domestic—could follow.

July 06, 2020

## From Tribalism to Tribalization

It was probably for the first time that a definite action plan for tribal welfare figured in a presidential address to both the Houses of Parliament on June 20. It is all to the good.

There was a time when small-scale industries had not graduated into the domain of a significant curriculum in the portals of leading educational institutes. Part of the reason was the lack of not only the ability to read but also that of instructional material. Then there was also no way forward on the unique characteristics of the management of tiny, medium and small scale enterprises. Many management functionaries erroneously believed that management principles, when reduced in size and domain, would be valid for tiny, medium and small industries.

Slowly as instructions focussed on entrepreneurship in a given sector, it grew in academic maturity, research contributed and the area picked up. It became abundantly clear that SMEs had unique characteristics. To feel the pulse, a sense about the nature of the area was needed. Similar is the story with tribal studies. That there has been little change in the plight of the tribals—most critically in their existence—is obvious. The tribals, take for example the Miris, who opted out of the tribal way of life and linked up with the mainstream, became the poster boys of tribal welfare. This, however, did more harm than good because these were precisely the very people who would not go back to the tribal environment and pick up the ways of life there. They got lost in the urban way of life and became part of the teeming millions. There is nothing wrong with this per se. But it's just that what they gained by merging into the mainstream life did not filter back to the tribal world. But this is another story.

By and large, the popular image of a tribal is that of a half-clothed, dark complexioned individual with an unusual head gear, usually accompanied with drum beats and folk beats. There is nothing wrong with this. But the problem is that popular image is incomplete and it does not do any justice either qualitatively or quantitatively to the real profile of the tribal way of life. It is unfair to think of these men and women as lost in the woods, waiting for civilisation to absorb them. There are unique characteristics about the tribal way of life which people in the cities need to learn. It is indeed possible to see it as an alternate lifestyle model to what has happened in the name of urbanisation or mainstreaming.

If sustainability is a goal, then the tribal way of life has a huge message for the people and is worth emulating. The community system of administrative justice is certainly more expeditious than the 'English' system of administering justice. The broader point to be taken here is that the concept of 'tribalisation' is not congruent with being a savage or needing urbanisation. Tribalism is still a dominant theme in many parts of the country and the so-called urbanisation and industrialisation are a distant cry. Drive a few 100 kms from Itanagar and the truth will begin to dawn. There is nothing about Arunachal Pradesh which would remotely earn it the label of the so-called backwardness. Many parts of metropolitan cities across the world are more "backward" in operational terms. Hence, it is necessary to develop a scientific lens to view tribalism. The foresters' ability at satiation and bonding without consumerism is enviable to say the least. Most of them do not have the mentality of accumulating beyond needs.

It is important to recognise that there is huge diversity in tribal practices, within 20 plus States of the country having significant tribal population. Their cultures, food habits and rituals are unique. Thus, it is that with Minimum Support Price for minor forest products being on the verge of becoming a nation-wide movement, tribals are being empowered. It is important to recognise that there is no one standard size which can fit all. There are group-related issues, process related issues, product related issues, giving to each ethnic group its unique identity.

This diversity is also reflected in different State administrations, where different Government departments with separate names—ranging from Forest Departments to Tribal Welfare Departments—are charged with the responsibilities of looking after our native populace. One of the banes of tribal development has been the glib assumption that the time has come to lead them all to technical platforms. What needs to be continually kept in mind is that every technology has its own logic and imperatives. This includes machine acclimatisation, maintenance and repair facilities. Reaching out to the tribals through technology routes is one intervention but pushing them to imperative uses of technology is another story. The time has come for a design and delivery of an Indian Institute of Tribal Research and Management.

June 24, 2019

## Expressions of Success

Everyone wants to be successful. Almost everyone has some faith or belief in symbols and his/her socialisation orients him/her to read the meaning under the symbols and thereby flag external indicators of success. In itself, success is often self-consuming and often cripples one if not destroy him/her by setting newer goal posts. Consider the current election results. Nearly 350 MPs from the projected ruling combine have not even formally entered the Lok Sabha portals and the race for the next indicator of success, i.e. making it to further prominence by getting into the ministerial position, has become a matter of speculation and conduct. The media has been talking about the possibility of the Prime Minister taking oath—alone—on the day the Cabinet is to be sworn and that other Ministers would be sworn in later. Success, but for how long and how much?

Put it simply: To a large extent, success is an act of choice, a frame of mind and a vantage point of perception.

It's often how one looks at a situation, interprets and internalises it.

This is only part of the story. There are objective situations and externalities to it. Illustratively, if one doesn't have adequate shelter or enough food to eat, then clearly one is in the grip of poverty, no matter how one defines it. Of the many definitions of poverty, perhaps the simplest one to understand is that it is an involuntary deprivation of the basic facilities and amenities of life, as accepted in the community where one is embedded.

Caution needs to be exercised here without being confused. Different communities have different perceptions of amenities and basics of life. For some, a common toilet maybe a way of life and it doesn't occur to that person that personalised toilets are achievable. And even if that person sees it as achievable, it may not be an objective in his/her life to reach that level. Once this is established, the story of success intensifies and it is an escalating story. Like many human emotions—love, hate and irrationality—success is without boundaries. The more you succeed, the more you want. The more you want, the more you work for it. Getting there, and once having got there, one needs to learn how to pause or one starts resetting the goal post. There are two messages to be given. One is that success is a personalised experience. Second, success is embedded in a social framework of reference. If success walks on these two legs, both of them are important to understand.

One is as successful as one believes one to be.

As an undergraduate student of a top-grade university in a B-grade city, this writer, having achieved some prominence in grades, was part of a group playing host to a Minister, who had flown in to the city on a Government aircraft. He was of the same State as where this university was and when the Minister was asked to tell more about himself, it looked strange to the writer that while the Minister was in his mid-50s, he remarked: "What more could I want from life? I have got enough. How much can the son of a peasant get? I am, after all, a peasant's son."

It struck the writer odd then, it strikes odd even now. The Minister's framework of reference was a peasant (a *kisan*). The sense he conveyed was that in his scale of living and occupation, a peasant (*kisan*) was the bottom of the pyramid. Having become a Minister in the Central Government, he had not only changed professions, but arrived. Why the society should look up to a Minister is not difficult to guess, especially if it is resource scarce. This is the not the story the world over. Illustratively in Scandinavian countries, it will be difficult to make out on the streets, if somebody was a Minister or a mere peasant. Put simply, success appears not only in multiple shapes but also multiple sizes, colours and myriad manifestations.

The story rolls on. That there are social indicators of success has already been referred to above. This is a frame of reference, which cannot be wished away. The proposition is simple—success is an internal feeling of well-being, arising out of a conformity to a visualisation of a preferred state of being. It is also ensconced in a context of group, community and geographical habitat. In all cases, it is a consort of smugness, of achievement, so recognised by the individual and the community to which he/she affiliates.

Like all stories, there is more to come and the missing part of the narration above is that success always requires internal peace and external recognition. Success will require being a light to one self and that is as much a matter of personal growth as of external recognition.

May 27, 2019

## Unity of the People of India

The experience of India in developmental processes is a medley of different streams. Forms were at some point in time borrowed from the Soviet Union, aspirations on other occasions were borrowed from the United States, behavioral stereotypes were often borrowed from the United Kingdom, industrial models copied from Japan and social models were often attempts at shadowing the Chinese experience. One model which no significant economist—they were and still remain in charge of the planning process—ever espoused, was the Indian model.

They cannot be blamed because they were not taught this in places where they studied. Hence, new categories and constructs, which were unknown to the social dialogue before the 19th century, became a part of the social-intellectual dialogue, thereafter. Categories of religion began emerging in the political discourse ever since the end of the 1920s.

Identities began to shape and later on they hardened. If religion was the dominant construct, caste could not be far behind. A sense of deprivation often based on some seedbeds began arousing resentment among a section of the Hindus, say, illustratively among the 'Mahars'. There were, of course, other communities which could be counted for discrimination.

Similarly, amongst the Muslims, the plight of communities such as the 'Ansaris' and especially the 'Ghaus Ansaris' was equally pathetic. Many Christians made it a point to emphasise that they were Brahmin Christians and not so-called 'low-caste Christians'. The epidemic of feelings of social inequity spread like virulent virus. It got inextricably linked with a quest of identities.

Even the tribals were taken into the ambit of such paradigm and a 'Ho' wasn't amused when confused with a 'Munda'. The electoral process provided channels of consolidation to these identities. Thus, purpose was added to a slowly kindling identity battle.

It suited the colonists very well. If the purpose was to govern, it is so much easier to derive compliance from a fragmented set of subjects than one which is consolidated into one identity. The ideological battle of the 30s and the 40s of the last century was muted evidence of trying to subsume fragmentation under one ideology or the other.

Concurrently, the personality factor became an element in the polity.

This leads to icons like Veer Savarkar, Jawaharlal Nehru, S.A. Dange. Several others of lesser heights and smaller capacities were to throw their hat in the ring for an iconic status. The Vallabhbhai Patels, Sheikh Abdullahs, Shyama Prasad Mukerjees of the world were clear-headed on what they wanted and were skilled in leadership techniques but ultimately the factor of time either cheated them of it or beat them to it. None of the three or others like them were bigots, but were generously accused by those denigrators who did not like the cut off their face.

Enter an era of contending leaders in a context of global turmoil of World War II, a weakening imperial edifice, an army and a civil service widely infiltrated by people who believed that the British had no business, real or imagined, to be governing India. The rest, as they say, is history.

It was unusual how in none of the social discourse, there were any serious attempt to incorporate the tribal communities. The splendid writings of Napoleon Chagnon to Christoph Von Furer Haimendorf, notwithstanding, this made no significant impact on the political going-ons of British India.

The princely India shows a much better track record in this regard. 'Bhils' of 'Mewar' are only one of the communities which suffered no deprivation. Similarly, the princely states of Travancore, Cochin or of Baroda were at peace, dealing respectfully with the likes of 'Bhils' in their territories. It was another matter that, in any case, the so-called princely India was given a destiny which was overshadowed by the political turmoil of the river valley governance dispensations of the British.

The unfinished story is now asking for its completion. For the first time in independent India, eight per cent of this country's population, that lives in tribal enclaves, is being imbued consciously with economic clout and incorporated in the larger social discourse through the Van Dhan Scheme. The situation needs careful handling and nurturing.

June 04, 2018

## Changing Fundamentals and the Locus of Control

We are living in a universe which is changing in more fundamental ways than we realise. Among the most significant changes taking place is in the domain of identity of an individual; the family; gender relationships. The list can be added on.

Equally significant changes are taking place in the organisational life and the collective domain of the society. Obviously, people with charismatic traits or ability to significantly maneuver are in control.

They get away because the majority keeps quite. Those who can speak are labelled and side tracked or worse. This is not good for anyone. The nation states, the corporate world, governance processes, academic institutions have had their own share of triumphant individuals who know how to have their way.

There is a statement attributed to Edmund Burke "the only (thing) necessary for the triumph of evil is for good man to do nothing". Initially, the articulate or the maneuvering leader cashes in on emotions and aspirations of the people. He also plays on their fears and anxiety.

Unless he is truly wise, he covers all this in the name of managing 'risks' or setting the ethical equilibrium right. Eventually, a good number of right thinkers get chased away and small coteries emerge.

US presidential hopeful Donald Trump, according to some, is a good example of doing this at the national level, he chose David Riden to be his henchman in the Republican National Convention.

Reportedly, he warned the Americans of the possibility of a need to attack with assault weapons and bombs in the nation's capital and elsewhere; further, he insisted that leaders in the US who violated the Constitution may have to be done away with. Another prominent supporter is C.A. Bailey. He was, as reported, already indicted for charges related to weapons and child pornography. His 75 acres gated compound had a subterranean room stocked with grenades, tear gas and illegal machine guns.

This model is attempted to be replicated by some in organisations or in a family or a social conglomerate. It always back fires—though it may take time.

Sometimes it is topped up by high flown philosophy. American philosopher Richard Rorty in 1997 had indicated that people start talking of systems failure and why sting vigilance and strong men are required. The atmosphere he pleaded would be for eliminating "the smudge bureaucrats, tricky lawyers, overpaid bond sales man and post-modernist professors….."

Decision-making process are usurped by a few because many stick to their comfort zone. There is no substitute for structured and genuine communications where the most committed and diligent people don't have to retire to their shell because hot winds of harshness. It is the responsibility of everyone to keep sanity and good judgment alive and active.

Parts of India and many corporate are passing through such crises—amongst several others. The saving grace is of course that there are many good people still in key positions. They, through their wait for proactive decision-making and genuine collective code, tilt the scale in favour of sanity.

However, real equations are set by which decision-making domains are controlled by which type of leadership.

Kashmir is a good example of how a small percentage of people can occupy such large mental spaces. The Reserve Bank of India is yet another brilliant example of how monitory policies are handled in a reductionist manner to radiate uncertainty in so many intermediately financial institutions.

There is little hope of a turnabout unless a system is created where the organisation objectives are protected by those who genuinely care and do not believe in strong arm tactics. One of the most successful rulers of this country was Ashok who was credited with having an iron fest in a velvet glove.

Velvet is important because at the end of the day everyone is also an emotional existence. The way a collective answers this question is the essence of the successful survival and growth of any entity.

To deny it, is to deny the basic truth of life which is the sun neither rises in the west nor sets in the west, it is the earth which rotates around the sun!

September 02, 2016

## More than a Mantra is Needed for Results

We live in the era of mantras. People claim to have developed mantras even for 'leadership'! Initially, mantras were supposed to be the distillation of years of meditation and experimentation, and to use a modern parlance, established 'thought leaderships'. Now, references to mantras have become a part of sloganeering. This also serves a purpose. It keeps the issue alive. This can be said for the phrase, 'Skilling India'. Everyone is on to it. Nothing wrong with that but there is, however, a problem of over-exposure. Then there are other problems that follow. Too much of noise with little output becomes counter-productive. Couple this up with an almost endemic of sorts proneness to hyper-sensitivity. The confusion is confounded. In a special address to the annual general meeting of a constituent unit of a national body, this writer made a passing remark on the skill deficiency of many branch managers of banks. He highlighted the need to raise their level of diligence in handling codes, processing procedures, changing rules, regulations in interfaces with banking products and, above all, making legible entries where computers were not applicable.

The intensity of reaction from two members was instructive. One even claimed to have written a book on the issue, running into several hundred pages. This writer was not surprised at the hyper-sensitivity on display. Getting back to skill formation in a different domain, one can look at some figures. Since 2011-2012, the Armed Forces have lost 35 aircraft, 15 helicopters in crashes, killing around 50 people. Since January this year alone, two MiG-27s, two Jaguars, one Sukhoi-30 MKI and one MiG-21 have crashed. These figures could not have been reached because of technical snags alone. It is obvious that human element and skill element (or the lack thereof) have also been at play. While many in the media will go chasing repetitive reports on well-understood problems, the thundering silence on such cases of skill deficiency is bewildering. Illustratively, one can take up national skill Development Corporation. In 2011-2012, the target for skilling people was 1,60,000; the claim is that

1,81,691 were skilled, of which 1,44,238 were placed in jobs. The respective figures for 2012-2013 was 4,00,000 (target), 4,02,506 (skilled) and 2,16,741 (placed in jobs). Jai ho!

The golden age has arrived, however, there is a snag in this dated methodology of target-oriented planning. One does not know what is the standard of skills, to which those who were skilled, have been measured. One does not even know how robust the selection processes of placement was. This issue has not been raised even by the reincarnation of the Planning Commission, that is the National Institution for Transforming India-Aayog. Similarly, did one need a panel on railway reform to know that Indian Railways is over-staffed? And the solution to it is even more original.

Reportedly four multinational consultancy companies have been shortlisted to rationalise railway manpower. Years ago, panel after panel had made similar recommendations on many public sector units. Many consultants were raked in the fallouts of such prescriptive remedies. When the consultancy reports came in, Government after Government reportedly were of the view that people's livelihoods cannot be jeopardised for 'streamlining'. One is again tempted to say Jai ho!

Weather it is 'jai' or otherwise, a simple question begs an answer. How about focussing energies for defining identifiable standards for specific clusters of jobs? Why not support voluntary training programmes, encourage people to achieve those standards of skills, through their own initiative? Why not have well identified and tested methods of recruitment to make sure only the deserving get in? If standards are tweaked to provide employment, aircraft will crash, and railways will have disasters and many organisations will run into losses. Even the solvency of many banks will stand seriously threatened. Then, what will happen to the people savings and their means of living? Getting provoked is easy, writing prescriptions is even simpler, finding actionable remedies that will alleviate the problem another matter altogether. There is no danger of India becoming 'great' unless the issue of skill development is handled fair and square, and head on. This needs wisdom. The basic lessons are still in the Noah's Ark—we all are in the same boat. We must learn to pull the oars and pull it together.

June 26, 2015

## Developing a Global Talent Hub in India

One of the outcomes of great expectations is the impatience for results. For expectations, May 2014 was high water-mark. Rarely had one seen such high expectations by so many people who were so varied among themselves. This was good augury.

However, life has predictable cycles: High expectations, high impatience, low bandwidth and then the inevitable backlash. The national polity has not completed the cycle yet. Some structures seem to have changed but the preceding pattern seems to be continuing in parts.

There is a tacit statement on shortage of talent in India in certain areas. Consider the backgrounds of some of the persons inducted laterally into high-profile bureaucratic positions in the area of economics or national ayog. Their profile would fill with joy any diehard supporter of the Congress-led UPA. It is the same set of credentials and the same pattern of import of individuals who have achieved some amount of recognition abroad.

Perhaps, this is understandable. Perhaps this is an inherent part of the distinction between electioneering and governing.

The story rolls on. There were a set of people who had made it good during the UPA regime. They moved at the right time and swam with the stream. With their ability to watch the directions of the wind, they moved with the surging crowd. They made it rich with the times.

This too is understandable. After all, we live in an era where it is possible to run with the hare and hunt with the hound. Eminence, people acquire today, through the ability, not only to articulate and write, but also to be available to take the call when opportunities arise. The skill to package oneself in the right manner with the right political cliché is invaluable. This too can be forgiven.

What, however, the times will demand are selections that carry conviction. There is a need to project Indian standards. IBM became IBM because there was a general acceptance of the fact that computers need to be IBM compatible. If India is to take its legitimate position in the comity of the nations, it must, at least set the pace in half a dozen areas, to begin with.

The UPA spent a lot of time talking about India leading in the education field or IT. After 10 years of rule, we could not identify two dozen educational institutions which could claim people were flocking to it for admissions and teaching positions, from all over the world.

The truth of the matter is that even in the IT area we had very limited place, other than in low-end jobs. The greatness of a country lies in exerting a pull factor, globally, for its intellectual leadership. Governmental policies and positioning must enable this. It is an unfortunate fact of life that even in small habits of daily chores there is much be-labouring the point, an overkill, and pointless monitoring.

Illustratively, a normal citizen is obliged to carry multiple identities for every distinct and not-so-distinct Government activity. Unique ID has become so unique that there is almost competitive uniqueness.

The Aadhar Card carries an identity of a series of number; it has no connectivity with the passport that in turns has no connectivity with the Pan number. All three serve the same purpose of identification. The person is the same, the address is the same but each unit issues its own numbers.

The story does not end here. To pay tax, one needs different identities. To serve on a company board, there is an identification number for the directors, and yet another identification number for directors for boards of mutual funds. The list of identities is almost as large as the number of departments. The wise teach themselves not to raise these issues and the successful practice the art of explaining them away.

On the balance, to be acceptable to the establishment one must appear compliant, unthinking and responsive. This needs to change. Essentially to appeal to the powerful, one must appear to be acceptable rather than having the ability to move things forward. One hopes in the times to come some of this will change.

January 09, 2015

## Moving Towards Equal Responsibility for All

It doesn't take a genius to know that the basic difference between man and woman is biological. The difference reflects itself in varying endocrynological combinations. This has a serious relationship with hormones and, therefore, is an influencing factor on behaviour, energy and approach.

It's plausible to argue that to reduce this difference, there can be scientific social interventions. Behavioural interventions can also help the two genders cope with the influences of the endocrynological systems, better. This branch of study still has to be seriously taken to its logical conclusions. In the meanwhile, the pitch on woman's position and rights has become increasingly shrill. There are many reasons for this.

As always discomforts are known. The analysis of the causative factors is well understood. It is the solutions which are widely debated. While teaching in the UK in the early 1970s in one of the high brow 'red brick' universities, I watched with bewilderment from my office window, groups of women parading the campus and shouting slogans. They were also throwing into air their undergarments. It was a part of an equal rights protest. I am not quite sure whether such demonstrations achieved anything but they were widely discussed.

We, in India, have witnessed such sights. We have never had salary differential between male and female employees. These are significant indicators. However, there are other problems. Perhaps the most encouraging sign is the utter sense of abhorrence with which the news of affronts to women's dignity has been met.

But the problem is much larger than that. There is a global women's movement. The United Nations Entity for Gender Equality and the Empowerment of Women has seven women's empowerment principles. It has also focussed on the corporate sector. There is an attempt to get chief executive officers to sign a pact and agree to the guiding principles on business and human rights. Putting it simply, the UN Global Compact focusses on corporate sustainability of the respect and support for human rights.

The story however goes on. Excessive talk of rights creates its own problems. Witness the extension of the talk of fundamental rights in the Constitution of India. No one can or will contest the semenality of the fundamental rights. Yet, there can be no rights till there are duties.

Somebody's rights create a counterpart of duties.

We now have representatives from the civil society parading the streets with placards of various rights. Who will grant it to them? Once granted, who will enforce it? If enforced, how will the defaulters be punished? And indeed who will punish if the judge himself is guilty? The whole nation has become a huge platform for demanding rights.

Getting back to women's issues, it is absurd to deny that women have rights but to imply that they don't have any duties will be silly. People are not talking of it because politically it is all wrong.

There is a sunny side to the man-woman relationship. Femininity for millennia has basked in the male's adoration. Indeed, a man's adoration of femininity and his chivalry has been much celebrated. Between causing affront to a woman's dignity and chivalry, there needs to be a reconciliation of the fundamental principles. The woman's psyche has to be trained to constructively confront the affront. The male psyche has to be trained not to confuse adoration as an encumbrance.

Quite simply, mentoring at the early childhood/infancy stage is a small step in the direction of a solution. During several stages in the life-cycle, from infancy onwards, during adulthood, when one goes to work, there is a need for making the workplace recognise the biological, familial and social consequences of these differences. Women need not belong to the kitchen but somebody has to run the kitchen. The workplace has to recognise that a father's responsibility in parenthood is just as onerous as a mother's responsibilities.

A holistic typology of female and male roles needs to be integrated into work patterns. Sloganeering in the name of women and leadership may perhaps only strengthen tokenism and be as good as far as it goes. Technology has enabled the present generation to re-write the man-woman and environment relationship.

August 22, 2014

## Management Learnings and the Final of the Football World Cup

The Football World Cup finals concluded a few days ago. Argentina romped back to glory after decades. The victors were no doubt aided by the presence of a doyen in the field of football, namely Lionel Messi. He now ranks with Ronaldo among the legendary famous on the football field. The French captain, Hugo Lloris, covered himself with glory not only with a flair but also with the cool and balanced demeanour of a world class player and a captain. France's loss in the finals elicits a range of emotions, no doubt influenced by the people who hold those preferences. That's another story.

The management lessons of the game are significant. It was worth watching the game to understand not just teamwork but individual competency. The two go together through goal-directed activity.

Even to a layman, not quite conversant with the nuances of the game, a few aspects of over an hour of sheer delight are worth noticing. There is no substitute for teamwork. No one can win the game on their own. There are points in time when the individual efforts matter—like putting the ball in the opponents' net—but that too is the outcome of a series of precursor activities. What was remarkable was how each position of the team, from right out to the centre forward, to left out to the centre half, to the person playing in the back position, the goalkeeper, has his role defined. One has to play one's role as per their position in the team and enable others to do their job.

Be that as it may, there has to be excellence. In this case, in both the teams, each one was a powerful player in his own right.

The passing of the ball was immaculate. The shots were as powerful and as soft as the move required. It had to be done with accuracy, to the right person at the right place at the right time, and in the right split second of a decision. It was telling that there was no jostling for individual glory: both teams had outstanding players, each playing to his full competency.

These lessons are valid not only on the sports field but also in corporate houses, academic institutions, publication setups and wherever group activity is involved. Indeed, any organisation that has a group of people brought together to pursue a given objective, would do well to observe and interpret this final play. One remembers an outstanding Chairman of a major public sector organisation who designed his organisation's Management Development Programs with some mountaineering, rafting, apple picking, and other similar activities. This helped create a culture of teamwork and efficiency. This required not only a feeling of getting to know each other better, but also creating a team when required and nurturing it with involvement and forethought.

Ultimately, the Football World Cup final brought out a simple message: the game is not over till it is over, and one has to give one's best at all stages. Even when Argentina led 2-0 until the last 10 minutes of the game, France came back to even things up at 2-2. An inner enthusiasm for one's team identity was palpable and moving. Even those who know nothing about football found the spirit inspiring. In simple terms, the game stretched on and several milestones were passed before it was over. The organisers of such a contest obviously saw such a situation as a possibility. Accordingly, rules were devised to anticipate the issues and provide for possible resolution of the complex issues. This involved providing for extra time in the game and then penalty corners, to enable a resolution of a possible tie.

Irrespective of who won and who lost, the outstanding players stood out in their position as being leaders in their own right. The goalkeeper of Argentina was particularly outstanding and massive, and it did well to recognise him.

The message is simple: individual performance needs to be peer recognised. To be a leader is not to overshadow others worth but to nurture it through tenderness.

Generously appreciating the work of others is not difficult, it helps one's own growth.

All in all, the Football World Cup final was a visual extravaganza, a treatise on sports and team building. But one should have the eyes to see it and learn where learning gets redefined.

January 01, 2023

# 11

# Managerial Skills

## Now is the Need For a Reality Check

There are many ways in which decision-making can be structured or planning can be done. There are many ways in which the struggle for the control of the decision-making processes takes place. Ultimately, those who emerge victors in the various competing ways of doing something carry the day. The articulate in the group become cheer leaders and those who care or dare to oppose are either eliminated or left to languish or perish.

This happens in matters big and small. The last few weeks have seen the emasculation of an army which was proclaimed to be one of the finest equipped in the world. The current ruling elite in Afghanistan have made no bones about their distaste for matters such as democratically elected governance. They are in control and some of the mightiest powers in the world are ready to encourage this regime. Clearly, the jury has not even convened, let alone 'be out' for a decision. The international system has yet again proved its ineptness in sufficiently holding out values and making worthwhile moves to push for them. Even the so-called cause of women's rights in Afghanistan has not echoed much in any significant part of the world. Staunch proponents of gender equality can be seen occasionally demonstrating in some city, somewhere. Indeed, counter collectives reportedly have gathered of women in Afghanistan proclaiming, in effect, that the country's establishment's views on the status of women is indeed correct and must prevail. Philosophy has little scope to sort out a seemingly contentious views especially when there are few listeners. The international bodies including the United Nations are observing a thundering silence on this issue. Almost all of the global women's movements have suddenly dried up in the dreary desert sands of abject disinterest.

This is the story not just of women's rights. It is also the story of other human rights. The existence in China of alleged concentration camps, meant for certain religious minorities, is another subject of popular global neglect. Globally, even their co-religionists are rarely raising any attention about this. This is in sharp contrast to other kinds of concerns that are being raised. One wonders whether 'politics' predominantly determines what is flagged for attention and what is not. Like the gender movement, the cause of human rights for all, including minorities, is conspicuously marked by selective outrage. In the meanwhile, the expenditure on armaments amongst the so-called super powers continues to escalate.

Some media channels have been showing the might of certain super powers to link power of artificial intelligence and incredible destructive capacity of nuclear devices. The powerful nations write their own rule books. In the last three decades or so, proclaimed aggression has been practiced to eliminate the so-called 'weapons of mass destruction' and more. Reportedly, the armorial dash was for control of oil resources. The sheer ability to cover up crass commerce with lofty principles of progress seems to be the hallmark of many powerful. The time has come to realise some of the underpinning driving the truth of our times. Unless the truth is placed, squarely, on the table, any reversal of this sorry logic—where the powerful grab what they want with or without attempts at camouflage— is likely to continue.

September 16, 2021

## Confusion Compounded

It is obvious that skill development in servicing instruments has not kept up with the efforts put into pushing the demand for products Culture defines several behavioural traits and explains many social groupings. However, the concept of culture itself is elusive.

Many notable thinkers, including the likes of poet T.S. Eliot, attempted to define it but left the discourse incomplete. Herein comes the role of thought. The components of the definition of an idea or word may be elusive, incomplete or both. However, everyone knows with some approximation what it means when the word is used. The meaning becomes clearer when it is used in a context and there is a shared approximation in its use. However, this approach cannot work in a product maintenance situation.

From issues of verbal or ill-equipped fuzziness would arise a multiplicity of approaches to an obvious reality. Whereas this could work in matters of definition of "culture" this kind of mindset cannot work in matters of product specificity. That requires precision and the ability to diagnose with exactitude. However, characteristics which govern perception acquire the trappings of reality. They also become the assumptions of further logical exploration, as in the case of culture. Hence, a premise which by itself is an approximation becomes the foundation of logical derivations. It also, at times, becomes the bedrock of other definitions and work approaches.

An illustration would help explain the point. Any discussion on Indianness inevitably starts veering towards culture. Irrespective of differences of opinion, most people have a gut understanding of the making of an Indian. To put it more directly, an Indian and an Arab, in a conversation with each other, can be easily distinguished.

Further India (which has a defined identity and an amalgam of many subcultures with a substratum of identifiable traits) has no one city as its cultural capital. It just has an identifiable political Capital. India had several cultural conglomerates recognised as cultural centres through centuries. The plurality of definition works in this case but not in a product situation. Trouble arises when the mental conditioning of one situation starts permeating a totally different context. Confusion is compounded when this break does not impact sales of given products because the product that is being acquired is often for upping the "status index" rather than for efficiency of work

In France for example, the situation is different. Paris is not only its political capital but the cultural capital, too. Hence India and France even though identifiable nation States have different frameworks of cultural and techno-political operation. This has its impact on technological product orientation. The matter could be ignored if vagueness in culture did not influence the skill formation behaviour of another sector, that is maintenance of technological products.

Consider the all-pervasive drumming up which is going on in India on digitalisation. From Netflix to iPhones, from visualisation products to Information Technology ones, the market is flooded with numbers, brands and other varieties. The manufactures are laughing all the way to the bank because at any one point of time there can be five to six generations of say, either handsets or television sets available. People buy various products not necessarily out of any deep understanding of their defining features but also because of the status that goes with their acquisition. If you have two handsets of a given brand of different generations, both of them loaded with telephone numbers or ID details, both of them would be open to storing the data in the cloud. If the customer presses the key for "sync" a merging of the numbers or connect-catalogues would take place. If someone, then, called on a number both the phones would start ringing and then you might as well have only one handset.

The outlets, even in metropolitan cities, may not be able to handle this issue. One then proceeds to a given service centre where, possibly, a professionally-trained storekeeper has moved over as the technical head. S/he tries her/his best to work through trial and error. Sometimes this ability of stumbling through works, sometimes it doesn't. As a result, a serious amount of money invested in two handsets gets tied-up. Yet all this does not seem to affect sales. It is obvious that skill development in servicing these instruments has not kept up with the efforts of pushing the demand for the products. Yet few see this as a problem. Else the manufacturers, the distributors or the users would be attempting to sort out this major shortcoming in servicing. Is it possible that this culture of accepting the inability to define clearly and trying to survive by trial and error has permeated the product world, too? Is it possible that this absence of clarity of definitions and roles has given to the Indian market of technological products a strange veneer? The jury is yet to return with a solution to these complex contradictions and show the way to a composite approach.

January 04, 2021

## The Anatomy of Student Activism

On December 20, a weekly newspaper published from Delhi carried a photograph with the caption, "Citizens' anguish" and the sub caption read, "I am a Christian, my husband a Hindu and my daughter is Indian." It then referred to pages that carried details about the protests against the controversial Citizenship Amendment Act (CAA). Earlier, demonstrations on such themes were captioned as "students' agitation" by many media houses. By definition, CAA neither touches upon the veracity of those who are currently citizens of India, nor does it have anything to do with the "students." But captions on CAA have been catchy. If perusing a genuine cause, where is the need to seek subterfuge under inaccurate and misleading captions? "Student" is a word that has several shades of meaning. At the time of writing this article, this word already surfaced in the front page of newspapers for nearly a week numerous times. In fact, courtesy a major Central university in South Delhi, it has been making headlines for over a year now for all sorts of reasons, including physical intimidation of the Vice-Chancellor in his vehicle. The time has come to step back from the scene of action and take an objective look at the news stories that are made out of such events. What becomes a cause célèbre and what is allowed to peter away if not quietly, at least by default, needs some thought.

To understand any process, a historical look at how it grew across time will help. The first major national leader who mixed educational institutions with political movements was Mahatma Gandhi. Hence, sanctified with his precursor intervention, protests have been legitimised through various stages of growth. In the early 20th century, Gandhiji gave a call to the students to quit their educational institutions and join his movement.

Subsequently, he came to the conclusion that the premature entry into politics by the youth, who had not even obtained adulthood, was not fair for the growth processes. So, he went about setting up some "vidyapeeth(s)." Four of them were particularly notable.

Institutions with appellation of "national" also got currency and Bihar National College, Patna, was one of them. The purpose of these lines is not to track the evolutionary growth of these institutions but to highlight, from a social science perspective, that the capacity of these institutions so set up was lesser than the seat capacity of the institutions the students were supposed to quit. Thus, it is that a whole generation and more went into public movement with half-baked processes of learning. This can be a contentious line of thought and it may be premature to take a position on it.

However, one thing was subsequently clear: The leadership of the independence movement largely passed into the hands of relatively younger people, who had gone for their education to England and came back for their own reasons. Gandhiji, M.A. Jinnah and Jawaharlal Nehru were but a few such notables. Those with "desi" education had to make do with more supportive leadership roles. That again may be a topic fit for discussion some time later. Closer to the scene of action, after a relatively quiet 50s, where educational institutions were themselves few, began the process, which converted a lot of universities into an apprentice set-up for training in political leadership. There, many future political leaders-to-be, cut their teeth. To get back to the CAA-linked agitation, interestingly, the media carried stories of "student movements" from States where CAA would not even apply; to those where there were reported protests against their identity being inundated by the number of migrants; to crowds which were burning public property to agitate against implementation of the National Register of Citizens (NRC).

On December 18, one of the dailies published a two-column thumb nail on the history of "student protests" in India since independence. In the 10 movements listed, most of the areas mentioned for agitation had little or no correlation with student issues. Illustratively, it said that on February 9, 2016, the Jawaharlal Nehru University (JNU) "erupted" in protests over the 2013 execution of Afzal Guru. An "eruption" does not take place three years later. Geographically, it could have been that JNU and Afzal's name may have been highlighted, but clearly, it was not a student issue. On December 19, another daily discovered a "potential" student agitation in the so-called prestigious business school in Hyderabad. The plea is simple: There can be issues and issues for agitations. If peacefully conducted, anyone can demonstrate for anything. However, no service is rendered, to anyone worth a reputation by misleading glib captions such as "citizens' anguish" "student movement." It was indeed a student movement in the University of Sussex when the students demonstrated against the invite to Huntingdon to address the university. The merits of the agitation apart, it was truly a students' issue. Nobody's cause is served by misleading captions to omnibus issues. Campus life is sacrosanct. All heads of institutions know how to protect it. To be fair to the student community, the heads have a collective responsibility to protect the students from the vagaries of people pursuing political goals. Students should be left to study and equip themselves for life. If they choose to go "political" later on, that's another story. If some of them want to pursue social causes in an agitational mode, they should do it outside the campuses.

December 24, 2019

## Why Taking Risks is Essential

Risk management is a vantage point of perception, which has now become endemic. Almost nothing gets done without some reflection on the risks involved. Progressively, it is being remitted to the audit function. Yet, it is not bound by it. Concerted attempts are being made to widen and deepen its operations. Historically speaking, the area received the first formal limelight when corporate regulatory agencies made it mandatory to have a function with this "title" in all listed companies. The aim of risk management was to have a separate identity. It was envisaged that under his/her overall control, the risk management wing shall carry out its responsibilities and he/she would at least have the rank of an executive director of the company. If any listed company actually institutionalised the structure of this silo with all the nuances of risk a process, the experiment is yet to be documented. In the meanwhile, the area grew both in terms of quantum of attention and the range of activities. Skill formation in this area was still weak and not surprisingly, many with little understanding or insight, entered the domain.

The method followed was usually simplistic. The way of listing risks usually followed the narratives of some key people and their perceptions. It was then categorised into high moderate and low risks. The "juggernaut" rolled on and very often, there was more noise than light. What this method yielded by way of results was not clear to many. More complicated was the fact that there were no established standards against which its efficacy could be evaluated. Only a detailed review at a subsequent point of time could establish this. The process is still in the making

The "notable" consulting companies (especially those with non-Indian names and linkages) made a killing. Their demand was high. Special magical attraction was for such firms that had connects with the Atlantic rim institutions. More specifically, and professionally speaking, any delineation of "risks" should have followed an enunciation of risk management and mitigation policy at the board level. This in turn should have been followed up by the immediate next executive level to remarket, internally in the organisation, the areas of risk.

Areas of defined unpredictability and risks could have been identified and specific episodes could have been sighted, where risk was visible. This would have led to a robust delineation of the risk terrain. Customised training programme would then have to be designed to cover the foot soldiers of that area and above. This would have made the orientation and processes more professional and rigorous. No such thing happened in many cases and in several such cases, training programmes were launched in very general and commonsensical terms. Sometimes this was in imitation of what had been attempted in another organisation, in another cultural context. There were cases where this was done without a policy statement on the risk in place in the organisation.

Pointing this out by well-meaning professionals did not always yield results and was often discouraged by the top management, who were keen to demonstrate their conformity to a given directive. Incidentally, the directive, like any similar exercise, could have been only a statement of intent and could not have substituted for a policy statement. If there were people at the top, who saw this contradiction or were worried about it, they took care of not to show their anxiety.

In the process, perhaps, more damage than help was caused. But that's another story. Usually, the financial, economic and material indicators of risk got flagged. Illustratively, where relevant foreign exchange risk was listed. Similarly, if there was inflation, the trend was cited as a risk. Similarly, losses in inventory and poor quality products got listed as risks because market would not be tolerant to it. What was often left out was a broader risk of skill deficiency at multiple level of organisations or the sheer ineptness of the CFO. Few people understood the problems of a badly designed job description and even fewer saw it as a matter of great concern. The organisation flows were often not identified and, hence, the bottlenecks to productivity and results could not be pinpointed.

At the end of the day, risk management became fashionable but its integration to the overall strategy formulation was low. The situation was further compounded by the sheer absence of any assessment of the risk management process. The highest level of the organisation was happy to receive the "results". Perhaps, a decade or so down the line, it became obvious but there was a lot of effort with no commensurate outcome. The issue is still being tackled. In the meanwhile, the risk registers are being compiled. The risk matrices are being created and who knows, one may even begin to see a sense of direction sooner than later?

August 05, 2019

## Reality and Forecasts

Everyone likes to know the future. The trouble with forecast is that often one does not know how much it will go wrong and in which direction. Nevertheless, forecasting is a flourishing business that keeps thousands and thousands of people occupied. People forecast by looking at the palm, at the stars, at the forehead, at the horoscope, through planchets, through numerology, the list is endless. Of course, one should not forget the columnists, who rake in money by sounding wise and profound through forecasts, by reading trends and extrapolating selective data. It does not worry any one too much that very often, these forecasts go wrong.

Certain times are more propitious for forecasts. One such case is at the beginning of the year. It is interesting to note how by a simple calendar change of date, a 'New Year' has been converted into such a ritual of consuming, dining, wining, buying and celebrating. It is possible to argue that there is really no difference between December 31 of any given year and January 1 of the next year any more than there is between one date and another. Sun rises in the same way and time passes the same way. Even the number of hours is the same. Changing dates is a simple tool of measurement. It has been mystified to point a global festival.

Incidentally, like the Gregorian calendar, which has a December 31 and January 1, there are a number of other calendars in the world. So also, there are a number of other New Years. There is a Chinese new year. There is a Vikram new year. The list would include Vishu, Baisakhi, Bihu, Chetichand, Gudipadwa and this only from India. Other cultures have other new years. Some of these relate to agricultural harvest and people get into celebratory mode. December 31 and January 1 of the Gregorian calendar has no such agricultural connotation because it has spread to many climatic zones.

Like all rituals, it feeds upon itself and brings in celebrations and forecasts. For example, January 1 of a new year is used as an occasion to forecast yearly trends in politics, economics, city growth, science and technology and agriculture among others. It is made attractive with graphs, charts, photographs, cartoons and whatever else can catch attention. The process keeps feeding upon itself and multiplying. Aspiration is to rake more revenue. If one looks at the forecast of the beginning of the year and reviews them a little later, sometimes the forecasts come across as hilarious.

Consider a forecast of January 1, 2019 of a national daily with humongous circulation about 'politics' under the head 'the year that will be'. The write up there on page 10 of this daily read: "With the Lok Sabha elections looking truly open, amid intense efforts by various parties to set up alternative fronts and alliances, Delhi's political circle appears to have arrived at a consensus—era of coalitions will be back this year." (These words would be ash in the mouth of the author today).

The write up then reasons why, across the columns and then goes on to predict that three scenarios could play out. The BJP could remain the single largest party. It will then turn to its existing NDA allies and reach out to other potential partners for a wider coalition. This will mean compromise on its ideological agenda, on power distribution and cabinet berths, and, perhaps, even leadership... The Congress could substantially improve its performance. It if exceeds the 130-150 range, the party could even throw its hat in the game for leadership... On the other hand, the BJP may substantially shrink—say, losing over a 100 seats from its current tally… the Congress may improve to over 100-120 seats, but not gain enough to claim leadership. In this scenario, leadership could move to a non-Congress, non-BJP party, but the government would rest on the support of the Congress."

Now everyone knows how true this turned out to be! In economic terms, "fastest GDP growth status was not seen as benefitting India as in China's case today". China and the US (were to be locked) in a massive clasp of palms in a feasibly demonstrable show of strength. And, of course, nobody had any time to forecast about tribals, even while everything from continental drift in European Union to tariff warpath was being discussed.

An author even declared that 100-year life was firmly within (each) grasp.

Today, welfare of the weaker communities has clinched the day. The economically weaker sections of the society are playing a determining role. The tribals are determining not just welfare but fashions. Human life is shakier than ever because of a threatened epidemic of cancer, climate change and distributed ecosystems. While some are trying to re-write the social scripts, there is really nothing unique in it because each generation tries to do the same. So much for forecasts and so much for reality!

June 10, 2019

## Invectives, Anger and Chaos

Most of us love talking. As our level of agitation grows, we break away from our mother tongue and switch to English. The voice gets shriller, arguments become incoherent, and soon, intimidation enters the strategic options of the two contending parties. So long as both sides play dumb charades, there's no significant resolution of issues and no serious anxiety. Trouble begins when one side escalates unreasonableness, which usually ends in abuses. The other side may begin by keeping calm but ultimately succumbs to retaliation in face of continuous aggression. When this happens to people below 30 years of age, it can be written off, maybe wrongly, as immaturity. Beyond 30 years, it can only be foolhardiness and an invitation to the other party to dare. The bluff gets called sooner rather than later and then all hell is let loose. Even newspapers, dotted with tales of conflict, which began as verbal duels and punishments to some, have not helped others to learn from the sorry twist to sordid tales of invectiveness.

One might ask, why do two people of this description ever get together? Reasons can be many—they may be staying under the same roof, their communities and work may bring them together, in short it may be just about anything. The urge to command and have things one's way leads not only to counter-productive verbal duels, but at times, as indicated in earlier lines, to physical violence or even worse. What is narrated above is neither uncommon nor can it be laid at the doors of youthfulness. Nobody gains and yet very few, if anyone, learn. Such scenes are common everywhere. Looking at all this, one may well wonder if human beings are capable of significant evolution. Community life is no different—there it is called freedom of speech. Elections to five States are barely over, and the president of a national party has set the standards high on intimidation by claiming that he will not let the leader of the ruling party sleep. If that is his ambition, who can grudge it? Yet, it holds to reason that if perpetrators of such abuse had really nothing to gain, then such petty intimidations would hardly have been made.

The fact is, given a contentious situation, election or otherwise, wild rhetoric without any obvious agenda does seem to give some advantages to the demagogue of the day.

This is not a good example for the generation in a formative phase. Almost 15 or 20 years later, when they graduate to unbridled adulthood, they may even find vile invectives as normal or useful weaponry. In an era of lumpen assertiveness, misconstrued formulations on gender parity and search for identity without the responsibility to carry one's identity can be a suicidal proposition. It is not just a coincidence that endemic domestic and street violence is escalating. People, who would calmly drive past an accident-hit victim gasping for breath, or overlook a woman being physically harassed, suddenly become champions of reasonableness once their own interests are hurt. It may not be fashionable anymore to read religious texts for their sheer literary beauty or philosophical insights but to convert them into a denominational proposition of a campaign. However, the truth is that everyone is interested in finding out the truth and it hurts when one realises that s/he was wrong all along. It is precisely these double standards of running with the hare and hunting with the hound that can be disastrous. It is only when one realises the unreasonableness of one's logic that he/she will make amendments. There is no formula to cause this awareness.

Decision-making in communities, organisations and the nation seems to be a victim of this malaise.

The outcome is for everyone to see. The individual is struck with hypertension, communities are embroiled in sub-terranean tug-of-war, larger communities in vilification and the nation at large with unprecedented foul public discourse. This is a road to nowhere. A movement of self-analysis, introspection and objective thinking would clearly be in order. The trouble is our nation is so possessed with talks of piety, religiosity and fear of the divine, there seems to be few takers of personal growth, self-improvement with clear thinking. Pilgrimages will be undertaken and vows offered in anxiety or aspiration. Religious places spawn their own culture of petitioning the almighty. This covers everything from tying threads around the trees to making offerings in places of worship but one simple thing which can be done goes by default—and that is to think straight.

One should simply hold one's peace and not talk in a manner in which he/she doesn't want to be talked to.

The ironies of life, when they stop tickling, sometimes also cause tears to dry. Yet, life goes on.

December 24, 2018

## Flawed Decisions Proclaimed Legitimate

In 1954, a Presidential order accorded special rights and privileges to the citizens of Jammu & Kashmir. Indian citizens could not acquire immovable property in the former riyasat of Jammu & Kashmir. Effectively, therefore, the Constitution was refracted to provide for citizenship within a citizenship. Similar provisions, not labelled as "citizenship rights", do give original inhabitants of, say, Meghalaya and elsewhere in India, privileges which are akin. One can work in Meghalaya for decades and will still not have the right to buy property. That may be important, but is a separate point.

The catch lies elsewhere. Former Prime Minister Jawaharlal Nehru's fascination with the issues in Jammu & Kashmir is well-acknowledged. According to many, his facade of a democrat covered a hardcore reality of a self-willed leader. Irrespective of the controversies, the Maharaja of Jammu & Kashmir did sign the instrument of accession to India and that is what the Indian Independence Act required. Two realities queered the pitch. One part was the apparent dominance of the Muslim population in the Kashmir Valley. The second was the contiguity of border with Pakistan. Nehru adhered to give primacy to the sentiments of some in the Kashmir Valley and total neglect of the sentiments of the people of Ladakh.

The writer of these lines, while preparing for a keynote address on the history of freedom movement in Jammu & Kashmir, in 1978, came across a narrative. It went as follows: When Sheikh Abdullah as the then Prime Minister of Jammu & Kashmir, in his early years in that role, was asked if a plebiscite would not be in order, he reacted sharply. He was of the view that once he had agreed to the merger, what significance was the plebiscite? The writer recalls raising this with Sheikh Saab at a State dinner at Lal Chowk that year. His response was enigmatic and he had a counter question, "Don't you agree with my view?"

More to the point, with no Supreme Court ruling behind him, in 1954, Jawaharlal Nehru went to the then President to get orders according to special rights, as referred above for the citizens of Jammu & Kashmir, reference immovable property. Interestingly, the same order denies property rights to a woman who marries a person from outside the State. It applies to women in property matters and also applies to her heirs. Whether the women's rights movement had ever protested about this discriminatory provision of the order at any time in the last 65 years, it is this country's best-kept secret. As an afterthought, the protagonist of this clause have sighted two verdicts of the Constitution benches of the Supreme Court in 1961 and 1969, which cite Article 370 (1)(D) of the Constitution that entitles the President to pass Constitutional orders. If that is accepted, Indian democracy needs to be redefined.

This debate is unlikely to be resolved in a hurry. The latest mood seems to be to postpone the hearing of the petition challenging the Constitutional validity of Article 35A till early next year. Grounds can always be found. There are many other contradictions in the way legality is used to push the point of view of the politically powerful of the day, to an institutionalisation frame. Once institutionalised, stakeholders in the decision emerge, and to reverse it, becomes problematic.

The crux of the matter seems to be strengthening the right to appeal. Nationwide, institution-wide and indeed against any framework of decision-making, right to appeal is an elusive proposition in India. The annals of the media and public experience are replete with examples where the key decision-maker had his/her way because either people kept quiet in default or did not feel stimulated enough to raise the questions. Put simply, it means that a decision may push for a point of view but it does not necessarily serve the cause. This is not good for collective welfare.

Helplessness delivering compliance is a dubious approach. Ultimately it does cause a shake-up. This shake-up does not necessarily follow the generational cycle of human existence. Autocratic styles have carried the day and the perpetrator has never paid his wages of unfairness and has passed way before retribution caught up. That indeed is the dilemma of a person's ability to do right or wrong and the historical inevitability of the time it takes for the effects to incubate.

Clearly, at least while designing and running of our institutions, one should make every effort to follow certain ground rules of probity in decision-making. This is true of the Government working and, therefore, the Government institutions. It is equally true of private systems and private institutions. So often the decision is at the cost of the hapless individual who had a cause but not the means to see it through. This may prove to be one of the bigger enigmas of decision-making of our times.

September 03, 2018

## Independence Day Dialogue

By the time this column appears in print, a gush of commentaries on the Independence Day speech of Prime Minister Narendra Modi (duly clipped by the attention to the demise of Atal Bihari Vajpayee) would likely be on wane. A revisit may be useful. August 15, speech from the Red Fort, has a unique position. It is used to project the Government's plans, work-in-progress and achievements. Sometimes it is peppered with rhetoric, demagoguery, exhortations or projecting a moral high ground. It has also been used on occasions to announce measures which the Prime Minister considers expedient. Anyone who makes it to the position of a Prime Minister has probably earned this prerogative. Of all Prime Ministers this country has had, only one did not make it to such an event.

Concurrently, as the breadth and depth of the media grew, even before the Prime Minister reached his next appointment after the speech, panels on television channels are on it to do a critique of what he said or did not say, his intentions or what he should have said or the worthiness of his statements—the list is endless. Some anchors do it with wisdom and moderation, others use it to canvas their own political biases. Figuring on these panels is an outcome of what the channel considers a worthwhile investment to boost its TRP. Nevertheless, they do impact a narrative on where the nation is.

The enunciation from the ramparts and the commentary which follows may be termed as the Independence Day dialogue. This is a significant input to the socio-political narrative of the nation. This year's Independence Day speech, like all other years, followed the President's Address which came the preceding evening. The Prime Minister made a reference to it establishing a continuity. This was a methodical contribution. All discussions, noted Prime Minister's exquisite use of language, the use of poetry and idiom, underplay of statistical jargonaise. The Prime Minister's penchant in public communication is widely acknowledged. The gift of this ability produces huge largesse.

The spokesman for a national party—with acknowledged distaste for the Prime Minister—flagged this ability, at public speaking, as a great risky factor. This was neither necessary nor a contribution to the dialogue. In case of this Party, their love for denigrating the present Prime Minister usually follows use of denigrating words. The cause for denigration is then stated by them, later. Perhaps this Party does not realise that in this manner they are only building the image of the person they wish to denigrate.

However, it should be acknowledged that like any other entity they have the right to their own stupidity. The approach of articulating without prejudice has certain prerequisites.

One of them is it should ride honesty. The second is, it should be, to the extent possible, non-judgemental. More to the point, as the Prime Minister Narendra Modi's speech does set a national agenda, the 'omissions' become as potent as the statements. Education, as a topic was painfully conspicuous by its absence. There was probably only one sentence on it. This, one hopes, was an 'inadvertent' omission and not a lapse. It is another matter that even in the overall schema of this Government, educational policy and reform are not exactly its bright spot. The National Higher Education Commission Bill coming in the last year of its existence is yet to be tabled in Parliament. It is believed that the Education Minister has issued an informal Writ to autonomous institutions of excellence to the effect that while reconstituting their boards, names should not be repeated. It is another matter that same name can occur on more than one board of such institutions. The chairmen of various boards in their usual propensity to please, thus, carry forward the 'Writ of autonomy'.

Perhaps, the Education Minister can be forgiven for his lack of experience, if not naivety.

The yearly forex spend on education (2017-18) is estimated to be \$2.8 billion. It is an indicator of the worth, those who can afford and attribute to our educational systems. The expenses (2017-2018) of foreign students in India is estimated to be \$479 million as compared to \$557 million in 2015-16. Even forgetting what it says of us, surely there is such a thing as educational diplomacy. These tell-tale figures need a speedy policy intervention. There is another aspect of this year's dialogue which is worrying. There was little focus on ocean related efforts, besides a passing reference to 'blue economy'. Given the experiences of South China Sea or Maldives, almost no reflection on 'ocean related efforts' is unwise.

Yet that is not the miracle. The miracle is no one on the panels or in the commentaries thought it worthwhile to raise the above concerns. There seems to be an apparent consensus of the articulate and the influential to focus only on those themes which do rabble rousing. Perhaps a nation building dialogue requires more than being 'catchy'.

August 20, 2018

## Of Padmaavat and History

History is much talked of discipline. It is needed when one wants to give to the next generation in a family, a sense of identity. It is needed when any issue is to be resolved (seldom if ever there is an issue that comes up for resolution which has never been handled in some manifestation, earlier on). It is needed when growth of a process has to be documented. It is needed whenever there is an attempt to understand the whys and the where-ofs of something. It is needed for reinforcing and clarifying national identity. It is needed for many situations, including the positioning of any product, activity or a sector. Yes, it is needed also for making films on people and processes, which have a historical echo. The list is endless.

One can begin from the bottom of the list. The recent happenings around Padmaavati or Padmaavat (I am not quite sure which is a more authentic name for the more than two hours long of a rehash of a template which one has seen earlier on in Jodha Akbar/Bajirao Mastani and elsewhere). Whether all history has been knocked out of this film or not is now a moot point. The people, who promoted this film, have put in a pretty penny and want their money's worth. That is the bottom line. If it sells in the name of history, that's good. If it doesn't, that's also fine, so long as returns are not affected.

The key concern is the return on investment.

Simultaneously, with the release of this film, there were two other films showing in Delhi, at times in adjacent halls to the one in which Padmaavat was showing. One was a film called 'The Post', the second one was a film called 'The Darkest Hour'. 'The Post' dealt with a slice of history, dealing with four American Presidents—Dwight D. Eisenhower, Richard Nixon, John F. Kennedy, and Lyndon B. Johnson. Those interested can do an Internet search for the story. The movie, 'The Darkest Hour' dealt with the early months of the prime ministership of Winston Churchill. The story is again available on the Internet.

The craft of cinematography across the three films, 'Padmavat', 'The Post' and 'The Darkest Hour' is so critical that for those, who boast of the evolved nature of Bollywood, time has come, if ever, for a serious rethink.

Irrespective of the political meanings read into 'Padmaavat' and not so subtle attempts of the Director at a rather avoidable play with emotions, clearly, it is an extravaganza. If the dances of the lead character in 'Padmaavat' and 'Bajirao Mastani' were put on video clips, they would sell just as much without anyone making out centuries of difference and the many hundred kilometres of distance between the happenings and location of the two episodes of the dances.

In the film, 'The Darkest Hour', there is one episode of a few minutes where Churchill reportedly visited an underground station and even that is flagged as 'unhistorical' in the Internet version of the movie's story. The name of the game is credibility.

It is about time there was professionalism in the critique of an effort, just as there is a need for higher professionalism in the inputs to the effort.

If this is the state of the craft of cinematography, the media is not far behind. As the protagonist of the movement against 'Padmaavat' began to lose ground, allegedly, funded campaigns in media picked ground. One particular channel, a day before the release of the movie, spent half an hour of prime news time, pleading that there was nothing 'objectionable' in the movie. The question is about the status of the professional character of our narratives, our commentaries and indeed our agitations.

Ushering in professionalism is not an act of governance, it is a frame of mind of the populace. We as a people, have to do some soul searching to find out how come, in spite of so many boasts of the left, right and centre-oriented ideologies and rhetoric about our intellectual orientation, we are so gross in management: In this case of our entertainment business.

February 01, 2018

## Taking Our Citizens' Lives for Granted

Almost everyone is concerned about 'managing risks'. In the worth-celebrating movie 'Wednesday', there was a reference to how anyone heading out of home in the morning would be worried about whether he would come back safe in the evening. The number of mishaps which can happen, would range from accidents to street rage to terrorist outfall to an unknown catastrophe. The dependent family members are bound to be worried for the person who ventures out. The safety parameter within the household is also under a cloud. The lack of a network to attend to a medical catastrophe is so definitive that various families have a protocol of cross-checking through the day.

What is said in preceding lines cannot be news to anyone. The difficulty, however, is that in the inability to come to grips with a problem, there is a tendency to circumvent it. Hence, the problem doesn't get sorted out.

Indeed, some have exercised the choice of confronting the problem even if it means straining the personal relationships, but then this is not institutionalisation. Decoding this to an organisational level is even a bigger task.

The bald truth is that the risks which organisations run at the level of simple efficiency are a far bigger danger to their productivity and profitability than perhaps anything else.

Organisations are replete with illustrations of how people will not do a simple job on time, and with characteristic Indian ingenuity produce a whole clutch of reasons which would explain what prevented them from doing so. This concern does not figure—to the best of the knowledge of this writer—in the broadest of listings of items which come under risk management!

The upshot is, like it is seepage beneath the walls, and it corrodes the foundations silently till one day the wall itself collapses. The more talked-of areas of risks include everything from exchange risks to issues in industrial relations. It's all because it enables a programmed mitigation.

The risks to life and limb, however, are not confined to corporate sector alone and covers the entire gamut of the act of living itself.

Thus, it is that trauma care has become an increasingly important part of healthcare, and some figures will highlight the significance of the issue. India's total landmass is 32,87,263 square kilometres. This is broadly 2.4 per cent of the surface area of the world. The nature of habitation can be figured out on this base. Injury is the third commonest cause of death in all ages. It costs three per cent of the GDP. With the baseline being taken as 1990, the number of deaths from injury was 5.1 million.

Add to it, disabilities arising out of injuries, and one can figure out the magnitude of not only the lives affected but also the families put in jeopardy. The fatalities in the age bracket of 15 to 44 have been listed at 50 per cent. As per records, in 1998 alone, in the World Health Organisation region, it was estimated that 1.2 million people were killed in road traffic injuries. The deaths by cancer and heart disease were several times smaller. If one calculates the year of productive life lost due to injury, singularly, accounted for 40.8 per cent. All other diseases accounted for 24.8 per cent deaths; heart disease for 16.4 per cent and cancer for 18 per cent.

The figures speaks for themselves. The number of road deaths in India in 2005 was 98,254; in 2014 it was 1,41,526. Taking 2005 as the base, the rise was up by 2.99 per cent. Deaths from accidents rose from 2,57,936 (2002) to 4,31,556 in 2014.

Rail road accidental deaths in 2014 were up by 95.37 per cent compared to the preceding year. Need one say more: We have the dubious distinction of recording the highest number of deaths in the world, that is 14 per hour. And we have not even begun to talk of terrorist-related injuries. As one looks around the absence of trauma care facilities across the board through the hospitals in India, the challenge becomes even more daunting.

We hear of so many missions. One is entitled to ask: What mission can be higher than preserving life?

January 23, 2017

## Socialism has Little Relevance in India

In an interview early this week, given at an economic summit, economist Jagdish Bhagwati modestly claimed that he is 80 years old and cannot accept a role in the Government. "I fall asleep", he is reported to have said. However, he felt he had the nicest things to say about the Prime Minister.

That is nothing unusual, because a lot of people have nice things to say about the Prime Minister. What marked Mr Bhagwati's comment, however, the extent of praise. Mr Bhagwati had reportedly said, "Narendra Modi is the gift of God to India". Now, that is a fulsome comment.

Mr Bhagwati was also asked if he had spoken to Amartya Sen recently and he made a joke about it. That Mr Sen had got a Nobel Prize which Mr Bhagwati had not, was also brought up. The latter was sporting about it.

He also had nice things to say about his colleague from California who is now the Chairman of NITI Aayog. (Had he recommended?) He also had kind words for the NRI who is continuing as Governor of the Reserve Bank of India.

Concurrently, I noticed another news item about a group of American faculty members who had been invited to the Indian Institutes of Technology for stimulating the environment through some teaching. I could not help wonder what all of this totalled up to. It sounded so much like the UPA in action. Former Congress Minister Kapil Sibal would be such a satisfied man after having read all of this.

In the mid-1990s, Mr Bhagwati, with his gospel of foreign investments and open economy, was duly invited by the powers then close to the current powers to evangelise about a free economy. People like Vinay Bharat Ram, the founder of the Delhi Cloth Mill, sponsored his lectures.

Seminars were organised around Mr Bhagwati's thoughts. I happened to be invited to some of those seminars and dutifully attended as, I was expected to. I would do so again, today, if I was asked, but that is not the point.

The point is a simple one: The idea of socialism is a national mission enshrined in the vision of the nation, as represented by the

Constitution of India. This country is supposed to be a sovereign, democratic, socialist, secular republic. What is to happen to the concept of socialism if the likes of Mr Bhagwati and his ilk continue to so critically determine the policy frame?

Times change, so do needs. If the needs change, the philosophy and the policy has also to change. It's much better to accept this, if this be the case with reference to both open economy and so-called socialism. Living with contradictions causes much confusion and chaos. So far so good.

However, consider another aspect of the national mission as enshrined in the Constitution: The word 'secularism'. Think of the holy anguish with which many people talk when their understanding of secularism, is violated.

However, when it comes to economics there is a thundering silence from almost all political parties on the issue of socialism. No constitutional guarantee is then evoked. If there really is such unanimity on the issue of an open economy, then is it not about time that we amended the Constitution to drop the word 'socialist'?

This suggestion is not being made in mirth. This is a serious line of thought for preserving the reality contact and aspiration of the sanctified document called the Constitution of India.

However, we must also ask if this silence on socialism and the articulation on a given understanding of secularism rooted in nature of political formations in this country? Political parties are operationally based on caste, community, religious considerations, and not on the economic constructs or ideology. People are moved for participation in political processes on issues of identity and community interests.

Are we, by action, implying that there are no significant economic ideological divides in India; hence there is no need for political formations based on economic ideologies? So far as development is concerned, there is no political party which says it does not want development.

January 23, 2015

## Intent Expressed, Now Time for Suitable Action

The President's address to the joint session of Parliament has taken place. It was predictably a middle of the road, straightforward elaboration. The options on foreign direct investment, social equity, inflation control and more are distinct areas of concern, and there is nothing much to choose. Indeed, the overall thrust of the new regime, beyond the concerns voiced in the presidential address, seems to be on enhancing administrative efficiency.

This is an approach which is overdue and nobody will grudge it. The impact of this kind of talk on the ground conditions is a separate matter altogether. Well-intentioned resolutions and directives have an ugly habit of lapsing into conventional patterns of conduct. The new year's resolution, which many of us, make is a classical statement of intent which runs dry in practice.

A fact of the matter is, besides the intent, there has to be the capacity to keep it alive. The Cabinet Secretary, under extension himself, has been busy issuing what the media calls 'commandments'. The Prime Minister himself, between exhorting his various audiences and attending to his regular work, will need to find time to usher in a credible, evolved, and perceptively new dispensation.

That is going to need ingenuity beyond replicating the Gujarat model.

The Prime Minister seems to have begun well by recognising the role of tradition (where all successful innovation has to be embedded) and technology (which is a handy instrument of leveraging the world).

In the meantime, the number of people who are moving over from well-ensconced positions in a quasi-liberal westernised environment to new found enthusiasm for the Prime Minister's past achievements, is growing. This is natural, and in a world full of stylised jargon, it is always possible to use phrases like 'getting the country back on track', as labels for writings.

This is a dangerous tribe because it is adept at finding logic for whatever propels its social climbing. This, however, is inevitable in the power lanes of the national capital. They cannot be eliminated but they certainly can be guarded against.

The Union Cabinet itself is yet to be fully formed, and there is wisdom in putting it on slow fire. There is something to be said about the intellectuals and the intellectual centres which have failed to generate policy options or contribute vigorously enough to the creation of a new dispensation for the country.

It is not amusing as to how, within the overall framework of debates and development, endless talk of diversity, richness of Indian natural resources and natural endowments, the discussion on the way forward is so repetitive. Endless jugglery with rates, GDPs, FDI figures, much of the dialogue is so grooved as to be almost predictable.

Consider a simple fact of the Indian coastline. Its vastness and richness is no news, yet in developmental planning, one is still to hear of ocean resources in a significant way. It makes no difference whether they deal with geological resources of minerals or edible resources of sea weeds and plants or marine resources. Life of the average Indian does not seem to incorporate this perspective. The sea resource industry alone is capable of affecting the prosperity patterns of the inhabitants of the coastal hinterland exponentially. Yet, whereas there has been some talk of fisheries development, there remains so much more to be done for other sea resources. There are other treasures from the sea besides shrimps and prawns.

The Government has been talking of tourism, and in the entire coastal line of India it is difficult to find a major world class water sports resort. From snorkeling to being at peace in the observation of sea creatures remains an activity still to be born in this country.

There is a need not only to remove the blinkers but to widen our frameworks of reference. This has to be converted into a national movement of upliftment. Perhaps Swami Vivekananda in his inimitable style had foreseen such a day, when he gave the slogan "Uthishthta, jaagrata prapya varan nibodhata" (Arise, Awake, Rest not till you have achieved!)

The Indian subcontinent is blessed with resources and talent. But these have to be galvanised through a focussed skill development programme with indigenous standards.

June 13, 2014

## Modern Day Leaders Must Stoop to Conquer

Context is its culture. It comprises *desh* (territory) and *kal* (the time). Culture is often perceived as the acceptable pattern of setting relationships, managing work and the values of the doable and the not-so-doable. Culture is all this and more.

Culture is also the definition of the optimal style acceptable to a group of people for its functioning. This is not necessarily confined to operation. It can also cover the aspiration. It is this aspirational platform towards which organisations, groups, and individual actions has to move. This is the role of the leader and the facilitator.

This road cannot be traversed without the help of the *guru*—who may be the leader himself or a facilitator who has to put together the group. Often, such a person is labelled as a trainer. Willy-nilly a facilitator/trainer's position is the role that people look for in organisations. While this common perception may not be inaccurate, it is certainly incomplete.

A leader can be found anywhere from Government cadres to political parties. Indeed the biggest contribution to this concept has often been from the Armed Forces. This is understandable because the services often operate in an environment of do or die. The price of not carrying others along can be heavy.

This enables us to recognise that it is never possible to operate without a cohesive group. One needs to recognise that creating a team, therefore, is not an idealistic luxury but an operational necessity for consistent execution. It is possible to confuse this with 'team building' or creating a harmonious group. That it will have to be minimally so, is true to an extent. However, the core concern remains: What kind of harmony and what does it entail?

Harmony would be needed in work methods and not in terms of individual likes and dislikes. Similarly, to achieve this harmony, the task content will need to be identified and to the extent possible, broken up into its constituent components. This is an operational necessity. These days, almost nothing gets done with single specifications. Different domains have to be molded together and integrated.

Consider the operation of an IT company. It requires systems specialist, content writers, model developers, those who test out the model and a person putting all this together. It will be rare to have a content developer who is equally good in developing a code. Hence, teams become an operational necessity.

Often team building has been seen as a behavioural issue where people are taught to be decent and understanding. Unfortunately, while behavioural dimensions are important, they do not go far enough. One often requires integration of specialties for a team to meet its goal. This kind of integration is needed almost universally, from election campaigns to dealing with vendors.

The leadership function, therefore, has become increasingly synergistic. Today's leader has to lead in today's context. In an era of spiralling aspirations and conflicting worldviews, it is important to factor in people's aspiration to get work out of them in an integrated manner. Spend time orienting leaders to be understanding and helpful is important, but does not go far enough.

Ultimately, a team will hold together only so far as the people see it as a vehicle of fulfilling their aspiration and their need. To this extent, a leader may have to forgo to his claim to credit and project the members of the teams as achievers. Simply, put he may have to stoop to conquer because he cannot leave the goal unachieved.

January 24, 2014

## Let Innovation be a Life Principle

Innovation is the applied aspect of creativity. It has been available in modern literature for over a century-and-a-half. It has had its own share of prominence in different parts of the world in different times. It has been a particular favourite for entrepreneurial actions in all seasons. In the last few decades, it has acquired almost universal applicability and now everything has to be 'innovative'. That's clearly a high goal to achieve.

It is so because without ensuring the routine, innovation cannot happen. Unfortunately 'routine' is a lot like the hygiene factor—crucial but often taken for granted. Yet, even standard performance at the routine-level is a far bigger challenge than attempting innovation. The trouble is discussing performance on the 'routine' is unglamorous. Discussing performance on innovation is fashionable.

Be that as it may, innovation is often understood as the attempt to do the same thing in a quicker, different or more elegant manner. Unfortunately, this cannot be carried out in a time-bound manner. Indeed, there would be no parameters to this change unless the core technology concerned becomes obsolete.

Innovation and creativity has its time-honoured classification. Perhaps there is a case to revisit it. By the same token, talk of creativity and innovation is often catapulted to significance by the patronage it receives from political processes.

Let us first take up the issue of classification of creativity and innovation. In the popular discourse, two classifications are found—scientific creativity and artistic/literary creativity. Scientific creativity has predictive validity. The techniques are time-tested and the results can be forecast.

They include a number of methods which work through, among other things, permutation and combination. Techniques such as forced matching, attributes listing, checklist of questions, morphological synthesis are well tested also. One can always create new products or services through them.

As differentiated from scientific creativity, literary creativity is less predictive. Often it is a dyadic situation— either it happens or it does not happen. One has to wait for inspiration—poems and outstanding creative performances are based on it. It is true that art also has a form. For example, poems have meters and dance routines have structures. Yet any great performance in the form of poetry, dance, painting and more is different when inspired—an inspired rendering is different from a customised rendering. The difference between scientific creativity and artistic creativity lies in the recognition of measurements and standards.

There is also yet another class of creative action. It is neither literary nor scientific but it is simply there. One knows the route to being different, useful and much more elegant, not because there is scientific method or one has been inspired, but because one has experienced so much and observed so well, that the instinct is at work. Let's call this 'informed creativity'. The sixth sense—if there be any such thing—takes over and one feels one's way through confusion and experimentation to something worthwhile. If one has to feel one's way through innovative products, services and indeed lifestyle one has to use all of this and indeed select which approach to creativity and innovation works best.

It would be stating the obvious to say that 'innovation' has had huge political patronage in last decade or so, and one name that is often associated with it is that of Sam Pitroda. The doubting Thomases will obviously ask for a tally and checklist of the achievements of such people. That however, is another story. The burden of this piece is to establish the primacy and relevance of innovation as a life principle.

August 09, 2013

## Progress and Risk-Taking

Life is full of risks; from walking the staircase to crossing the road to eating food and, indeed, much else. One is always confronted with risks. There is always a distinct possibility of slipping on the steps just as there is a possibility of being knocked down on the road by a vagrant person or a vehicle. The food may always have some latent contamination or a virus which could not be screened. In the present era of possibilities of 'intensifying' the surface of the vegetables/fruits; one is always running the risk of buying fresh fruits or vegetables which are corrosive to the body. The list can be multiplied and with it the anxieties which accompany the awareness of this possibility. Since the chances of eliminating these possibilities to a zero level are impossible; one has to develop a threshold of what caution dictates and leave the rest to providence and much else.

The message is simple, the only way of living is doing the best one can to mitigate the risks and train oneself to ignore the rest. The second step is important because if one does not do that unnecessary stress, is the outcome. The formulation may be simple to state but it takes effort to practise. Mind control is not always easy.

Thus, it is that there is a need for widening and deepening the range of skills at the early childhood level and gradually making it a more informed process as one goes on. There are very few institutions—formal or informal—which are helping to do it.

The role of parenthood in this is critical. As one grows older and parents fade away, the role of institutions and self-development become more critical. Unfortunately, the matter is not receiving sufficient attention, the way of dealing with it needs to be institutionalised. It is even more worrying that the awareness of the need of a formal response to this concern, is at the best weak and possibly waiting to be recognised.

The Covid experience is but one example of how one seeks to protect oneself from a virus which is yet to be fully programmed. In February 2021, in most parts of the world, the virus was declared dead and yet in a few months' time it came back with a bang. In the last few weeks, this pandemic has been declared to be over in many parts of the world and yet, it is there in an ugly form in certain pockets. Covid is not the only virus. There are issues of hygiene related to just about anything one wears, eats or sleeps with. The writer of these lines has a distinguished doctor friend who advised that the important thing is to protect the bed. Translated into action, it simply meant not sitting on it with random clothes and bathing before sleeping. It is difficult to say, how the doctors follow the prescriptions which they write. But that is a separate point. It is more relevant to recognise that doctors have by virtue of their training and profession the competence to write a protocol on the upkeep of the body. The tricky part is the doctors agree to a threshold of information only up to a point and thereafter there are always variations, depending upon the experience of the doctor and his range of exposure/awareness of that kind of risk. Hence, the focus is on the individual.

A joyful individual basically, positive in the orientation need not go splitting hairs. A commonsensical approach like in business decisions is the best way forward.

It is known that most business decisions mean grappling with a range of variables which are either unknown or at best an interpretation of past experiences. Yet businesses have nurtured human civilisation since time immemorial. There is intuition, instinct and foresight in everyone. An educated, informed and sensitive mind is the best guarantee of success.

Overemphasis can and must be controlled in favour of a joyful and positive approach to oneself, others and life itself. This is the message which needs to be spread essentially by practising what one would want others to do. Leading by example is the best way forward and mutual respect and bonding facilitates this.

This text began with talking of risks. Popularly, professionals have viewed entrepreneurship as risk-taking for-profit maximisation. This is the essence of entrepreneurship. It was so since time immemorial and continues to be so today. Any community which has an appetite for healthy risk taking will be an entrepreneurial community. Entrepreneurship was at the root of human progress and continues to be so. One has to inculcate and encourage this spirit from early childhood to all stages of life.

Risk taking is a recognition of realities of human life and how it can be seen as a positive input for not only pushing the boundaries but enriching personal lives and growth possibilities of groups.

Over generations, incoming of technology has added newer dimensions to this fascinating journey. It is at the core of human progress. It covers everything from microbe hunting to explorations of the space.

December 01, 2022

# 12

# Business Policy

## The dark world of bright crystals

Business is fickle because, like the rising sun, an emerging success is always welcomed and the declining sun is ever-abjured. At the end of the day, there is a lot of jostling to continue to be successful and brand oneself as such. There are instances in post-Independence India where a public system was rapaciously ransacked by voracious and cunning individuals to get an initial breakthrough in the circle of wealth. Interpretation has it that in the most successful of such ravaging for years, nothing was unknown. What was happening was almost in the knowledge of those who cared to know. Even the so-called culprits were known. But no one was really booked because if you booked one of the key functionaries, he/she knew too much. Once they spilt the beans it would cause convulsions in the close circles and nobody knew who would be affected. So at the end of the day, a new business house was born and some flourishing careers in the corporate and governance circles were re-enforced. A few of the vulnerable known to flourish in any regime thrive even today.

The moralist can go into convulsions and the Romanist can thump his chest but the colt had bolted. This cannot be the place to discuss the morality and worse, of such a scenario. Someday if not in an economic history book, this episode would make a successful narrative of a novel. That's another story. The basic proposition remains that lucre is always dirty. The dictionary defines it as a monetary reward or gain. It is more than that. It is the end pursued by many minds. Whether it is dirty or not, doesn't seem to affect many in any substantial sense. Not very long ago there was a movie called 'Blood Diamond'.

Those who know of it would recall how it made a theme of the kind of exploitation of the human body and more that went into diamond mining. The message was simple, that those who buy these diamonds lubricate the coffers of unscrupulous businessmen who have no conscience. The story does not end there. The high and the mighty, in their search for the distinctive, lubricate the business of the unscrupulous. The public reaction to the information can only be of the type that, however, is material to actual ground conditions. If the movie made any dent on the overall attraction of the business or reformed the processes, the message is still to come in. Such movies and related writings on this theme are neither unique nor once in a lifetime. It's like a parallel stream. The business does what it does. The objector does what he/she has to.

The art lies in recognising that such writings or presentations, even cinematic, help to contain the problem, because at least something is being set in motion to do so.

Unfortunately, ethics in enterprise is a very limited domain, even in business schools. The emphasis seems to be more on proper bookkeeping, integrity of documentation and simple morality of truthfulness and more. There can be nothing wrong with that. However, there are other core issues. It doesn't happen only in diamonds. It has to do with matters big and small, including child labour. There was a newspaper report of crystals colonising Tucson in February 2019. This was the month of the Tucson gem shows, perhaps the largest crystal expo in the world. A very large species of businessmen, from new-age enthusiasts to major wholesalers would number amongst the customers and there are no prizes for guessing that the US and Europe dominate the users. They include everything, from museums to crystal healers, yoga centres to wellness retailers. This is a specific fallout of the wellness fever which has swept the world. Go to any city or aspiring city and one business which is on the uptake is that of crystals and gems. There is nothing wrong with that. The only thing is that in a world where so many things are being converted into revenue items, there is little surprise that being social media-friendly lubricates business. Aesthetics, combined with cosmic spirituality, is a heady cocktail. Healing crystals are a great rage and when anything becomes such a trend, passions, the like of which can only be selectively discussed, enter the scene. Today there is a crystal for every occasion. The celebrities, the collectors, the investors are all into it.

Predictably, the concept of ambient energy enters the scene. Yet, the fate of miners of crystals, even in the age of rose quartz, reminded one of scenes from the 'Blood Diamond'. There is almost a conspiracy of silence because enthusiastic patrons of all kinds of causes, from the most obvious to more subtle ones, are a dime a dozen. However, there appear to be very few applying scrutiny to the crystal industry. There is no certification of fair trade in crystals. Transparency schemes, the likes of which are there for gold and diamond, are yet to enter the crystal industry in any significant way. Perhaps one day, management experts will wake up to the sorry state of affairs and the despicable conditions of some of the poorest of the poor involved in the mining for crystals. Perhaps they will make an issue of matters of human dignity and sound working conditions, if not of terrible business practices. Hope that day comes soon.

January 06, 2020

## An Opportunity to Reinvent

At the time of writing these lines, news had just come that the Jammu & Kashmir administration will host a three-day global investors' summit from October 12 in Srinagar. Part of it will also be held in Jammu. An MoU has been signed by the Jammu & Kashmir Trade Promotion Organisation and the Confederation of Indian Industries (CII) to organise and manage the event. Supposedly, the meet will give the State an opportunity to showcase its approach and a possibility of it entering the global market in a major way. It will also presumably put to rest some anxieties that have arisen due to recent changes in the functioning of the State. It should be a useful occasion to familiarise those who are interested in knowing the potential of the natural resources of this idyllic State and its infrastructure. This should not be a template meet like the ones that have been held in Tamil Nadu, Uttar Pradesh or West Bengal. Reasons for this are different. Natural resources found in Jammu & Kashmir are unlikely to be found in any other Indian State.

And it's not just the horticulture and a wide range of agricultural products but also raw materials and the perception thereof.

Consider the case of Taiwan, a small island in the East Asian region—small enough not to have any significant raw material but is large enough to innovate with foresight.

Ceramic products of this nation is celebrated globally for their design and finesse. They range from tea cups to plaques. Their quality sets its own standards. Couple this with the place Taiwan has earned in the world of information technology, which is also the key to its incredible prosperity. The knowledgeable are aware that Taiwan has resources of foreign exchange in excess of its needs. Indeed, it also has all the problems of plenty.

Learning from the example of Taiwan can be a source of policy challenges in its own right.

The hills of the Kashmir Valley and the rugged terrain of Udhampur or of the Kathua region hold a huge potential of literally converting the hill dust to aesthetic and functional products. What is needed is raw material and the vision to redesign products out of it.

Some of this is already being done. It is now possible to buy from the markets of Kashmir tea sets or dinner sets, which are a visual and utilitarian delight. The only deficiency is that they do not have brand value. Whether the proposed investors' summit will be able to plug this gap is an interesting question, to which, time alone can provide the answer. Clearly, it has to do much more than just famous names descending in the Valley to lend celebrity value to an area, which has already been reeling under severe challenges of mental recalibration. At this stage of development, equal attention needs to be paid to reconstructing mindsets as well. Locals were earning a livelihood and had the propensity to multiply the business under the pre-August 6 dispensation. The uninitiated would have to be helped to trust the new dispensation. They would begin to believe when results start rolling.

The unmatched skills of artisans in Jammu & Kashmir in Pashmina shawls and the sheer hard work on different types of base material have a rich potential of being converted into useful and marketable products. This can have a global demand, too. It can also leverage the income potential of a region, which is not always identified with prosperity but is always known for its acumen. Talking of tourism and fruit production is to talk about costs as well as gainful employment of a substantial part of the population. However, a much more significant dimension of the State's economy is its potential in aesthetics and revenue generation, supported by business-friendly policies of the Government. What is needed is infrastructure for connectivity, which is now beginning to bloom. The skilled as well as unskilled manpower now has a lot of opportunities knocking at its door. They hold the potential of being unprecedented in its boom. Investment in this region and the coupling of the potential with possibilities may well open a new chapter for their trouble-riddled existence.

Hopefully, Ladakh will not be left out from the focus of the investment summit. With its own version of aesthetics and knowledge management of tribal products, this region has an untold story of humongous dimension. In a joint initiative, the Tribal Cooperative Marketing Development Federation of India (TRIFED) is organising a Aadi Mahotsav or National Tribal Festival in the third week of August. This is the first of its kind. It knocks at the door of immense possibilities. In a wonderful country like India, sky is not the limit of innovation and rediscovery. If it can soar anywhere, it can soar in India. Jammu & Kashmir may just be a fitting locale of TRIFED's next frontier. The global investors meet could possibly pick up threads from there, too.

August 19, 2019

## Nurture Neglected Businesses

Forest wealth is one of the biggest assets for India. It needs application of principles, creativity and innovation in the same scale and intensity as has been done in the larger R&D section of manufacturing and services. Application of the principles of subtraction, modification, addition, alteration and more of the creativity process to the sequence of modification of the produce will add value to the product. To illustrate, substracting the content of sulphur in hydro carbon products makes the petrol less polluting. The principles of creativity and innovation do not end with such transformations alone. They include practices of attribute listing, forced matching, synectics and the list can be long.

The inability to institutionalise these interventions on forest products like tamarind and chiraunji among others has come in the way of product value addition. It is everyone's loss—from the general public, who would have gained from the medicinal property of tamarind to the gatherer, who gets less remunerative prices.

It does not need a genius to realise that *Sal* leaf can be used for *dona* making or indeed peeling together all petals for popular use. This would have been hygienic and economical for the user and remunerative to those who collect. In fact, *Sal* seed, which is generally used for oil extraction, can be used as a bio fuel. Putting together cow dung on shafts of the corn plant or the bare paddy plants and drying them has served useful service in bringing light to areas where electricity may not have reached. Local innovation plays a crucial role in making life not only more bearable but also joyful. Organised R&D, which is often a fallout of formal education, has by and large not shown much awareness for such interventions of innovation at the grassroot level. It does not need a genius to know that tamarind seed powder is an input in the medical sector and can also be used for talc and starch purposes.

Similar is the story of *Mahua* seeds, which can yield bio fuel. They can have good usage, say in proportion of 20 per cent in petroleum fuel for vehicles. There is nothing against Western paradigm of research. Similarly, there can be nothing against R&D

efforts. But the plea in these lines is to widen the ambit of R&D in a manner which is a win-win situation for all. The Tribal Cooperative Marketing Development Federation of India (TRIFED) is trying to attempt at this. However, the world of possibilities is so large that resource of one institution cannot possibly plug the gap. Indeed, it will be very difficult even for an institution, which is commercially oriented. To do this, R&D is needed. This will give large-scale benefits to make it not just commercially viable but remunerative for all stakeholders. For some strange reason, businesses do not see this as an opportunity.

This is not the only sector which has defaulted in larger processes of Indian industry and business. A young graduating engineer with a management degree will not seek employment in a unit manufacturing, say of the industrial alcohol in the rural sector. Even though he may be given a sprawling farm house or extensive club facilities and support to commutations to towns and more, he will still be reluctant. His first choice will remain employment in the larger sector say of FMCG, IT or finance division in a metropolis. It does not matter to him that living conditions over there are often harsh, requiring him to travel long distances and long hours in inhospitable conditions. Daily chores keep gnawing at whatever cushion time he can snatch from ever expanding office hours.

Such is human nature: It is often riddled with contradictions and attracted towards the incoherent. Trying to keep up with the trend, many keep chasing at a mirage of comfort. These are subtler issues of orientation and acclimatisation of value systems which gain approval. Social climbing in circles, where one seeks acceptability, is a push factor. Tribal welfare and interventions may even make business sense but being bereft of social glamour, they have very little pull factor. The argument of going to the tribal areas to do some good to the communities is a facetious one—it is neither true nor fair to the tribal world. So the talent in dominant percentages does not move in the right direction in significant numbers. Without this talent intervention, communities in not so fashionable areas don't reap the harvest of technology at a sufficient scale. This needs serious thought. Unfortunately, snazzy economist paradigms and a large percentage in corridors of power have found little time to address these issues.

Indeed, many of the tribal products can fuel favourites of the urban communities, for example *chiraunji* seed, which is popular in many areas, including Jharkhand and is a useful input to the ice cream industry. Perhaps in the business of the linkages indicated above, all are left the poorer by the neglect.

July 22, 2019

## Unconventional but Effective Measures

The financial markets are in a state of churning—in more senses than one. The present times are seminal. Simultaneously, multiple moves are being made. Even in the best of times it is only the rare and the gifted who see with clarity the implications of their action in cognate or distant areas. In normal times such line of vision is a rarity.

Consider the case of ports and the banks—these are two seemingly unrelated areas but they have a cusp. There is an attempt, and rightly so, to create Special Economic Zone (SEZ) around some ports. The writer of this article recalls his experience as a consultant at the Dubai Port Authority in a similar area. In case of India, the SEZ development is projected to begin with around Jawaharlal Nehru Port Trust. For this, 277 hectares are to be put aside.

This zone is about five kilometres away from the port. The target is to develop 100 acres by December. Various global manufacturing companies are interested. The chief executive officer of the JNPT, SEZ, S. Sittarasu, has a reputation of competence. For competence to show results in such an environment, the powers of the special planning authority need to be bestowed on the SEZ. Here, the Maharashtra Regional and Town Planning Act, 1966, would get into play. The steps appear obvious but can get complicated.

A parallel look at the shipping industry will also bring to fore postures which would need to be reconciled. If one keeps in mind that 95 per cent of India's trading, by volume, and 70 per cent by value is moved through maritime resources, then the importance of shipping is obvious. Yet, the type of vessels which are used by shipping firms are essentially second-hand acquisitions, acquired internationally. Gaps in the Indian capacity in shipping gets a further twist with Goods and Services Tax (GST).

GST has predictably raised various issues of tax burden on the Indian shipping companies. If things continue as they are, a major concern is going to be the levy of five per cent Integrated Goods and Service Tax (IGST). This would cover both inter-State supply of goods and services and imports.

The implication for capital cost and working capital is obvious. It would have been challenging to foresee these contradictions before they started surfacing.

The domain expertise, sector for sector, simply cannot be handled without domain knowledge. There is, however, a practical limit to access the very extensive list of domain expertise that would be required for operationalising the concept of GST on the ground. It is a fit case for giving sufficient time for the industry bodies to react. Unfortunately, far too much time was lost on political squabbles. Sorting out the operational economic and financial knots too needs time.

Unfortunately, the experience at squabbling doesn't seem to have ended. The brave words of disagreement from the Finance Minister of West Bengal, Amit Mitra, coming in May end, are too well known for repetition. Putting it in simple terms, there seems to be several grey points in the operationalisation of GST.

Reference had been made earlier on this text to the banking sector. Interestingly, the S&P Bombay Stock Exchange banking index has flagged the rise in its index by over 30 per cent. The key player seems to be Yes Bank, IndusInd Bank, Axis Bank, Kotak Mahindra bank, HDFC etc. One can go looking for the Public Sector Undertaking (PSU) banks and their growth patterns. The impaired loan of PSU bank stood at 13.4 per cent while it stood at 4.4 per cent for the private banks. Clearly, more rationalisations are in order.

To sum up, if the foregoing contradictions are placed on a bed of unrelated and at times 'sudden appearance factors', the complexity is compounded. Consider the infusion of cash in the market by payment of arrears of the Seventh Pay Commission. Consider the sudden welcome break of the monsoon beginning with the showers on the shores of Kerala.

The cash infusion will cause a boom at several places, including in the auto sector. The rains would lead to higher take of the agricultural produce. Scenes can and do the change. There is a need to put all this together for a cohesive public policy coupled with quick action. It needs a specialised mechanism, methodology and a group of exceptionally gifted people to work in harmony.

June 05, 2017

## How Entrepreneurship Evolved for the Better

Entrepreneurship means different things to different people. A part of the problem is that everyone does not quite see that it can be perceived differently to what they see as elements of entrepreneurship. The word itself originated in France in the end of 18th century where a person, who made his fortunes by seeking wealth, often by the dint of his might, made it good.

Times were different then. The French polity itself was in a turmoil. Those who could not make it good went out of France to different parts of the French empire to generate wealth.

Clearly, this was a model which was not unique to the French. However, as the concept spread, it became increasingly common to use the word 'entrepreneur' for people who made fortunes by their outgoing and risk-taking nature.

Quite simply, risk-taking for profit maximisation became the core definition of an entrepreneur or indeed entrepreneurship.

It was clearly overlooked that ever since the Homo-sapiens became conscious of stocking up or accumulating assets for a lean period, there has been a practice of entrepreneuring. It is important to recognise that risk was manifold. It meant competition with others who may be trying to do the same thing.

There would be the risk of life and limb from the animals, if one was trying to stock up food for the winter or the rainy season. There would be risk from the element and nature and the list goes on.

It should be clear from the above description that any lifestyle which did not have assured wages for defined services could broadly be termed as entrepreneurship.

In the early Indian literature, in different languages, including Tamil, Sanskrit and various dialects, which had a literary manifestation, there is both text and poetry eulogising risk-taking for profit maximisation.

In an euro-centric world, it may be worth emphasising that though the crusades of the 11, 12, 13, 14 centuries, the quickest way to get rich for many Europeans was to join the attacking Armies which saw victory over the West Euro-Asian empires as there life mission. This was both obvious and popular.

In the modern times, however, like in many areas, the problem has grown deeper and wider. Today, entrepreneurship is practiced with numerous permutations and combinations of business and ownership.

There are the multinational organisations. At times they are in a proprietary mode and on other occasions, they are in a partnership mode, sometimes private sometimes quasi-private. The list is again long.

Governments in many parts of the world have found it convenient to respond to the problem of employment through talk of self-employment and support in various manners.

Entrepreneurship can be of various categories. There are nations where the entrepreneur and his firm is classified as cottage, small, medium and large. This categorisation can also vary from region-to-region.

In some parts of the world, a number of people who are employed, become a category for classification. In other parts of the world, the amount of money invested becomes the cut-off point.

The basis of such categorisation is not to be taken lightly because it becomes the touchstone of the distinguishing characteristics of the scale of entrepreneurship.

Since governmental support and institutional favours are a factor of the type of entrepreneurship one visualises, as being worthy of support, the defining index may have a very significant relation with the nature of growth of small enterprises.

This support can tilt the favour significantly in favour of one class of entrepreneurship or another. Again there is a possible classification of entrepreneurial venture through the life cycle approach. There may be starts up, they may be medium size enterprises nudging sickness or growing well. Indeed, they may be large entrepreneurial enterprises tending to burst into the powerful businessman's circle.

That the present Government in India seems to be pushing for start-ups is clearly a multi-pronged strategy of development, the core of which seems to be to provide means of livelihood to the young and the aspiring class. Like many things this need not be stated, but what is understood—without being stated—is perhaps the most powerful statement.

May 27, 2016

## Ignore Political Gossip, Talk Development

There is something strange about the public discourse in India, where much time is spent on political discussions and little time given to alternative models of development. When this writer raised this issue with a group of researchers and academics, he was told that this was because India was a resource-scarce country.

This writer did not know what to make of the response because India is not a 'resource scarce' nation. Consider energy—so long as the sun shines on any patch of land, India cannot have a resource-scarce experience.

So far as water is concerned, the number of Indian rivers is so large that it is enough to provide adequate water with planning. This is not without even taking the oceans into consideration.

Twenty years ago, Singapore was fully dependent on Malaysia for its water needs. Today, it meets three-fourths of its drinking water demand on its own. Through desalination, Singapore has almost eliminated its dependence on others for potable water.

Kerala, with a coastline that is 640 km long and whose depth rarely exceeds more than 66 km at any point, has an almost perennial water shortage. Almost three-fourths of its potable water drains into the sea.

There is a lot that is said of the cultural diversity of Kerala and much on its land issues. There is nothing wrong with this. What is equally true is the sheer inadequacy of effort to harness Kerala's water resources, either through storage or desalination.

There is not adequate space in the social discourse on the water problem or the energy problem. Of course, complaints are there, but what is missing is the significant, impact-making search for solutions.

The proposition is simple: There are serious doubts in assuming India to be a resource-scarce situation. It is, therefore, obvious that the disproportionate spaces occupied by political issues in the public mind cannot be explained by a 'resource-rich' situation.

Another group of self-styled thinkers, when confronted by this writer on such a situation of eschewed emphasis on political issues, tried to explain it away by saying that politics in India gets huge attention because it is one of the quicker ways of social climbing; perhaps also a quicker way of getting rich. This writer had no means of analysing the statement.

The third reason they gave is even more ingenious. They felt that politics had great value in a country where formal avenues of engagement and entertainment were short. Be that as it may, any undue emphasis on any one aspect of collective life is not good for the whole.

If discussions on development and the options for growth are few in public discourse, that is not good news. Elsewhere in Asia, there is a different slant in the media—both printed and electronic.

Indeed the kind of discussions, seminars and symposiums that are held in our country are also typical. A cursory look at their topics is easy to analyse in terms of biases. The focus is on favourite themes of the contemporary powers that be.

'Pura', as a concept, faded out with the eclipse of former President APJ Abdul Kalam. Celebrating diversity, as a concept, faded with former Prime Minister Manmohan Singh. Examples are many.

These are often attempts often to seek political dividends from existing power centres and not necessarily a genuine enquiry into a line of thought. Unless this is corrected, politics will continue to be the prima donna of public discourse.

Constant discussion on the struggle of power also comes out of a situation where there is little faith in systems and procedures. It gives undue importance to processes which have little to do with developmental thinking. It can do little good and its capacity to do harm is large. Even for a significant and purposeful struggle for power, it has to be informed and dynamic in nature.

Without losing one's contact with reality and one's own roots, one has to be open to inputs from the experiences and learnings of others. The same is valid for good thoughts to come from all sides. It is then that meaningful social discourse takes roots and leads to a purposeful search for direction.

May 29, 2015

## Public-sector Units are Family Jewels

Interest in the public-sector is on the upswing. The reasons are many. Given the tattered state of the Government treasuries (both at the Centre and the States), obviously there is a huge urge to source for funds.

Compulsion of economic need has led to some action, in areas which were earlier beyond the domain of civil discourse. The reference is to black money. At least the first step has been taken to shatter this glass ceiling.

Similarly, the temptation to sell the shares of public-sector companies is large. There are few successful public-sector enterprises. The Rajasthan Minerals and Metal Corporation is one of the notable exceptions. Many of the Government's enterprises serve the purpose of providing creature comforts and perquisites to public figures of bad political fortunes but important political profiles. However, the worth of State Government public enterprises even with divestment will be little.

The case of Central Government undertakings is somewhat different. Many have their eyes on Maharatnas, Navratna and Miniratnas. The truth is that these agencies provide the source of support and indulgence to the ruling power elite. Their guest houses and their transport support are used and, of course, they provide sponsorships to the preferred activities of the political elite.

Recall the over Rs. 10 crore contribution of a Maharatna to the All India Football Federation not so long ago, because a politically powerful person of the day wanted it to be so. Hence, the divestment of even the successful Central Government undertakings is going to be few and cautious.

Yet, another source of income for the Government is the land in possession of public enterprises such as the Railways, the Port Trusts and more. Here there is huge potential but also the scope for mischief is enormous. Recall sale experiences of some specialised hotels under the infrastructure-related ministries some years ago.

Hence, the functioning of the public enterprises is one of the key inputs to the state of the economy. This is both a positive indicator and a loaded one.

One aspect of State functioning which has not received adequate attention is the traditions which they inherited in the domain of administrative action or commercial operations. Consider the case of Rajasthan till the merger of Principalities. It had a large number of Princedoms which were got merged. The extant systems of administration were superseded by a civil administration which had little percolation to pre-industrial habitats. The results are there for all to see.

Many Principalities of Rajasthan were well administered; there happiness quotient was significant. The post-integration administration had little use of these practices.

There are other stories in other States. Earlier this month I was in Hyderabad, in the older part of the city, which reeks of deprivation and penury. I was staying at the Falaknuma Palace on a small hilltop which reeked equally of opulence and prosperity. A jewel of the Nizam dynasty, it is now run by the India Group of Hotels for profit.

To understand this contrast between penury and prosperity one has to understand how the Asaf Jah rulers functioned from 1724 to 1950. The Nizams accumulated wealth with great diligence while much of Telangana populace grovelled in poverty. The last Nizam, Osman Ali Khan, was reputed to be the richest man in the world. Notwithstanding the leakages, his jewels were acquired by the Government of India at a price of nearly Rs. 250 crore after much legal wrangling.

People have narrated examples of how investments of Andhra origin now lay threatened in Hyderabad under the new dispensation, after the bifurcation of the State.

As of today, even private investments are internally threatened and in the last decade or so, business houses have shown a huge propensity to invest abroad.

The public sector has, in many ways, been cannibalised for varied commercial purposes. Units which have survived and are successful today are now threatened with sale. Small palliatives provide temporary succour. Time has come to re-invent administration. Mere reforms may prove pyrrhic.

July 11, 2014

## Task of Building a Strong and New India Lies Ahead

Different adjectives are used for the times we are living through. Up-market expressions currently in vogue include 'churning', 'samundramanthan', 'turbulence' and more on these lines. When delivered in a Western environment with cocktails flowing, and degrees from Oxbridge or Harvard being the common denominator, such expressions are particularly impressive. Heads shake despondently and the front foot is tapped with great wisdom. In-depth analysis is offered and carefully calibrated agreements and disagreements are exchanged, in a know-all atmosphere. Then, the whole conversation is pushed in to oblivion more sooner than later.

But this is only one part of the story. From here, the affected domain is forks into two. One part does not adequately realise that turbulence is global and not exclusively Indian. The other part has never travelled without aide to register what life in the raw can be like.

Things are changing all over the world. The era of capitalism has undergone multiple forms. A few decades ago, it was about creating higher levels of comfort, but is now more concerned about nurturing ideas that can change lives.

Similarly, after the disintegration of the USSR, China became the face of communism. As is now widely realised, one of the many things significant about China is its ability to change prices of various items across the world. When there is turbulence at the foundation, the shaking of the leaves is only symptomatic.

New building materials, like new sources of energy, are redefining life. Old palaces are not only passé but fit only for use as offices or resorts. The fast-moving, consumer goods firms stand transformed and the consultant does not have a clue about the paradigm that has changed so dramatically.

Tata Nano cars may not be a success in India but similar models across the world are encouraging innovation in fuel-consumption and emission technology. The fuel ecosystem has moved on to use of gas. In Gujarat alone cost efficiency of industries have gone up by about 32 per cent with gas use. Across the world, people are looking to the heritage variable for alternative models.

In India, while we believe that for 67 years we have worked to create a secular state, the reality is of 'competitive communalism'. The world over communities are breaking barriers for better internal egalitarianism; in India, the state is erecting barriers to social egalitarianism. The world is talking of creating new labour opportunities and new market values; in India, we like to provide political harvest to inherited castes.

The cocktail circles will be largely oblivious to the state of the roads in the unfashionable parts of India. Forget the romanticised version of the countryside, even the national highways in many parts are in a poor state. Take the case of NH-34. Say in West Bengal, between Dhalkola to Raiganj, roughly a 65 to 75 km stretch, the condition of the highway is such when one starts on that road, he does not know how he will emerge at the other end. I went to this unfashionable part of the world, a few days ago.

The surer and more sensible way of negotiating this stretch is through the villages of Nangor, Rotela, Tajpur and Bombichi. The enterprising drivers plunges into unknown village roads to beat the traffic jams, which can last several days.

This is not turbulence; it is discordance. One could have used a stronger word. And herein lies the job of building an India which is true and strong. And I hope, this will happen some day.

December 27, 2013

## Education must be as Local as it is Global

Industrial revolution in its present incarnation is an ongoing process that began around the third quarter of 19th century. It is different from several industrial revolutions that preceded it as there has always been a break in the continuity of those other revolutions. It is this longitudinal perspective on the evolution of industrial revolutions that is necessary to appreciate what is currently happening.

However, it is a latitudinal perspective on industrial revolution that could make it is still more interesting a phenomenon to observe. A good question to ask would be how has the industrial revolution affected different parts of the world? It is here that a comparative perspective is not only helpful but also critical to understanding some of the processes. The effect of the industrial revolution, say, in Brazil is different from the effect of the industrial revolution in China. Indeed each of the BRIC countries have been affected differently. The comparative study of the impact of the industrial revolution in different parts of the world throws up a very interesting paradigm which needs to be examined.

Exploring it would show that impact of industrial revolution in different parts of the globe in the primary and secondary stages have a wide range of variation. This variation tends to be smoother and made common in the tertiary or the maturity phase.

Thus it is, that, in the primary and the secondary stage of impact, the political orientations are wide and the debate on the frameworks of social interventions are large. They often convert themselves into political battles and in the tertiary situation, modes of governance become more important instrument of channelising energy.

By the same token if a given region does not experience any industrial revolution then political norms are bound to be different and the developmental trajectory would be quite unique in that region. Perhaps impact of industrial revolution is one of the largest symbolic variables in studying social unrest, turmoil or trajectory of the developmental processes. This would also affect the nature of knowledge management in each territory and the structure and the processes of educational interventions.

Illustratively, it is difficult to move directly from agrarian society to a knowledge-based economy. The chaos can be many times more confounding if the sources of curriculum and content of learning is imitative of what is taught in industrial or post-industrial societies. The sheer irrelevance of what is sought to be taught in the educational institutions of a society to what it needs will cause dissonance. It will be so in managing aspirations and creating a situation where use of such learning is forever crippling to an individual's ability to adapt to local conditions.

There is a case, therefore, to revisit the curriculum and the method of instruction keeping in mind not only an international reference point but also the demands of the local context. Even so there are classical postulates which remain the postulates of 'learning to learn' and define characteristics of a good human being. These would continue to be relevant.

Also, there needs to be a recognition of the process that the objectives, while being defined in material terms, cannot overlook the objectives in rarified terms, of happiness or a sense of fulfilment.

The material and the contentment component have a third variable which gets intertwined with the rest of the processes and that demand is of security. Obviously, material well-being and emotional happiness cannot flourish in an atmosphere of insecurity. This perspective can be appreciated, but how to achieve it remains a core planning objective. Somewhere, the ability to anticipate, mitigate and manage risks becomes important. However, dealing with risks as a concept, is itself a relatively new territory of exploration. To that extent, the intellectual challenge and excitement of today is as large and intense as it was in the renaissance period.

July 26, 2013

## When the hills Came Crashing Down

There is something about the continuing depredation in Uttarakhand which does not seem right. Barring the heroic efforts of the Armed Forces, which have indeed been of epic proportions, there is little that gives a sense of hope and confidence.

Earlier this week, it was reported that a meeting would be held to decide if the tragedy in Uttarakhand could be called a 'national disaster'. I have no means to know if such a meeting was called, but a friend of mine who moves in the right circles, counselled me that "it does not matter. It is not going to affect the flow of funds." If that is all that is to be said, then by that logic the concept of a 'national disaster' is in itself a misnomer. Nothing ever need be termed a 'national disaster'.

Public sector units which are known to cough up money when a convention is held or when sponsorship is required, have, however, been conspicuous by their business-as-usual-approach. (Of course, the condition for making donations usually is that someone influential must ask them to do so.) Be it among the Maharatnas, Navratnas or Mini-ratnas, the silence is thundering. Is it because no one powerful, in their reckoning, has asked them to donate towards relief activities?

The story does not end here. The Union Minister for Home Affairs is concerned about individual States and their leaders carrying out relief operations in Uttarakhand —as if the relief operations are so heavily subscribed that there is no scope for un-invited entrants!

As for the Chief Minister of Uttarakhand, he has said that there were no violations of green laws and that little can be done if there is a cloudburst. Further, he threatened that 'developmental activities' (presumably as defined by him) will not cease. Uttarakhand, he argued, is a frontier State with Chinese roads coming right up to the border.

Perhaps there was some piece of logic here that remains unclear, because one was under the impression that the issue at hand was illegal construction on river beds and flood banks. Who said anything about roads?

Also, someone should have asked the Chief Minister if the cloudbursts were really such an unheard of phenomenon or if the flash floods had never happened before? Why then did his hilly State have no preparation at all?

If only the chances of something bad happening are to determine the nature and extent of pre-cautionary measures taken to protect oneself against it, then fire extinguishers installed in many places are a waste. Indeed, any fire station should only have the number of fire trucks that is directly proportional to the number of times that they have actually been used to put out a fire.

There are thousands trapped in the mountains, with no access to aid. To understand the poignancy of the situation, one must ask how one would have reacted if their loved ones were lost in that region and one had no way of knowing about their welfare.

The media has been replete with reports of how the high-and-mighty have been using their influence to ensure their friends and family members enjoy priority in evacuation efforts. But why not use that same influence to push the Uttarakhand administration to take proactive action in the next round of relief efforts?

A good beginning would be to at least recognise one's lapses and stop sounding glib about it. Various explanations and speculations abound about the disaster.

A newspaper report claims that the huge flow of water around Srinagar in the State was caused by the authorities opening a tunnel on June 16. On the same night, Kedar valley above Srinagar was deluged. The theory goes that flooding in Kedarnath was caused by lightning strikes on a glacier, which let out a huge amount of water that was locked inside. Clearly, some answers are still needed.

June 28, 2013

## Let's Work for Gross National Happiness

The times that we live in are complex to the point that only a high degree of maturity and knowledge can show the way. The energy considerations are an obvious point of reference. The global reality is driving up prices and putting pressure on enterprises.

To control cost, a focus on raw material and process efficiency is no longer enough. One needs to carefully manage, besides energy, other valuable natural resources that enable one's business and existence. From taking people to work or delivering products to customers, or making office and data centre operate with efficiency, one has to manage resources that are largely hidden from sight.

What is needed is an integrated approach to tangible and intangible resources. One needs to move towards a holistic understanding of sustainability. This cannot be confined to a focus on energy and environment only. The developmental idea has to be fuller and complete. To reconcile various contending pressures into a unified focus is the challenge of the times.

The increasing quantum of waste and pollution and the rising prices of raw materials are well-recognised problems. There is a growing recognition of the threat caused by green house gas emissions which have brought the world to a critical point, where actions in each and every region of the planet have widespread effect.

The demands on national governance are changing because the nature of challenges is changing. The solution would lie in technology infusion, infrastructure development, financial infusion and proactive capability development.

The poverty of large masses of people has worrying human dimensions. The fruits of development are eschewed and no one enjoys them in their fullness. The economies of need are beginning to dominate the developmental debate. If one out of three cannot afford two square meals a day, and education of the next generation remains a luxury, then security and peace are bound to be at crossroads.

There are also other concomitant results of poverty, absence of education, poor education and uneven distribution of wealth. Competency, in such a context, cannot grow as required. If competency does not grow, development and ultimately gross national happiness will be a casualty.

The objective is to create core competencies in major areas which also enable production and availability of quality goods. A shift in the paradigm of development is needed to manage the change better. The focus cannot be solely on the tangible. There is a never changing characteristic of human resources and social behaviour which often overrule the efforts that ignore them. The social fabric can lead to devastating circumstances.

The multiple social identities of Indians are forever being reinforced for the cultivation of power. This has a dangerous potential of spinning out of hand. While they may fare well in the light of electoral politics, there is a need to check their growth. This is what developmental planning must also include. But this needs maturity and knowledge and sobriety too. The continuous multiplication of social identities may hinder the collective progress of society.

Technology has a powerful hand in social regulation. This has to be carefully nurtured. The power of social networks is also in speeding up word-of-mouth exchanges. There is a need to contain the tinting of the content at each exchange.

What is challenging is not only the ease with which panic can be introduced but the rapid change in social fabric that it can bring about. It is relatively easy to react and respond to the existing social structure. But when matters are in a state of flux, it is another situation altogether.

Pre-emptive localised strategies which balance the system that keep global enterprises efficient must be explored. Gross national happiness has to be the ultimate gainer.

May 31, 2013

## Changes in Time Sequence and the Relevance of the Insights therefrom

Any civilization can be periodised in different manners. The easiest, simplest, and perhaps, the most widely used, categorization is through period-marking political power. Thus, there is talk of emperors, kings, and territories. There is nothing wrong with this.

Perhaps one can think of the basis of periodization which can make it be more complete.

This realisation is not new because it led to concepts such as 'Dark Ages', 'Renaissance', and more. Again, there is a limitation. The limitation is that the experiences of the dominant power become defining elements of periodization, and what was true for European powers may not be true for what was then happening in Latin America, Asia, or Australia. Further analyses can be given, but they do not necessarily substantiate the point any better.

Another dimension used in periodicing, in history is the use of the 'dominant material' or element in a given period.

Thus, one learns of the Stone Age, the Iron Age, and more. These categories also go a distance, but they are good only as far as they go.

History of business is no exception to the pattern noted above. Any civilised community needs business to survive. This is so because no element or component of a society is ever fully self-sufficient. Illustratively, if one grows cereals, one still needs vegetables, and if one grows both cereals and vegetables, one would need to be able to store them and, therefore, elements and materials from which shelter can be built, would need to be obtained. Hence, there is always a need for something that can be traded for what one can give. Exchanges have their own compulsion.

That is the Root of Business.

The history of business is the history of these exchanges in chronological order. One of the common characteristics of the study of history is the study of "exchanges" in time sequence. Various categorisations of history emerged because there were different kind of exchanges. Each sector of human activity had its own periodization.

The Homo sapien is a common thread, but the needs of the Homo sapien are large. Accordingly, different versions and variants of histories emerge.

It is a pity that historiography as a craft has not captured this point sufficiently. This is not a reflection on the state of the craft of historiography, but on the state of the dominant concerns in history. As enumerated above, it can be prudent to take up the use of 'metal' or 'material' as a basis for creating periodization.

If one could take a leap from this point of perception to the present, the experience could be both fascinating and instructive. A history of modern times will talk of world wars, the struggle of freedom movements, the emergence of global and regional conglomerates, the birth of international bodies, and more. But what one has missed, is the history of the tribal worlds across the globe.

Whether it be tribes of the Maya region or Asiatic region, United States, Canada, or Tribal communities in the deep, colder climes of Europe; tribal communities in Asia or Australia—one cannot help but be struck by their continuity of existence and perception. One marvels at their ability to distil life lessons, which they not only deciphered but preserved. This could well be part of the subjects of research for the understanding of modernism.

This is so because no element of the modern world has the continuity, depth, or reach which the tribal world has. If at all there is a lesson to be learnt from the experiences of history, one has to go back to the understanding of how these tribal worlds have survived and grown. Even when being threatened, they have kept alive their production systems, strategic systems, or businesses. There is an urgent need to understand this. This can be very useful in put to the perspective for understanding changes in time sequence.

Business history of this perspective will indeed enrich the insights on how to conduct future businesses and make it more worthwhile.

September 01, 2023

## Some Policy Perspectives at a Micro Level of Livelihood and Economy

There is a story of the agricultural sector beyond slogans: the story is real because it is affecting the distribution of money in the rural sector as well as the cropping pattern. It goes somewhat like the following narrative:

Following the market pattern, productivity of the soil and the nature of the irrigation pattern, there can be a switch from cereal cultivation to cash crop cultivation and vice versa. At a micro level, it may not appear to be a very significant switch, whether from cereal to cash crop or cash crop to cereal. However, as the skill changes, the switch becomes a significant factor in the economy. This is so because availability and utilisation pattern of the cereal and the cash crop are not interchangeable.

Illustratively, rice or pulses are cereals, whereas sugarcane or spices are examples of cash crops. Both, cereals and cash crop cultivation have their exclusive skill profiles. As such, the switch from one to the other has a double edged potential and very often affects the overall supply situation. Magnify the scale, and the problem becomes enormous.

Yet another element in the sequence is 'livelihood', which in certain cases is dependent on support services like carpentry, blacksmithing, electrical maintenance, and more. This sector may be called the tertiary sector. A shift from cereals to cash crops or vice versa can cause significant shake ups. A shift from growing crops to rendering services in the tertiary sector can cause convulsions in the professional equilibrium. The return on effort in the tertiary sector is significantly higher and more enduring. The income from cultivation, whether cash crops or cereals, is lower, and hence the takers are fewer.

As already mentioned above, the return from cash crop cultivation is higher and richer than the return from cereal cultivation. Hence, the hierarchy of the pull factor for eligible youth seeking livelihood, is dominated by the tertiary sector, followed by livelihood in the cultivation of cash crops, followed by seeking livelihood in the cultivation of cereals. Such a demand side may not necessarily be in sync with requirements of a balanced economy.

Indeed, the realities of the national economy would also vary from region to region. In certain regions, there may be a shortage of cash crops of a certain variety, while in another region there may be a shortage of certain types of cereals. Net-net, there may be an overall shortage of takers in the tertiary sector. This is where the buck stops, and considered intervention becomes necessary. The logic of the market need not necessarily overlap with the logic of the economic needs. A given region may be short on agricultural products but may have an adequate supply of manpower in the tertiary sector. Clearly, the numerical imbalance will create further maldistribution of numbers across sectors with shortages in one segment and surpluses in another.

This cannot be handled at the central level or, at times, even at the state level. This has to be handled at the local level through thought through policy and regulation. Such interventions at the local level with policy perspective are an uncommon phenomenon. There is a need to put this in position.

The result is twists and turns from the supply side to the demand side, with little resonance in social reality. One family with three earning adults may succumb to the economy pressures, if each of the three adults has different earnings because of the choices of the segment. This can range from producing cereal crops to cash crops to work in the tertiary sector. This kind of economic transience would result in unplanned migrations. The result can be manifold including decrease in the value of land, thereby causing reverberations in the social fabric at the local level.

The outcome is obvious: there is a serious possibility of distortion in the local economy, disturbing the economic viability or indeed the health of the social economic systems at a local level. This is a situation that cannot be ignored. Such a situation requires long-term patience sustained thinking with action in operational terms.

It would require effective local-level research analysis leading to a package of responses. These responses could be in the form of market facilities, subsidised rates of procurement, or even the setting up of a cooperative to determine and control the supply chain requirement.

However, before any or all of this can happen, a consensus will have to be created for this kind of proposition. This would need support at the local level. The local educational institution and the administration heads would need to work together for this proposition. They would need to be far-sighted and responsible enough to design and implement it from concept to commissioning. Significant effort is needed, there is very little option.

May 01, 2023

## Changing Times and Timing Change

It is common sense to recognise that everything changes. People change, context changes, the environment changes, even the nature of the material changes over a period of time. It is, therefore, important to have some insights into understanding how to cope up with change. The more complex problems are those that have to do with the internal changes within us, about us and above all changes in the way we think. These are subtle and at times elusive propositions. The trickier aspect is the search of continuity in this change.

When it touches business, it acquires ramifications which can be quite fundamental and at times shattering. The almost abrupt extinction of a product line can be devastating not just for the line of business but also the well-being of the affected parties, including the investors. A case in point would be how the recording-disc-manufacturing and indeed the industry itself got phased out. Not only convulsions were caused across a cross-segment of the population—both user and otherwise—but so much data was equally abruptly lost. If any messages were distilled out of this experience it has still to reach the public domain.

Life has a unique attribute to keeping on with the movement itself, often ignoring those who fall by the wayside. To say that this is sad would be perhaps one of the most grotesque understatements of the times.

Life requires not only keeping up with the changes but with keeping pace with it. It is the second which is the bigger challenge of the era one lives in.

There are other forms of changes. The importance of minerals in the global economy was never so large as in the present set up. The importance of minerals is nearly as old as human civilisation and for millennia it has been one of the cornerstones of so-called progress. Zinc and Copper mining goes back thousands of years. Gold and Diamond have, also, been the cornerstones of the means of storing wealth. Other examples can be found. The oncoming of the industrial revolution widened and deepened the quest of minerals and metals. A point seems to have been reached where what was first written off as barren, arid and desolate is today being acquired for control in an unprecedented manner. It is what lies hidden beneath the surface of the earth is what is being chased. It is not as if every piece of land has some rich deposits but that the possibility that every piece of land may have some concealed riches that captures the imagination. The story goes on especially in parts of the earth which have a structure going back into thousands of millennia.

As the climate change becomes an experience of household existence there are other deeper changes taking place. The ice in the Arctic is reported to be melting. Huge chunks of ice are reported to be floating through the oceans to unknown destinations. That itself is an unprecedented phenomenon. The full possibilities of this process have yet to be grasped.

In the meanwhile, the grab for territory in the Arctic region has already gone up. Eight nations have, reportedly, a presence there. For the rest of Arctic, jostling is underway. There is perhaps, some reluctance to declare, monitor and ensure that remaining of the Arctic gets institutionalised as 'common territory'. New bidders are, reportedly, wanting to enter that domain and how it will unfold remains to be seen. Closer to the 'lay of the land' is the story of the 'lay of the land'. The nations who have got there earlier seem to be keen to preserve their dominance.

It is common assumption that the land structure of the Arctic's must have unique minerals and metals. Indeed there may be minerals there of a unique variety which may have unprecedented use. The possibilities are huge.

Climate change therefore, is amongst other things rewriting the future of human growth. New disciplines will emerge and new lifestyles will be around the corner. In all this, the search for constancy, familiarity and the cosiness of the known may become increasingly limited in potential and possibility. These are unprecedented times of change. The basic question remains what would be the limits of human change: physical, emotional, cognitive or more? It is possible that life scripts themselves may need redrafting.

Business will only remain a subset of this. The context requires the recognition of the seminality of the current times. It is not only that the fittest will survive—which is true—but also, that there may be new forms of survival.

Being human will require the emotional wherewithal and the ability to hold each other's hand through all this.

September 01, 2022

# Index